IN SEARCH OF OURSELVES

selected and edited by **Malcolm Ross**, M.A., PH.D., F.R.S.C.,
Professor of English Literature and Dean of Arts
at Trinity College, University of Toronto,

and **John Stevens**, M.A., Professor of English
at the College of Education, University of Toronto

J. M. DENT & SONS (CANADA) LIMITED, TORONTO

ISBN 0-460-92616-0

Printed and bound in Canada by The Bryant Press Ltd.

Acknowledgments

The editors and publisher of this volume gratefully acknowledge permission to reprint the following copyright material:

"What I Believe", from *Two Cheers for Democracy* by E. M. Forster. Reprinted by permission of Edward Arnold (Publishers) Ltd.

"Marrakech" by George Orwell, from *The Collected Essays of George Orwell*. Reprinted by permission of Martin Secker & Warburg Ltd.

"That Day at Hiroshima", from *Human Relations in a Changing World* by Alexander H. Leighton, published by E. P. Dutton & Co., Inc. Originally published in *The Atlantic Monthly*. Copyright © 1946, Alexander H. Leighton. Reprinted by permission of Russell & Volkening, Inc.

"The Killers" (Copyright 1927 Charles Scribner's Sons; renewal copyright © 1955) is reprinted with the permission of Charles Scribner's Sons from *Men Without Women* by Ernest Hemingway.

"One, Two, Three Little Indians", from *The Yellow Sweater and*

Other Stories by Hugh Garner. Reprinted by permission of the author.

"The Rockpile", reprinted from *Going to Meet the Man* by James Baldwin. Copyright © 1948, 1951, 1957, 1958, 1960, 1965 by James Baldwin and used with the permission of the publishers, The Dial Press, Inc.

"Ha'penny" is reprinted with the permission of Charles Scribner's Sons from *Tales from a Troubled Land* by Alan Paton. Copr. © 1961 Alan Paton.

"The Macbeth Murder Mystery" by James Thurber. Copyright © 1942 James Thurber. From *My World—And Welcome to It*, published by Harcourt, Brace & World, Inc. Reprinted by permission of Mrs. James Thurber.

"My Oedipus Complex", from *The Collected Stories of Frank O'Connor*. © Copyright 1952 by Frank O'Connor. Reprinted by permission of the author.

"Charles", reprinted from *The Lottery* by Shirley Jackson by permission of Farrar, Straus & Giroux, Inc. Copyright 1948, 1949 by Shirley Jackson.

"My Discovery of England" by Stephen Leacock. Reprinted by permission of Mrs. Donald Nimmo.

"America at Last", reprinted by permission of G. P. Putnam's Sons from *America at Last, The American Journal of T. H. White*. Copyright © 1965 by International Authors, N.V.

"The Unfading Beauty: A Well-Filled Mind" by John Ciardi. Reprinted from *Glamour*; Copyright © 1959 by The Condé Nast Publications Inc.

"Odour of Chrysanthemums" by D. H. Lawrence, from *The Complete Short Stories of D. H. Lawrence*, published by William Heinemann Limited. Reprinted by permission of Laurence Pollinger Limited and the estate of the late Mrs. Frieda Lawrence.

"The Wedding Gift" by Thomas Raddall. Reprinted by permission of the author.

In this anthology, the editors have retained the original American spellings in stories by American authors.

Contents

PART ONE HUMANITY AND INHUMANITY

PART TWO THE OUTSIDERS

PART THREE MEN AND WOMEN

PART FOUR MAN AND HIS SYMBOLS

Introduction

WE USUALLY THINK of literature and the other arts as expression – the expression of thought and feeling and attitude about life, about the world, about man's destiny in the world – and beyond it. Certainly the great themes of man's hope and man's fate recur in literature from age to age and find expression in writers as distant in time as Milton from Ernest Hemingway or as distant in place as Alan Paton from Hugh MacLennan. But from age to age and from place to place, man's convictions about his world and his destiny change. And there are whole periods of literature in which the expression of values resting on clear conviction about the nature and destiny of man gives way to the question mark, to a search, sometimes desperate, always intense, for new ground upon which to take a stand.

In our own age, an age both shattered and shaped by political, scientific, and philosophical revolution, inherited convictions and beliefs have not been abandoned nor have they been preserved without agony of mind and heart, and not without that fearful inner quest which breaks below the surface of idea and attitude to the very nerve ends of being.

It is as though man, before taking off to the distant stars or to new realms of value, has paused to ask himself *who he is*. And he dwells on that word "is". He is concerned, perhaps as never before, with what it is to *be*.

In this brave new age we are, then, really "in search of ourselves". Not selfishly – or not always selfishly. We are in search of our identity, the identity of our human kind. Thus we probe the human condition. We reach, through the imagination, into the marrow of Alan Paton's outcast African boy and, closer to home, into the congealed pain of James Baldwin's Harlem family or Hugh Garner's "Little Indians". We try on the colour of skins other than ours; we break out of the human skin altogether to catch at the mystery of being alive with O'Flaherty's "Hawk"; or, with Faulkner's "Bear", we seek and find the measure of our manhood.

Indeed, with writers as different as D. H. Lawrence, S. I. Hayakawa, Wallace Stegner, John Updike, and Ernest Hemingway we search out the human condition. And we search out as well our specifically human capacity — our capacity for love, for terror, for pity, for evil, for joy. And our capacity for survival.

The stories and essays here are in the main contemporary. The most notable pieces from the past presented here are the excerpts from essays by John Milton and John Stuart Mill, speaking to us from different times and in different voices of man's ceaseless quest for freedom. How different in tone — and conviction — is the voice of our elder contemporary E. M. Forster with his "two cheers only" for democracy and his uniquely modern search for purpose in the thick of purposelessness. And how very different still is the tone and the faith of another modern man — Graham Greene, with his story of a quest, ancient but ever new.

In form, our stories range from simple narrative to prose poem, our essays from the outer edge of story style to the inner edge of philosophical speculation. There are many tones and shades in the book, from the humour of Leacock to the horror of Hiroshima. For we go in search of ourselves down many different paths and in all kinds of weather.

Throughout the text we have tried to suggest in terms of both stories and essays, various thematic and technical relationships and points of contrast for use in class discussion. Our sets of "questions" are meant to suggest various approaches to the interpretation of the material. Other and different approaches will occur to the reader.

M. R.
J. S.

IN SEARCH OF OURSELVES

PART ONE
HUMANITY AND INHUMANITY

E. M. FORSTER

b. 1879

What I believe ✥ ✥ ✥

It is worth noting at the outset that this statement of belief, or rather this affirmation of a set of values, was written in 1939 and therefore at a moment when all the humane and liberal achievements of Western civilization were about to be put to the test. The fanatical tribes were on the march, mad prophets of power and violence cried out for conquest and for blood. It was a time for inventory and for re-assessment. Where could we take our stand? Which of our inherited notions about God and man and society could meet the test and endure? Where could we turn to find the source and assurance of strength? Forster writes as a reverent agnostic: "I do not believe in Belief." But his scepticism is the very opposite of cynicism as he explores the human capacity for love and for creativity and thereby reaffirms a faith in the ultimate dignity and decency of man. And while he disavows any belief in the Belief of Christians, we might profitably ponder the degree to which the author's mind and spirit have been moulded by that very Belief. Forster's most significant novels are *A Room with a View* (1908), *Howard's End* (1910), and *A Passage to India* (1924). "What I Believe" appears in his collected essays *Two Cheers for Democracy* (1951).

I DO NOT BELIEVE in Belief. But this is an age of faith, and there are so many militant creeds that, in self-defence, one has to formulate a creed of one's own. Tolerance, good temper, and sympathy are no longer enough in a world which is rent by religious and racial persecution, in a world where ignorance rules, and science, who ought to have ruled, plays the subservient pimp. Tolerance, good temper, and sympathy — they are what matter really, and if the human race is not to collapse they must come to the front before long. But for the moment they are not enough, their action is no stronger than a flower, battered beneath a military jack-boot. They want stiffening, even if the process coarsens them. Faith, to my mind, is a stiffening process, a sort of mental starch, which ought to be applied as sparingly as possible. I dislike the stuff. I do not believe in it, for its own sake, at all. Herein I probably differ from most people, who believe in Belief, and are only sorry they cannot swallow even more than they do. My law-givers are Erasmus and Montaigne, not Moses and St. Paul. My temple stands not upon Mount Moriah but in that Elysian Field where even the immoral are admitted. My motto is: "Lord, I disbelieve — help thou my unbelief."

I have, however, to live in an Age of Faith — the sort of epoch I used to hear praised when I was a boy. It is extremely unpleasant really. It is bloody in every sense of the word. And I have to keep my end up in it. Where do I start?

With personal relationships. Here is something comparatively solid in a world full of violence and cruelty. Not absolutely solid, for Psychology has split and shattered the idea of a "Person" and has shown that there is something incalculable in each of us, which may at any moment rise to the surface and destroy our normal balance. We don't know what we are like. We can't know what other people are like. How, then, can we put any trust in personal relationships, or cling to them in the gathering political storm? In theory we cannot. But in practice we can and do. Though A is not unchangeably A or B unchangeably B, there can still be love and loyalty between the two. For the purpose of living one has to assume that the personality is solid, and the "self" is an entity, and to ignore all contrary evidence. And since to ignore evidence is one of the characteristics of faith, I certainly can proclaim that I believe in personal relationships.

Starting from them, I get a little order into the contemporary chaos. One must be fond of people and trust them if one is not to make a mess of life, and it is therefore essential that they should not let one down. They often do. The moral of which is that I must, myself, be as reliable as possible, and this I try to be. But reliability is not a matter of contract – that is the main difference between the world of personal relationships and the world of business relationships. It is a matter for the heart, which signs no documents. In other words, reliability is impossible unless there is a natural warmth. Most men possess this warmth, though they often have bad luck and get chilled. Most of them, even when they are politicians, *want* to keep faith. And one can, at all events, show one's own little light here, one's own poor little trembling flame, with the knowledge that it is not the only light that is shining in the darkness, and not the only one which the darkness does not comprehend. Personal relations are despised today. They are regarded as bourgeois luxuries, as products of a time of fair weather which is now past, and we are urged to get rid of them, and to dedicate ourselves to some movement or cause instead. I hate the idea of causes, and if I had to choose between betraying my country and betraying my friend, I hope I should have the guts to betray my country. Such a choice may scandalize the modern reader, and he may stretch out his patriotic hand to the telephone at once and ring up the police. It would not have shocked Dante, though. Dante places Brutus and Cassius in the lowest circle of Hell because they had chosen to betray their friend Julius Caesar rather than their country Rome. Probably one will not be asked to make such an agonizing choice. Still, there lies at the back of every creed something terrible and hard for which the worshipper may one day be required to suffer, and there is even a terror and a hardness in this creed of personal relationships, urbane and mild though it sounds. Love and loyalty to an individual can run counter to the claims of the State. When they do – down with the State, say I, which means that the State would down me.

This brings me along to Democracy, "even Love, the Beloved Republic, which feeds upon Freedom and lives." Democracy is not a Beloved Republic really, and never will be. But it is less hateful than other contemporary forms of government, and to that extent it deserves our support. It does start from the assumption that the individual is important, and that all types are needed to make a civilization. It does not divide its citizens into the bossers and the bossed – as an efficiency-regime tends to do. The people I admire most are those who are sensitive and want to create something or discover something, and do not see life in terms of power, and such people get more of a chance under a democracy than elsewhere. They found religions, great or small, or they produce literature and art, or they do disinterested scientific research, or they may be what is called "ordinary people", who are creative in their private lives, bring up their children decently, for instance, or help their neighbours. All these people need to express themselves; they cannot do so unless society allows them liberty to do so, and the society which allows them most liberty is a democracy.

Democracy has another merit. It allows criticism, and if there is not public criticism there are bound to be hushed-up scandals. That is why I believe in the Press, despite all its lies and vulgarity, and why I believe in Parliament. Parliament is often sneered at because it is a Talking Shop. I believe in it *because* it is a talking shop. I believe in the Private Member who makes himself a nuisance. He gets snubbed and is told that he is cranky or ill-informed, but he does expose abuses which would otherwise never have been mentioned, and very often an abuse gets put right just by being mentioned. Occasionally, too, a well-meaning public official starts losing his head in the cause of efficiency, and thinks himself God Almighty. Such officials are particularly frequent in the Home Office. Well, there will be questions about them in Parliament sooner or later, and then they will have to mind their steps. Whether Parliament is either a representative body or an efficient one is questionable, but

I value it because it criticizes and talks, and because its chatter gets widely reported.

So Two cheers for Democracy: one because it admits variety and two because it permits criticism. Two cheers are quite enough: there is no occasion to give three. Only Love the Beloved Republic deserves that.

What about Force, though? While we are trying to be sensitive and advanced and affectionate and tolerant, an unpleasant question pops up: does not all society rest upon force? If a government cannot count upon the police and the army, how can it hope to rule? And if an individual gets knocked on the head or sent to a labour camp, of what significance are his opinions?

This dilemma does not worry me as much as it does some. I realize that all society rests upon force. But all the great creative actions, all the decent human relations, occur during the intervals when force has not managed to come to the front. These intervals are what matter. I want them to be as frequent and as lengthy as possible, and I call them "civilization". Some people idealize force and pull it into the foreground and worship it, instead of keeping it in the background as long as possible. I think they make a mistake, and I think that their opposites, the mystics, err even more when they declare that force does not exist. I believe that it exists, and that one of our jobs is to prevent it from getting out of its box. It gets out sooner or later, and then it destroys us and all the lovely things which we have made. But it is not out all the time, for the fortunate reason that the strong are so stupid. Consider their conduct for a moment in the Nibelung's Ring. The giants there have the guns, or in other words the gold; but they do nothing with it, they do not realize that they are all-powerful, with the result that the catastrophe is delayed and the castle of Walhalla, insecure but glorious, fronts the storms. Fafnir, coiled round his hoard, grumbles and grunts; we can hear him under Europe today; the leaves of the wood already tremble, and the Bird calls its warnings uselessly. Fafnir will destroy us, but by a blessed dispensation he is stupid and slow, and creation goes on just outside the poisonous blast of his breath. The Nietzschean would hurry the monster up, the mystic would say he did not exist, but Wotan, wiser than either, hastens to create warriors before doom declares itself. The Valkyries are symbols not only of courage but of intelligence; they represent the human spirit snatching its opportunity while the going is good, and one of them even finds time to love. Brünnhilde's last song hymns the recurrence of love, and since it is the privilege of art to exaggerate, she goes even further, and proclaims the love which is eternally triumphant and feeds upon freedom, and lives.

So that is what I feel about force and violence. It is, alas! the ultimate reality on this earth, but it does not always get to the front. Some people call its absences "decadence"; I call them "civilization" and find in such interludes the chief justification for the human experiment. I look the other way until fate strikes me. Whether this is due to courage or to cowardice in my own case I cannot be sure. But I know that if men had not looked the other way in the past, nothing of any value would survive. The people I respect most behave as if they were immortal and as if society was eternal. Both assumptions are false; both of them must be accepted as true if we are to go on eating and working and loving, and are to keep open a few breathing holes for the human spirit. No millennium seems likely to descend upon humanity; no better and stronger League of Nations will be instituted; no form of Christianity and no alternative to Christianity will bring peace to the world or integrity to the individual; no "change of heart" will occur. And yet we need not despair, indeed, we cannot despair; the evidence of history shows us that men have always insisted on behaving creatively under the shadow of the sword, that they have done their artistic and scientific and domestic stuff for the sake of doing it, and that we had better follow their example under the shadow of the aeroplanes. Others, with more vision or courage than myself, see the salvation of humanity ahead, and will dismiss my conception of civilization as paltry, a sort of tip-and-run game. Certainly it is presumptuous to say that we *cannot* improve, and that Man, who has only been in power for a few thousand years, will never learn to make use of his power. All I mean is that, if people continue to kill one another as they do, the world cannot get better than it is, and that since there are more people than formerly, and their means for destroying one another superior, the world may well get worse. What is good in people — and consequently in the world — is their insistence on creation, their belief in friendship and loyalty for their own sakes; and though Violence remains and is, indeed, the major partner in this muddled establishment, I believe that creativeness remains too, and will always assume direction when violence sleeps. So, though I am not an optimist, I cannot agree with Sophocles that it were better never to have been born. And although, like Horace, I see no evidence that each batch of births is superior to the last, I leave the field open for the more complacent view. This is such a difficult moment to live in, one cannot help getting gloomy and also a bit rattled, and perhaps short-sighted.

In search of a refuge, we may perhaps turn to hero-worship. But here we shall get no help, in my opinion. Hero-worship is a dangerous vice, and one of the minor merits of a democracy is that it does not encourage it, or produce that unmanageable type of citizen known as the Great Man. It produces instead different kinds of small men — a much finer achievement. But people who cannot get interested in the variety of life, and cannot make up their own minds, get discontented over this, and they long for a hero to bow down before and to follow blindly. It is significant that a hero is an integral part of the authoritarian stock-in-trade today. An efficiency-regime cannot be run without a few heroes stuck about it to carry off the dullness — much as plums have to be put into a bad pudding to make it palatable. One hero at the top and a smaller one each side of him is a favourite arrangement, and the timid and the bored are comforted by the trinity, and, bowing down, feel exalted and strengthened.

No, I distrust Great Men. They produce a desert of uniformity around them and often a pool of blood too, and I always feel a little man's pleasure when they come a cropper. Every now and then one reads in the newspapers some such statement as: "The coup d'état appears to have failed, and Admiral Toma's whereabouts is at present unknown." Admiral Toma had probably every qualification for being a Great Man — an iron will, personal magnetism, dash, flair, sexlessness — but fate was against him, so he retires to unknown whereabouts instead of parading history with his peers. He fails with a completeness which no artist and no lover can experience, because with them the process of creation is itself an achievement, whereas with him the only possible achievement is success.

I believe in aristocracy, though — if that is the right word, and if a democrat may use it. Not an aristocracy of power, based upon rank and influence, but an aristocracy of the sensitive, the considerate, and the plucky. Its members are to be found in all nations and classes, and all through the ages, and there is a secret understanding between them when they meet. They represent the true human tradition, the one permanent victory of our queer race over cruelty and chaos. Thousands of them perish in obscurity, a few are great names. They are sensitive for others as well as for themselves, they are considerate without being fussy, their pluck is not swankiness but the power to endure, and they can take a joke. I give no examples — it is risky to do that — but the reader may as well consider whether this is the type of person he would like to meet and to be, and whether (going farther with me) he would prefer that this type should *not* be an ascetic one. I am against asceticism myself. I am with the old Scotsman who wanted less chastity and more delicacy. I do not feel that my aristocrats are a real aristocracy if they thwart their bodies, since bodies are the instruments through which we register and enjoy the world. Still, I do not insist. This is not a major point. It is clearly possible to be sensitive, considerate, and plucky and yet be an ascetic too, and if anyone possesses the first three qualities, I will let him in! On they go – an invincible army, yet not a victorious one. The aristocrats, the elect, the chosen, the Best People – all the words that describe them are false, and all attempts to organize them fail. Again and again Authority, seeing their value, has tried to net them and to utilize them as the Egyptian Priesthood or the Christian Church or the Chinese Civil Service or the Group Movement, or some other worthy stunt. But they slip through the net and are gone; when the door is shut, they are no longer in the room; their temple, as one of them remarked, is the Holiness of the Heart's Affection, and their kingdom, though they never possess it, is the wide-open world.

With this type of person knocking about, and constantly crossing one's path if one has eyes to see or hands to feel, the experiment of earthly life cannot be dismissed as a failure. But it may well be hailed as a tragedy, the tragedy being that no device has been found by which these private decencies can be transmitted to public affairs. As soon as people have power they go crooked and sometimes dotty as well, because the possession of power lifts them into a region where normal honesty never pays. For instance, the man who is selling newspapers outside the Houses of Parliament can safely leave his papers to go for a drink and his cap beside them: anyone who takes a paper is sure to drop a copper into the cap. But the men who are inside the Houses of Parliament – they cannot trust one another like that, still less can the Government they compose trust other governments. No caps upon the pavement here, but suspicion, treachery, and armaments. The more highly public life is organized the lower does its morality sink; the nations of today behave to each other worse than they ever did in the past, they cheat, rob, bully, and bluff, make war without notice, and kill as many women and children as possible; whereas primitive tribes were at all events restrained by taboos. It is a humiliating outlook – though the greater the darkness, the brighter shine the little lights, reassuring one another, signalling: "Well, at all events, I'm still here. I don't like it very much, but how are you?" Unquenchable lights of my aristocracy! Signals of the invincible army! "Come along—anyway, let's have a good time while we can." I think they signal that too.

The Saviour of the future—if ever he comes—will not preach a new Gospel. He will merely utilize my aristocracy, he will make effective the good will and the good temper which are already existing. In other words, he will introduce a new technique. In economics, we are told that if there was a new technique of distribution, there need be no poverty, and people would not starve in one place while crops were being ploughed under in another. A similar change is needed in the sphere of morals and politics. The desire for it is by no means new; it was expressed, for example, in theological terms by Jacopone da Todi over six hundred years ago. "Ordina questo amore, O tu che m'ami," he said; "O thou who lovest me—set this love in order." His prayer was not granted, and I do not myself believe that it ever will be, but here, and not through a change of heart, is our probable route. Not by becoming better, but by ordering and distributing his native goodness, will Man shut up Force into its box, and so gain time to explore the universe and to set his mark upon it worthily. At present he only explores it at odd moments, when Force is looking the other way, and his divine creativeness appears as a trivial by-product, to be scrapped as soon as the drums beat and the bombers hum.

Such a change, claim the orthodox, can only be made by Christianity, and will be made by it in God's good time: man always has failed and always will fail to organize his own goodness, and it is presumptuous of him to try. This claim—solemn as it is—leaves me cold. I cannot believe that Christianity will ever cope with the present world-wide mess, and I think that such influence as it retains in modern society is due to the money behind it, rather than to its spiritual appeal. It was a spiritual force once, but the indwelling spirit will have to be restated if it is to calm the waters again, and probably restated in a non-Christian form. Naturally a lot of people, and people who are not only good but able and intelligent, will disagree here; they will vehemently deny that Christianity has failed, or they will argue that its failure proceeds from the wickedness of men, and really proves its ultimate success. They have Faith, with a large F. My faith has a very small one, and I only intrude it because these are strenuous and serious days, and one likes to say what one thinks while speech is comparatively free: it may not be free much longer.

The above are the reflections of an individualist and a liberal who has found liberalism crumbling beneath him and at first felt ashamed. Then, looking around, he decided there was no special reason for shame, since other people, whatever they felt, were equally insecure. And as for individualism – there seems no way of getting off this, even if one wanted to. The dictator-hero can grind down his citizens till they are all alike, but he cannot melt them into a single man. That is beyond his power. He can order them to merge, he can incite them to mass-antics, but they are obliged to be born separately, and to die separately, and, owing to these unavoidable termini, will always be running off the totalitarian rails. The memory of birth and the expectation of death always lurk within the human being, making him separate from his fellows and consequently capable of intercourse with them. Naked I came into the world, naked I shall go out of it! And a very good thing too, for it reminds me that I am naked under my shirt, whatever its colour.

QUESTIONS

1. Why does the author say he "dislikes" faith?
2. What does he mean by saying that he lives in an "Age of Faith"?

3. Why would he rather betray his country than betray a friend?

4. Why is there no occasion to give *three* cheers for Democracy?

5. Do you agree with Forster's notion of what constitutes "civilization"?

6. What does he mean by telling us he is "not an optimist"? Is he a pessimist?

7. How does Forster reconcile his notions of democracy and aristocracy?

8. Explain the role of Forster's "Saviour of the future".

9. Do you think Forster's liberal and individualist values are strong enough and compelling enough for the world of the 1960's? Explain any disagreements you may have with the author.

GEORGE ORWELL

1903-1950

Marrakech ✥ ✥ ✥

George Orwell (pen-name for the English writer Eric Blair) is best known for his novels *Animal Farm* (1945) and *Nineteen Eighty-Four* (1949), but he also wrote vigorous essays on literature and politics. This one comes from *Such, Such Were the Joys* (1953). Like E. M. Forster's "What I Believe", "Marrakech" was written in 1939 under the shadow of the Second World War. And like Forster, Orwell runs against the current of the times which glorified the state; he places highest value on the individual human life, regardless of race. He penetrates the surface gaiety of the North African resort town, a favourite of both Europeans and Americans because of its quaint, medieval flavour, and sees the plight of the permanent inhabitants of its native quarter. In the concluding paragraphs he seems to prophesy the troubled Africa of our own generation.

AS THE CORPSE went past the flies left the restaurant table in a cloud and rushed after it, but they came back a few minutes later.

The little crowd of mourners — all men and boys, no women — threaded their way across the market-place between the piles of pomegranates and the taxis and the camels, wailing a short chant over and over again. What really appeals to the flies is that corpses here are never put into coffins, they are merely wrapped in a piece of rag and carried on a rough wooden bier on the shoulders of four friends. When the friends get to the burying-ground they hack an oblong hole a foot or two deep, dump the body in it and fling over it a little of the dried-up, lumpy earth, which is like broken brick.

No gravestone, no name, no identifying mark of any kind. The burying-ground is merely a huge waste of hummocky earth, like a derelict building-lot. After a month or two no one can even be certain where his own relatives are buried.

When you walk through a town like this – two hundred thousand inhabitants, of whom at least twenty thousand own literally nothing except the rags they stand up in – when you see how the people live, and still more how easily they die, it is always difficult to believe that you are walking among human beings. All colonial empires are in reality founded upon that fact. The people have brown faces – besides, there are so many of them! Are they really the same flesh as yourself? Do they even have names? Or are they merely a kind of undifferentiated brown stuff, about as individual as bees or coral insects? They rise out of the earth, they sweat and starve for a few years, and then they sink back into the nameless mounds of the graveyard and nobody notices that they are gone. And even the graves themselves soon fade back into the soil. Sometimes, out for a walk, as you break your way through the prickly pear, you notice that it is rather bumpy underfoot, and only a certain regularity in the bumps tells you that you are walking over skeletons.

I was feeding one of the gazelles in the public gardens.

Gazelles are almost the only animals that look good to eat when they are still alive, in fact, one can hardly look at their hindquarters without thinking of mint sauce. The gazelle I was feeding seemed to know that this thought was in my mind, for though it took the piece of bread I was holding out it obviously did not like me. It nibbled rapidly at the bread, then lowered its head and tried to butt me, then took another nibble and then butted again. Probably its idea was that if it could drive me away the bread would somehow remain hanging in mid-air.

An Arab navvy working on the path nearby lowered his heavy hoe and sidled slowly towards us. He looked from the gazelle to the bread and from the bread to the gazelle, with a sort of quiet amazement, as though he had never seen anything quite like this before. Finally he said shyly in French:

"*I* could eat some of that bread."

I tore off a piece and he stowed it gratefully in some secret place under his rags. This man is an employee of the Municipality.

When you go through the Jewish quarters you gather some idea of what the medieval ghettoes were probably like. Under their Moorish rulers the Jews were only allowed to own land in certain restricted areas, and after centuries of this kind of treatment they have ceased to bother about overcrowding. Many of the streets are a good deal less than six feet wide, the houses are completely windowless, and sore-eyed children cluster everywhere in unbelievable numbers, like clouds of flies. Down the centre of the street there is generally running a little river of urine.

In the bazaar huge families of Jews, all dressed in the long black robe and little black skull-cap, are working in dark fly-infested booths that look like caves. A carpenter sits cross-legged at a prehistoric lathe, turning chair-legs at lightning speed. He works the lathe with a bow in his right hand and guides the chisel with his left foot, and thanks to a lifetime of sitting in this position his left leg is warped out of shape. At his side his grandson, aged six, is already starting on the simpler parts of the job.

I was just passing the coppersmiths' booths when somebody noticed that I was lighting a cigarette. Instantly, from the dark holes all round, there was a frenzied rush of Jews, many of them old grandfathers with flowing grey beards, all clamouring for a cigarette. Even a blind man somewhere at the back of one of the booths heard a rumour of cigarettes and came crawling out, groping in the air with his hand. In about a minute I had used up the whole packet. None of these people, I suppose, works less than twelve hours a day, and every one of them looks on a cigarette as a more or less impossible luxury.

As the Jews live in self-contained communities they follow the same trades as the Arabs, except for agriculture. Fruit-sellers, potters, silversmiths, blacksmiths, butchers, leather-workers, tailors, water-carriers, beggars, porters — whichever way you look you see nothing but Jews. As a matter of fact there are thirteen thousand of them, all living in the space of a few acres. A good job Hitler wasn't here. Perhaps he was on his way, however. You hear the usual dark rumours about the Jews, not only from the Arabs but from the poorer Europeans.

"Yes, mon vieux, they took my job away from me and gave it to a Jew. The Jews! They're the real rulers of this country, you know. They've got all the money. They control the banks, finance — everything."

"But," I said, "isn't it a fact that the average Jew is a labourer working for about a penny an hour?"

"Ah, that's only for show! They're all money-lenders really. They're cunning, the Jews."

In just the same way, a couple of hundred years ago, poor old women used to be burned for witchcraft when they could not even work enough magic to get themselves a square meal.

All people who work with their hands are partly invisible, and the more important the work they do, the less visible they are. Still, a white skin is always fairly conspicuous. In northern Europe, when you see a labourer ploughing a field, you probably give him a second glance. In a hot country, anywhere south of Gibraltar or east of Suez, the chances are that you don't even see him. I have noticed this again and again. In a tropical landscape one's eye takes in everything except the human beings. It takes in the dried-up soil, the prickly pear, the palm tree, and the distant mountain, but it always misses the peasant hoeing at his patch. He is the same colour as the earth, and a great deal less interesting to look at.

It is only because of this that the starved countries of Asia and Africa are accepted as tourist resorts. No one would think of running cheap trips to the Distressed Areas. But where the human beings have brown skins their poverty is simply not noticed. What does Morocco mean to a Frenchman? An orange-grove or a job in Government service. Or to an Englishman? Camels, castles, palm trees, Foreign Legionnaires, brass trays, and bandits. One could probably live there for years without noticing that for nine-tenths of the people the reality of life is an endless, back-breaking struggle to wring a little food out of an eroded soil.

Most of Morocco is so desolate that no wild animal bigger than a hare can live on it. Huge areas which were once covered with forest have turned into a treeless waste where the soil is exactly like broken-up brick. Nevertheless a good deal of it is cultivated, with frightful labour. Everything is done by hand. Long lines of women, bent double like inverted capital L's, work their way slowly across the fields, tearing up the prickly weeds with their hands, and the peasant gathering lucerne for fodder pulls it up stalk by stalk instead of reaping it, thus saving an inch or two on each stalk. The plough is a wretched wooden thing, so frail that one can easily carry it on one's shoulder, and fitted underneath with a rough iron spike which stirs the soil to a depth of about four inches. This is as much as the strength of the animals is equal to. It is usual to plough with a cow and a donkey yoked together. Two donkeys would not be quite strong enough, but on the other hand two cows would cost a little more to feed. The peasants possess no harrows, they merely plough the soil several times over in different directions, finally leaving it in rough furrows, after which the whole field has to be shaped with hoes into small oblong patches to conserve water. Except for a day or two after the rare rainstorms there is never enough water. Along the edges of the fields channels are hacked out to a depth of thirty or forty feet to get at the tiny trickles which run through the subsoil.

Every afternoon a file of very old women passes down the road outside my house, each carrying a load of firewood. All of them are mummified with age and the sun, and all of them are tiny. It seems to be generally the case in primitive communities that the women, when they get beyond a certain age, shrink to the size of children. One day a poor old creature who could not have been more than four feet tall crept past me under a vast load of wood. I stopped her and put a five-sou piece (a little more than a farthing) into her hand. She answered with a shrill wail, almost a scream, which was partly gratitude but mainly surprise. I suppose that from her point of view, by taking any notice of her, I seemed almost to be violating a law of nature. She accepted her status as an old woman, that is to say as a beast of burden. When a family is travelling it is quite usual to see a father and a grown-up son riding ahead on donkeys, and an old woman following on foot, carrying the baggage.

But what is strange about these people is their invisibility. For several weeks, always at about the same time of day, the file of women had hobbled past the house with their firewood, and though they had registered themselves on my eyeballs I cannot truly say that I had seen them. Firewood was passing – that was how I saw it. It was only that one day I happened to be walking behind them, and the curious up-and-down motion of a load of wood drew my attention to the human being beneath it. Then for the first time I noticed the poor old earth-coloured bodies, bodies reduced to bones and leathery skin, bent double under the crushing weight. Yet I suppose I had not been five minutes on Moroccan soil before I noticed the overloading of the donkeys and was infuriated by it. There is no question that the donkeys are damnably treated. The Moroccan donkey is hardly bigger than a St. Bernard dog, it carries a load which in the British Army would be considered too much for a fifteen-hands mule, and very often its pack-saddle is not taken off its back for weeks together. But what is peculiarly pitiful is that it is the most willing creature on earth, it follows its master like a dog and does not need either bridle or halter. After a dozen years of devoted work it suddenly drops dead, whereupon its master tips it into the ditch and the village dogs have torn its guts out before it is cold.

This kind of thing makes one's blood boil, whereas – on the whole – the plight of the human beings does not. I am not commenting, merely pointing to a fact. People with brown skins are next door to invisible. Anyone can be sorry for the donkey with its galled back, but it is generally owing to some kind of accident if one even notices the old woman under her load of sticks.

As the storks flew northward the Negroes were marching southward – a long, dusty column, infantry, screw-gun batteries, and then more infantry, four or five thousand men in all, winding up the road with a clumping of boots and a clatter of iron wheels.

They were Senegalese, the blackest Negroes in Africa, so black that sometimes it is difficult to see whereabouts on their necks the hair begins. Their splendid bodies were hidden in reach-me-down khaki uniforms, their feet squashed into boots that looked like blocks of wood, and every tin hat seemed to be a couple of sizes too small. It was very hot and the men had marched a long way. They slumped under the weight of their packs and the curiously sensitive black faces were glistening with sweat.

As they went past a tall, very young Negro turned and caught my eye. But the look he gave me was not in the least the kind of look you might expect. Not hostile, not contemptuous, not sullen, not even inquisitive. It was the shy, wide-eyed Negro look, which actually is a look of profound respect. I saw how it was. This wretched boy, who is a French citizen and has therefore been dragged from the forest to scrub floors and catch syphilis in garrison towns, actually has feelings of reverence before a white skin. He has been taught that the white race are his masters, and he still believes it.

But there is one thought which every white man (and in this connection it doesn't matter twopence if he calls himself a socialist) thinks when he sees a black army marching past. "How much longer can we go on kidding these people? How long before they turn their guns in the other direction?"

It was curious, really. Every white man there had this thought stowed somewhere or other in his mind. I had it, so had the other onlookers, so had the officers on their sweating chargers and the white N.C.O.'s marching in the ranks. It was a kind of secret which we all knew and were too clever to tell; only the Negroes didn't know it. And really it was like watching a flock of cattle to see the long column, a mile or two miles of armed men, flowing peacefully up the road, while the great white birds drifted over them in the opposite direction, glittering like scraps of paper.

QUESTIONS

1. Sum up in a sentence or two Orwell's main thesis in this essay.

2. Although this is a journalistic essay that attempts to illumine a real situation, Orwell writes as an artist, arranging his ideas and using images that will have a persuasive impact on his reader. In the opening three paragraphs, how does he arrest your attention and enlist your sympathy?

3. In order to enlist sympathy for a victim the writer must use restraint; the reader tends to resist a too strident demand for his pity. Pick out an incident narrated in the body of the essay and show that it is a restrained appeal to the reader's power of sympathy.

4. The initial image of the flies is not isolated. Show that Orwell weaves this image into his essay as a descriptive theme or motif. What effect does the repeated use of this image produce?

5. Orwell's style has been described as "fast, clear, grey, bitter prose with its arguing ring and satirical asides". A specific illustration of this aspect of his style is to be found on page 18; "After a dozen years of devoted work it suddenly drops dead, whereupon its master tips it into the ditch and the village dogs have torn its guts out before it is cold."
   (a) Write down another short passage which illustrates the quoted description of Orwell's style.
   (b) Try to explain why the passage you have chosen has clarity and bite.

6. (a) In what way is the final portion of the essay prophetic?
   (b) Explain the possible symbolism of "the great white birds".

ALEXANDER H. LEIGHTON

b. 1908

That day at Hiroshima ✥ ✥ ✥

In various military headquarters of the world's great nations, computers calculate and re-calculate the permutations of missile strategy. The statistics of death that they produce look clean enough in the reports, but actually killing large numbers of people is a messy reality. The account below of the first primitive success in nuclear war on August 6, 1945, reminds us that man is flesh and does not die cleanly, as a cypher on a page. Alexander Leighton is a social psychiatrist, a scientist who studies diseases of the mind as they are reflected in the behaviour of society. From 1944 to 1945 he was a member of an American Military Intelligence research team that was to investigate Japanese morale and to find out what might be achieved by psychological warfare. After Japan's collapse he became a member of the United States Strategic Bombing Survey to evaluate the psychological effects on the Japanese of the bombers' work. The following essay is from *Human Relations in a Changing World* (1949), a book that resulted from his experiences in Japan.

I

WE APPROACHED Hiroshima a little after daybreak on a winter day, driving in a jeep below a leaden sky and in the face of a cold, wet wind. On either side of the road, black flat fields were turning green under winter wheat. Here and there peasants worked, swinging spades or grubbing in mud and water with blue hands. Some in black split-toed shoes left tracks like cloven hoofs. To the north, looming close over the level land, mountains thrust heavy summits of pine darkly against the overcast. To the south and far away, the bay lay in dull brightness under fitful rain.

"Hiroshima," said the driver, a GI from a Kansas farm, who had been through the city many times, "don't look no different from any other bombed town. You soon get used to it. You'll see little old mud walls right in the middle of town that wasn't knocked down. They been exaggerating about that bomb."

Within a few miles the fields along the road were replaced by houses and shops that looked worn and dull yet intact. On the road itself people straggled to work, some on bicycles, most of them on foot – tattered and bandy-legged old men, girls with red cheeks and bright eyes, ancient women under towering bundles, middle-aged men looking stiff in Western business suits. In one place there were several Koreans together, the women easily distinguished from the Japanese by their white blouses and the full skirts that swung as they strode. At a bus stop a crowd stood waiting in a line long enough to fill a train. Half a mile farther on we passed the bus, small, battered, and gray, standing half obliterated by the cloud of smoke that came from the charcoal burner at the back while the driver stood working at its machinery.

Children of all ages waved, laughed, and shouted at us as had the children in other parts of Japan.

"Haro-goodabye! Haro-goodabye!"

"Jeepu! Jeeeepu!"

Like the children of Hamelin to the piper, they came rushing, at the sound of our approach, from doorways and alleyways and from behind houses, to line up by the road and cheer. One little fellow of about six threw himself into the air, his little body twisting and feet kicking in a fit of glee.

The adults gazed at us with solemn eyes or looked straight ahead. They were more subdued than those I had seen elsewhere in Japan. The children seemed different, possessed by some common animation denied their elders – an animation which impelled them toward the occupation forces, toward the strong and the new.

Presently a two-story trade school appeared, with boards instead of window glass, and then a factory in the same condition. Soon there were shops and houses all along the way with windows missing. A house came into view with its roof pressed down, tiles scattered, and walls bulging outward. A shop with no front, like an open mouth, showed its contents, public and private, clear to the rear window.

The road turned to the Ota River, where the tide was running out and boats lay heaved over the beach. A bridge ended suddenly like a headless neck. Now every house and shop was damaged and lay with only one end or a corner standing.

Then all the buildings ceased and we came as if from a forest out on a plain, as if from tumult into silence. Imagine a city dump with its smells of wet ashes, mold, and things rotting, but one that runs from your feet almost to the limits of vision. As is often the case with level and desolate places on the earth, the sky seemed close above it. The predominant colours were red and yellow, crumbles of stone, bricks, red earth, and rust. Low walls made rectangles that marked where houses had stood, like sites of prehistoric villages. Here and there in the middle distance, a few large buildings stood about, buttes in the rubble of the plain.

"You see them?" said the driver, as if it were a triumph for his side. "The bomb didn't knock *them* down."

Running like ruler lines through the waste were black roads surprisingly dotted with people, some on foot and some in carts of all sizes drawn by man, woman, horse, or cow. Clothing was old and tattered and of every combination from full European to full Japanese. People looked as if they had grabbed what they could from a rummage sale.

Occasionally, blending like protective coloration with the rubble were shacks built out of fragments of boards and iron. Around them were vegetable gardens, for the most part full of *daikon,* Japanese radish. A few more pretentious sheds were going up, shining bright yellow with new boards.

We slowed down to go around a piece of cornice that lay partly across the road like a glacial boulder, and from somewhere in a band of children who cheered and called to us came the gift of a tangerine that landed on the floor of the jeep. Wondering at them, I picked it up and put it in my pocket.

When crossing a bridge, we could see down through the swiftly running water to the stones and shells on the bottom. This clearness gave a feeling of odd contrast to the disorder of the land. We passed a number of trees burned black but still holding up some leafless branches as if in perpetual winter.

The drive ended at a large building that was still standing, a former bank, now a police headquarters, where I had an appointment with the chief to arrange for office space and guides. The driver said, as he got out. "This is it."

II

One hears it said that, after all, Japanese cities were really a collection of tinderboxes, while American urban centers are made of stronger stuff. In Hiroshima there were many buildings of types common in the United States and some, prepared against earthquakes, far stronger. The engineers of the U.S. Strategic Bombing Survey concluded from their examination that "the overwhelming bulk of buildings in American cities would not stand up against an atomic bomb bursting at a mile or a mile and a half from them." To this must be added the realization that the bomb dropped at Hiroshima will be considered primitive by future standards.

The bank building which housed the police headquarters was a well-made structure of stone, three stories high. Through an imposing entrance my interpreter and I went past tall and solid metal doors that were bent inward like cardboard and no longer usable. The lobby was large and high, but dark because it had no window glass and the openings were boarded to keep out the wind. Through poor light there loomed the white face of a clock up on one wall, its hands pointing to 8:10—the time it had stopped on August 6.

In the years when that clock had been going, Hiroshima

had been a city, at first unknown to Europe and America, then a source of immigrants to the United States, and finally an enemy port. It lay on a delta between the seven mouths of the Ota and was traversed by canals and an ancient highway that connected Kyoto in the east with Shimonoseki in the west. Close around the city stood mountains covered with red pine, while before it stretched the bay, indented with headlands and spread with islands, in places narrow and steep like a fjord. In shallows near the shore, rows of poles stool as if in a bean patch, set in the sea to anchor oysters and to catch edible seaweed passing in the tide. In deeper water, fishing boats with hawkish prows and planked with red pine were tending nets. A few fishermen used cormorants to make their catch.

Hiroshima had expanses of park, residences, gardens, orange and persimmon trees. Since there had been much traveling back and forth by relatives of immigrants to California, the influence of the United States was marked. On main streets there were movies and restaurants with façades that would have fitted into shopping districts of Bakersfield or San Diego.

But Hiroshima was also ancient. Its feudal castle raised a five-story keep that could be seen a long distance over the level land of the delta. There were three large temples and many smaller ones and the tombs of the Asano family and of the wife and son of the leader of the Forty-seven Ronin, Oishi-Yoshio. There were also Christian churches, whose bells mingled with the temple gongs and the honking of auto horns and the rattling of trolleys.

The people of the city had earned their living by buying and selling farm produce and fish, by making mountain pines into boats for the fishing fleet of the Inland Sea, by meat packing, rubber processing, and oil refining, by making textiles from the cocoons of wild silkworms, by brewing rice and grape wine, by manufacturing paper umbrellas, needles, *tabi* socks, small arms, metal castings, and by working in utilities and services such as electricity, transportation, schools, and hospitals.

During the war there was an increase of industrialization, and plants grew up, chiefly in the outskirts.

There was a famous gay district with little streets along which a person walking in the night could hear laughter, the twang of the *shamisen,* and geishas singing.

The university had been an active cultural center but also stressed athletics, particularly swimming. There were sometimes mass aquatic exercises when hundreds of students would swim for miles, strung out in the bay in a long line with boats attending.

Although not a fortified town, Hiroshima was a major military command station, supply depot, and staging area because of its protected position and because of Ujina Harbor with access to the Pacific, the Sea of Japan, and the East China Sea. More than a third of the city's land was taken up with military installations, and from the harbor troopships left for Korea, Manchuria, China, and the southern regions. However, toward the end of hostilities, most of the shipping had ceased because of sinkings in the Inland Sea.

The population of Hiroshima was given as well over 300,000 before the war, but this was reduced by evacuation, before the atomic bomb fell, probably to about 245,000. It is still not certain how many the bomb killed, but the best estimate is from 70,000 to 80,000.

III

About seven o'clock on the morning of August 6 there was an air-raid warning and three planes were reported in the vicinity. No one was much disturbed. For a long time B-29's flying over in small numbers had been a common sight. At some future date, Hiroshima might suffer an incendiary raid from masses of planes such as had devastated other Japanese cities. With this possibility in mind there had been evacuations, and firebreaks were being prepared. But on this particular morning there could be no disaster from just three planes.

By 7:30 the "all clear" had sounded and people were thinking again of the day's plans, looking forward to their affairs and engagements of the morning and afternoon. The castle keep stood in the sun. Children bathed in the river. Farmers labored in the fields and fishermen on the water. City stores and factories got under way with their businesses.

In the heart of the city near the buildings of the Prefectural Government and at the intersection of the busiest streets, everybody had stopped and stood in a crowd gazing up at three parachutes floating down through the blue air.

The bomb exploded several hundred feet above their heads.

The people for miles around Hiroshima, in the fields, in the mountains, and on the bay, saw a light that was brilliant even in the sun, and felt heat. A countrywoman was going out to her farm when suddenly, "I saw a light reflected on the mountain and then a streak just like lightning came."

A town official was crossing a bridge on his bicycle about ten miles from the heart of the city when he felt the right side of his face seared, and thinking that he had sunstroke, he jumped to the ground.

A woman who was washing dishes noticed that she felt "very warm on the side of my face next the wall. I looked out the window toward the city and saw something like a sun in bright color."

At a slower pace, after the flash, came the sound of the explosion, which some people have no recollection of hearing, while others described it as an earth-shaking roar, like thunder or a big wind. A black smoky mass, lit up with color, ascended into the sky and impressed beholders with its beauty. Red, gold, blue, orange, and many other shades mingled with the black.

Nearer to the city and at its edges, the explosion made a more direct and individual impact on people. Almost everyone thought that an ordinary bomb had landed very close to him, and only later realized the extent of the damage.

A man who was oiling the machinery in a factory saw the

lights go out and thought that something must be wrong with the electricity. "But when the roof started crumbling down, I was in a daze, wondering what was happening. Then I noticed my hands and feet were bleeding. I don't know how I hurt myself."

Another, who was putting points on needles, was knocked unconscious, and when he came to, found "all my surroundings burned to the ground and flames raging here and there. I ran home for my family without knowing I was burned around my head. When I arrived home, our house was devastated and destroyed by flames. I ran to the neighbors and inquired about my family and learned that they had all been taken to safety across the river."

An invalid who was drinking tea said, "The tin roof sidings came swirling into my room and everything was black. Rubble and glass and everything you can think of was blasted into my house."

Said a woman, "I was in the back of the house doing the washing. All of a sudden, the bomb exploded. My clothes were burned off and I received burns on my legs, arms, and back. The skin was just hanging loose. The first thing I did was run in the air-raid shelter and lie there exhausted. Then I thought of my baby in the house and ran back to it. The whole house was knocked down and was burning. My mother and father came crawling out of the debris, their faces and arms just black. I heard the baby crying, and crawled in and dug it out from under the burning embers. It was pretty badly burned. My mother carried it to the shelter."

In the heart of the city death prevailed and few were left to tell us about it. That part of the picture has to be reconstructed, as in archeology, from the remains.

The crowd that stood gazing upward at the parachutes went down withered and black, like a burned-out patch of weeds. Flames shot out of the castle keep. Trolleys bulging with passengers stopped, and all died at once, leaving burned figures still standing supporting each other and fingers fused to the straps. The military at their barracks and offices were wiped out. So too were factories full of workers, including students from schools, volunteers from neighboring towns working on the firebreaks, children scavenging for wood, the Mayor's staff, and the units for air-raid precaution, fire, welfare, and relief. The larger war industries, since they were on the fringe of the city, were for the most part not seriously damaged. Most of the personnel in the Prefectural Government offices were killed, though the Governor himself happened to be in Tokyo. In hospitals and clinics, patients, doctors, and nurses all died together, as did the priests and pastors of the temples and the churches. Of 1,780 nurses, 1,654 were killed, and 90 per cent of the doctors in Hiroshima were casualties.

People who were in buildings that sheltered them from the instantaneous effects that accompanied the flash were moments later decapitated or cut to ribbons by flying glass. Others were crushed as walls and floors gave way even in buildings that maintained their outer shells erect. In the thousands of houses that fell, people were pinned below the wreckage, not killed in many cases, but held there till the fire that swept the city caught up with them and put an end to their screams.

A police chief said that he was in his back yard when the bomb went off. He was knocked down and a concrete wall fell over him, but he was able to dig himself out and go at once toward the police station in the bank. "When I arrived at the office, I found ten policemen, some severely wounded. These were evacuated to a place of safety where they could get aid. We tried to clean up the glass from the windows, but fire was spreading and a hot southerly wind was blowing. We used a hose with water from a hydrant and also formed a bucket brigade. At noon the water in the hydrants gave out, but in this building we were lucky because we could pump water from a well. We carried buckets up from the basement to the roof and threw water down over the building. People on the road were fainting from the heat and we threw water on them too and carried them into the one room in the building that had not been affected by the bomb. We applied oil and ointment to those who had burns.

"About 1:00 p.m. we began to apply first aid to the people outside, since the fire seemed under control as far as this building was concerned. A doctor came to help. He himself was wounded in one leg. By night this place was covered by a mass of people. One doctor applied all the first aid."

A doctor who was at a military hospital outside Hiroshima said that about an hour after the bomb went off, "many, many people came rushing to my clinic. They were rushing in all directions of the compass from the city. Many were stretcher cases. Some had their hair burned off, were injured in the back, had broken legs, arms, and thighs. The majority of the cases were those injured from glass; many had glass imbedded in the body. Next to the glass injuries, the most frequent were those who had their faces and hands burned, and also the chest and back. Most of the people arrived barefooted; many had their clothes burned off. Women were wearing men's clothing and men were wearing women's. They had put on anything they could pick up along the way.

"On the first day about 250 came, who were so injured they had to stay in the hospital, and we also attended about 500 others. Of all of these about 100 died."

A talkative man in a newspaper office said that the most severely burned people looked like red shrimps. Some had "skin which still burned sagging from the face and body with a reddish-white skin underneath showing."

A reporter who was outside the city at the time of the explosion, but came in immediately afterward, noticed among the dead a mother with a baby held tightly in her arms. He saw several women running around nude, red from burns, and without hair. Many people climbed into water tanks kept for putting out fires and there died. "The most pathetic cases were the small children looking for their parents. There was one child of about eleven with a four-year-old on his back, looking, looking for his mother in vain."

Shortly after the bomb fell, there was a high wind, or "fire storm" engendered by the heat, that tore up trees and, whirling over the river, made waterspouts. In some areas rain fell.

The severely burned woman who had been washing when the bomb fell said that she went down to the river, where "there were many people just dripping from their burns. Many of them were so badly burned that you could see the meat. By this time it was raining pretty badly. I could not walk or lie down or do anything. Water poured into the shelter and I received water blisters as well as blisters from the burns. It rained a lot right after the bomb."

Although the fire burned for days, the major destruction did not take very long. A fisherman out on the bay said, "I saw suddenly a flash of light. I thought something burned my face. I hid in the boat face down. When I looked up later. Hiroshima was completely burned."

IV

Hiroshima, of course, never had been prepared for a disaster of the magnitude which overtook it, but in addition the organized sources of aid that did exist were decimated along with everything else. As a result, rescue had to come from surrounding areas, and soon trucks and trains were picking up the wounded, while hospitals, schools, temples, assembly halls, and tents were preparing to receive them. However, the suburbs and surrounding areas were overwhelmed by the rush of immediate survivors out of the bombed region and so, for about a day, help did not penetrate far into the city. This, together with the fact that survivors who were physically uninjured were stunned and bewildered, resulted in great numbers of the wounded dying from lack of aid.

The vice-mayor of a neighboring town that began receiving the wounded about 11:30 in the morning said, "Everybody looked alike. The eyes appeared to be a mass of melted flesh. The lips were split up and also looked like a mass of molten flesh. Only the nose appeared the same as before. The death scene was awful. The patient would turn blue and when we touched the body the skin would stick to our hands."

Those who ventured into Hiroshima were greeted by sights they were reluctant to describe. A businessman reported: "The bodies of half-dead people lay on the roadside, on the bridges, in the water, in the gardens, and everywhere. It was a sight no one wants to see. Practically all of these people were nude. Their colour was brownish blackish and some of their bodies were dripping. There was a fellow whose head was half burned so that I thought he was wearing a hat." Another man said, "The bodies of the dead were so burned that we could not distinguish men from women."

In the public parks great numbers of both wounded and dead were congregated. There were cries for aid and cries for water and there were places where unidentifiable shapes merely stirred.

In the late afternoon, aid began to come farther into the city from the outer edges. Rice balls and other food were brought. From their mission up the valley a number of Jesuits came, and one of them, Father Siemes, gave a vivid and careful description of what he had seen, when he was later interviewed by members of the Bombing Survey in Tokyo. He said, "Beneath the wreckage of the houses along the way many had been trapped and they screamed to be rescued from the oncoming flames. They had to be left to their fate."

On a bridge, he encountered a procession of soldiers "dragging themselves along with the help of staves or carried by their less severely injured comrades. Abandoned on the bridge there stood with sunken heads a number of horses with large burns on their flanks.

"Fukai, the secretary of the mission, was completely out of his mind. He did not want to leave the house when the fires were burning closer, and explained that he did not want to survive the destruction of his fatherland." He had to be carried away by force.

After dark, the priests helped pull from the river two children who suffered chills and then died. There was a sand-spit in the river, covered with wounded, who cried for help and who were afraid that the rising tide would drown them. After midnight, "only occasionally did we hear calls for help."

Many patients were brought to an open field right behind Hiroshima station, and tents were set up for them. Doctors came in from the neighboring prefectures and from near-by towns such as Yamaguchi, Okayama, and Shimane. The Army also took part in relief measures, and all available military facilities and units were mobilized to that end.

A fisherman who came to Hiroshima to see what had happened said, "I cannot describe the situation in words, it was so pitiful. To see so many people dead was a terrible sight. Their clothes were shredded and their bodies puffed up, some with tongues hanging out. They were dead in all shapes."

As late as the second day the priests noted that among cadavers there were still many wounded alive. "Frightfully injured forms beckoned to us and then collapsed."

They carried some to the hospitals, but "we could not move everybody who lay exposed to the sun." It did not make much difference, anyway, for in the hospitals there was little that could be done. They just lay in the corridors, row on row, and died.

A businessman came into Hiroshima on the third day. "I went to my brother's house in the suburbs and found that all were wounded but none killed. They were stunned and could hardly speak. The next day, one of the four children died. She got black and blue in the face, just as if you had mashed your finger, and had died fifteen minutes after that.

In another half hour, her sister did the same thing and she died also."

The wife of a soldier who had been with the Hiroshima troops said, "My husband was a soldier and so he was to die, but when it actually happened, I wondered why we did not all go with him. They called me and I went to see. I was to find him in the heap, but I decided against looking at the bodies. I want to remember him as he was — big and healthy, not some horribly charred body. If I saw that, it would remain forever in my eyes."

A police chief told how the dead were collected and burned. "Many could not be identified. In cases where it was possible, the corpses or the ashes were given to the immediate family. Mostly, the cremation was done by the police or the soldiers, and the identified ashes were given to the family. The ashes of those not identified were turned over to the City Hall. There still are boxes in the City Hall. Occasionally even now one is identified, or is supposed to be identified, and is claimed."

The destroyed heart of Hiroshima consisted of 4.7 square miles, and the best estimates indicate that the mortality rate was 15,000 to the square mile. For many days funeral processions moved along the roads and through the towns and villages all around Hiroshima. The winds were pervaded by the smell of death and cremation. At night the skies were lit with the flames of funeral pyres.

V

Very few of the people we interviewed at Hiroshima attempted to make a play for sympathy or to make us feel guilty. The general manner was one which might be interpreted as due either to lingering apathy and absence of feeling consequent on shock, or to reserve which masked hate. It was probably a mixture of both, in varying degrees in different people. But on the surface everyone appeared willing to co-operate and oblige.

An official of a near-by small town thought that "if America had such a weapon, there was no use to go on. Many high school students in Hiroshima who were wounded in the raid spoke incoherently on their deathbeds, saying, 'Please avenge that raid for us somehow.' However, most of the people felt that since it was war, it was just *shikata ga nai,* could not be helped. But we were unified in the idea that we had to win the war."

A newspaper reporter said that after the bomb fell, some felt that this was the end, while others wanted to go on regardless. "Those who had actually experienced the bomb were the ones who wanted to quit, while those who had not, wanted to go on."

The wife of a soldier killed in the blast said, "Though many are resentful against America, I feel no animosity. It was an understood war and the use of weapons was fair. I only wonder why they didn't let the people know about this bomb and give us a chance, before bombing us, to give up."

A police chief believed that the general reaction among the people was one of surprise and a feeling that "we have taken the worst beating, we have been the goats." He said, "They felt that America had done a terrible thing and were very bitter, but after the surrender they turned on the Japanese military. They felt they had been fooled, and wondered if the military knew that the bomb was coming and why they did not take steps. The bomb made no difference in the fighting spirit of the people: it drew them together and made them more co-operative. My eldest son was killed, but I felt that it was destiny that ruled. When I see people who got away without any injury, I feel a little pang of envy naturally, but I don't feel bitter toward them."

Poking in the ruins one day, I came on the stone figure of a dog, one of that grinning type derived from China which commonly guards the entrances to temples. It was tilted on its pedestal but undamaged, and the grin gleamed out as if it were hailing me. Its rakish air and its look of fiendish satisfaction with all that lay around drew me on to inspect it more closely. It was then apparent that the look was not directed at me, but out somewhere beyond. It was, of course, only a piece of stone, and it displayed no particular artistic merit; yet in looking at it I felt that I was a clod, while it had a higher, sentient wisdom locked up within.

The look and the feeling it inspired were familiar and I groped to remember where I had seen it before other than on temple dogs. The eyes were creased in a fashion that did not exactly connotate mirth, and the lips were drawn far back in a smile that seemed to blend bitterness, glee, and compassion. The word "sardonic" came to mind, and this led to recognition and a realization of terrible appropriateness.

All who have acquaintance with the dead know the curious smile that may creep over the human face as *rigor mortis* sets in, a smile of special quality called by doctors *risus sardonicus*. The dog had this look, and it seemed to me probable that some ancient Oriental sculptor, in seeking an expression for temple guardians that would drive off evil spirits, had taken this death grin as his model, and thus it had come down through hundreds of years to this beast looking out on Hiroshima.

Many a soldier has seen this face looking up at him from the field of battle, before he himself was wearing it, and many a priest and doctor has found himself alone with it in a darkened room. As with the dog, at first the look seems at you, and then beyond you, as if there lay at last behind it knowledge of the huge joke of life which the rest of us feel vaguely but cannot comprehend. And there is that tinge of compassion that is as dreadful as it is unknowable.

As I continued to study this stone face, it began to appear that the grin was not directed at the waste and the destruction around, at the red and yellow and the smells, any more than it was at me. It was not so much a face looking at Hiroshima as it was the face of Hiroshima. The carved eyes gazed beyond the rubble, beyond the gardens of radishes and fields of winter wheat, beyond the toiling adults and the rippling children with their tangerines and shouts of "Haro-goodabye!" surging up with new life like flowers and weeds spreading over devastation, beyond the mountains with red pines in the blue sky, beyond all these, over the whole broad shoulder of the world to where, in cities and towns, watches on wrists and clocks on towers still ticked and moved. The face seemed to be smiling and waiting for the harvest of the wind that had been sown.

There was one woman in Hiroshima who said, "If there are such things as ghosts, why don't they haunt the Americans?"

Perhaps they do.

QUESTIONS

1. (a) Without actually pleading a cause directly, the author of this essay is trying to persuade us to make certain judgments. What are they?
   (b) In what way is his purpose like Orwell's in "Marrakech"?

2. Assign a descriptive title to each of the five sections of the essay, so that your five titles together will suggest how the essay is organized.

3. Explain why the Kansas GI's sceptical comments make an effective lead-in to the main part of the essay.

4. Why does Leighton devote most of section II to describing Hiroshima as it was before the bomb?

5. Understatement or restraint is a technique by which a writer may arouse an emotion in his reader while denying it to his style. He concentrates on unvarnished statement, letting the facts speak for themselves. Or, if he uses an image, it may even seem callous, as with this one on page 28: "The crowd . . . went down withered and black, like a burned-out patch of weeds." By referring to sections III and IV show that Leighton uses understatement in developing an atmosphere of increasing horror.

6. The essay draws to a concluding focus on the stone dog. What does this statue symbolize?

7. (a) Compare Leighton's use of narrative, exposition, and description with Orwell's use of these elements in "Marrakech".
(b) Compare the use of restraint or understatement in the two essays.
(c) Compare Leighton's use of the leering stone dog in this essay with Orwell's use of the great white birds in "Marrakech".

8. The author deals with the profoundly disturbing subject-matter of this essay in a cool, detached style with no obvious display of his own personality. Still, the kind of man he is does appear. What are your impressions of him? Explain.

ERNEST HEMINGWAY

1898-1961

The killers ✤ ✤ ✤

Only seven characters appear in this story, but they embody a whole society in which killers move about their business unhindered. The story is one of several in which Nick Adams, the adolescent in "The Killers", progresses from a state of innocence to a state of maturity in which he reconciles himself to the evil in the world by a deeper understanding of himself. The other Nick Adams stories are included in *The Short Stories of Ernest Hemingway* (1955). It is his novels that mainly account for Hemingway's fame and for his being awarded the 1954 Nobel Prize for literature. Of these the best known are *The Sun Also Rises* (1926), *A Farewell to Arms* (1929), *For Whom the Bell Tolls* (1940), and *The Old Man and the Sea* (1952). But Hemingway first made his mark on modern literature with two publications of short pieces written while he was living with other expatriate Americans in Paris, *Three Stories and Ten Poems* (1923) and *In Our Time* (1924). Many of the stories in these two collections dealt with the First World War, in which Hemingway had served on the Italian front as an ambulance driver; and all of the stories treated the themes of violence and death. Perhaps the severity of his own wounds suffered during the war, and the witness of so much suffering, made themes other than man's grapple with death seem trivial. More than the themes themselves it was the spare, vigorous style that made critics like Edmund Wilson sit up and take notice. In the first review of Hemingway ever printed, Wilson noted of *In Our Time:* "... behind the cool, objective manner, it constitutes a harrowing record of the barbarities of the period in which we live." In "The Killers", from *Men Without Women* (1927), this cool, objective manner has so pruned away comment and description that the story reads almost like a play.

THE DOOR of Henry's lunchroom opened and two men came in. They sat down at the counter.

"What's yours?" George asked them.

"I don't know," one of the men said. "What do you want to eat, Al?"

"I don't know," said Al. "I don't know what I want to eat."

Outside it was getting dark. The street-light came on outside the window. The two men at the counter read the menu. From the other end of the counter Nick Adams watched them. He had been talking to George when they came in.

"I'll have a roast pork tenderloin with apple sauce and mashed potatoes," the first man said.

"It isn't ready yet."

"What the hell do you put it on the card for?"

"That's the dinner," George explained. "You can get that at six o'clock."

George looked at the clock on the wall behind the counter.

"It's five o'clock."

"The clock says twenty minutes past five," the second man said.

"It's twenty minutes fast."

"Oh, to hell with the clock," the first man said. "What have you got to eat?"

"I can give you any kind of sandwiches," George said. "You can have ham and eggs, bacon and eggs, liver and bacon, or steak."

"Give me chicken croquettes with green peas and cream sauce and mashed potatoes."

"That's the dinner."

"Everything we want's the dinner, eh? That's the way you work it."

"I can give you ham and eggs, bacon and eggs, liver –"

"I'll take ham and eggs," the man called Al said. He wore a derby hat and a black overcoat buttoned across the chest. His face was small and white and he had tight lips. He wore a silk muffler and gloves.

"Give me bacon and eggs," said the other man. He was about the same size as Al. Their faces were different, but they were dressed like twins. Both wore overcoats too tight for them. They sat leaning forward, their elbows on the counter.

"Got anything to drink?" Al asked.

"Silver beer, bevo, ginger-ale," George said.

"I mean you got anything to *drink*?"

"Just those I said."

"This is a hot town," said the other. "What do they call it?"

"Summit."

"Ever hear of it?" Al asked his friend.

"No," said the friend.

"What do you do here nights?" Al asked.

"They eat the dinner," his friend said. "They all come here and eat the big dinner."

"That's right," George said.

"So you think that's right?" Al asked George.

"Sure."

"You're a pretty bright boy, aren't you?"

"Sure," said George.

"Well, you're not," said the other little man. "Is he, Al?"

"He's dumb," said Al. He turned to Nick. "What's your name?"

"Adams."

"Another bright boy," Al said. "Ain't he a bright boy, Max?"

"The town's full of bright boys," Max said.

George put the two platters, one of ham and eggs, the other of bacon and eggs, on the counter. He set down two side-dishes of fried potatoes and closed the wicket into the kitchen.

"Which is yours?" he asked Al.

"Don't you remember?"

"Ham and eggs."

"Just a bright boy," Max said. He leaned forward and took the ham and eggs. Both men ate with their gloves on. George watched them eat.

"What are you looking at?" Max looked at George.

"Nothing."

"The hell you were. You were looking at me."

"Maybe the boy meant it for a joke, Max," Al said.

George laughed.

"*You* don't have to laugh," Max said to him. "*You* don't have to laugh at all, see?"

"All right," said George.

"So he thinks it's all right." Max turned to Al. "He thinks it's all right. That's a good one."

"Oh, he's a thinker," Al said. They went on eating.

"What's the bright boy's name down the counter?" Al asked Max.

"Hey, bright boy," Max said to Nick. "You go around on the other side of the counter with your boy friend."

"What's the idea?" Nick asked.

"There isn't any idea."

"You better go around, bright boy," Al said. Nick went around behind the counter.

"What's the idea?" George asked.

"None of your damn business," Al said. "Who's out in the kitchen?"

"The nigger."

"What do you mean the nigger?"

"The nigger that cooks."

"Tell him to come in."

"What's the idea?"

"Tell him to come in."

"Where do you think you are?"

"We know damn well where we are," the man called Max said. "Do we look silly?"

"You talk silly," Al said to him. "What the hell do you argue with this kid for? Listen," he said to George, "tell the nigger to come out here."

"What are you going to do to him?"

"Nothing. Use your head, bright boy. What would we do to a nigger?"

George opened the slit that opened back into the kitchen. "Sam," he called. "Come in here a minute."

The door to the kitchen opened and the nigger came in. "What was it?" he asked. The two men at the counter took a look at him.

"All right, nigger. You stand right there," Al said.

Sam, the nigger, standing in his apron, looked at the two men sitting at the counter. "Yes, sir," he said. Al got down from his stool.

"I'm going back to the kitchen with the nigger and bright boy," he said. "Go on back to the kitchen, nigger. You go with him, bright boy." The little man walked after Nick and Sam, the cook, back into the kitchen. The door shut after them. The man called Max sat at the counter opposite George. He didn't look at George but looked in the mirror that ran along back of the counter. Henry's had been made over from a saloon into a lunch-counter.

"Well, bright boy," Max said, looking into the mirror, "why don't you say something?"

"What's it all about?"

"Hey, Al," Max called, "bright boy wants to know what it's all about."

"Why don't you tell him?" Al's voice came from the kitchen.

"What do you think it's all about?"

"I don't know."

"What do you think?"

Max looked into the mirror all the time he was talking.

"I wouldn't say."

"Hey, Al, bright boy says he wouldn't say what he thinks it's all about."

"I can hear you, all right," Al said from the kitchen. He had propped open the slit that dishes passed through into the kitchen with a catsup bottle. "Listen, bright boy," he said from the kitchen to George. "Stand a little further along the bar. You move a little to the left, Max." He was like a photographer arranging for a group picture.

"Talk to me, bright boy," Max said. "What do you think's going to happen?"

George did not say anything.

"I'll tell you," Max said. "We're going to kill a Swede. Do you know a big Swede named Ole Andreson?"

"Yes."

"He comes here to eat every night, don't he?"

"Sometimes he comes here."

"He comes here at six o'clock, don't he?"

"If he comes."

"We know all that, bright boy," Max said. "Talk about something else. Ever go to the movies?"

"Once in a while."

"You ought to go to the movies more. The movies are fine for a bright boy like you."

"What are you going to kill Ole Andreson for? What did he ever do to you?"

"He never had a chance to do anything to us. He never even seen us."

"And he's only going to see us once," Al said from the kitchen.

"What are you going to kill him for, then?" George asked.

"We're killing him for a friend. Just to oblige a friend, bright boy."

"Shut up," said Al from the kitchen. "You talk too goddam much."

"Well, I got to keep bright boy amused. Don't I, bright boy?"

"You talk too damn much," Al said. "The nigger and my bright boy are amused by themselves. I got them tied up like a couple of girl friends in the convent."

"I suppose you were in a convent."

"You never know."

"You were in a kosher convent. That's where you were."

George looked up at the clock.

"If anybody comes in you tell them the cook is off, and

if they keep after it, you tell them you'll go back and cook yourself. Do you get that, bright boy?"

"All right," George said. "What you going to do with us afterward?"

"That'll depend," Max said. "That's one of those things you never know at the time."

George looked up at the clock. It was a quarter past six. The door from the street opened. A street-car motorman came in.

"Hello, George," he said. "Can I get supper?"

"Sam's gone out," George said. "He'll be back in about half an hour."

"I'd better go up the street," the motorman said.

George looked at the clock. It was twenty minutes past six.

"That was nice, bright boy," Max said. "You're a regular little gentleman."

"He knew I'd blow his head off," Al said from the kitchen.

"No," said Max. "It ain't that. Bright boy is nice. He's a nice boy. I like him."

At six-fifty-five George said: "He's not coming."

Two other people had been in the lunch-room. Once George had gone out to the kitchen and made a ham-and-egg sandwich "to go" that a man wanted to take with him. Inside the kitchen he saw Al, his derby hat tipped back, sitting on a stool beside the wicket with the muzzle of a sawed-off shotgun resting on the ledge. Nick and the cook were back to back in the corner, a towel tied in each of their mouths. George had cooked the sandwich, wrapped it up in oiled paper, put it in a bag, brought it in, and the man had paid for it and gone out.

"Bright boy can do everything," Max said. "He can cook and everything. You'd make some girl a nice wife, bright boy."

"Yes?" George said. "Your friend, Ole Andreson, isn't going to come."

"We'll give him ten minutes," Max said.

Max watched the mirror and the clock. The hands of the

clock marked seven o'clock, and then five minutes past seven.

"Come on, Al," said Max. "We better go. He's not coming."

"Better give him five minutes," Al said from the kitchen.

In the five minutes a man came in, and George explained that the cook was sick.

"Why the hell don't you get another cook?" the man asked. "Aren't you running a lunch counter?" He went out.

"Come on, Al," Max said.

"What about the two bright boys and the nigger?"

"They're all right."

"You think so?"

"Sure. We're through with it."

"I don't like it," said Al. "It's sloppy. You talk too much."

"Oh, what the hell," said Max. "We got to keep amused, haven't we?"

"You talk too much, all the same," Al said. He came out from the kitchen. The cut-off barrels of the shotgun made a slight bulge under the waist of his too tight-fitting overcoat. He straightened his coat with his gloved hands.

"So long, bright boy," he said to George. "You got a lot of luck."

"That's the truth," Max said. "You ought to play the races, bright boy."

The two of them went out the door. George watched them, through the window, pass under the arc-light and cross the street. In their tight overcoats and derby hats they looked like a vaudeville team. George went back through the swing-ing-door into the kitchen and untied Nick and the cook.

"I don't want any more of that," said Sam, the cook. "I don't want any more of that."

Nick stood up. He had never had a towel in his mouth before.

"Say," he said. "What the hell?" He was trying to swagger it off.

"They were going to kill Ole Andreson," George said. "They were going to shoot him when he came in to eat."

"Ole Andreson?"

"Sure."

The cook felt the corners of his mouth with his thumbs.

"They all gone?" he asked.

"Yeah," said George. "They're gone now."

"I don't like it," said the cook. "I don't like any of it at all."

"Listen," George said to Nick. "You better go see Ole Andreson."

"All right."

"You better not have anything to do with it at all," Sam, the cook, said. "You better stay way out of it."

"Don't go if you don't want to," George said.

"Mixing up in this ain't going to get you anywhere," the cook said. "You stay out of it."

"I'll go see him," Nick said to George. "Where does he live?"

The cook turned away.

"Little boys always know what they want to do," he said.

"He lives up at Hirsch's rooming-house," George said to Nick.

"I'll go up there."

Outside the arc-light shone through the bare branches of a tree. Nick walked up the street beside the car-tracks and turned at the next arc-light down a side-street. Three houses up the street was Hirsch's rooming-house. Nick walked up the two steps and pushed the bell. A woman came to the door.

"Is Ole Andreson here?"

"Do you want to see him?"

"Yes, if he's in."

Nick followed the woman up a flight of stairs and back to the end of a corridor. She knocked on the door.

"Who is it?"

"It's somebody to see you, Mr. Andreson," the woman said.

"It's Nick Adams."

"Come in."

Nick opened the door and went into the room. Ole Andreson was lying on the bed with all his clothes on. He had been a heavy-weight prizefighter and he was too long for the bed. He lay with his head on two pillows. He did not look at Nick.

"What was it?" he asked.

"I was up at Henry's," Nick said, "and two fellows came in and tied up me and the cook, and they said they were going to kill you."

It sounded silly when he said it. Ole Andreson said nothing.

"They put us out in the kitchen," Nick went on. "They were going to shoot you when you came in to supper."

Ole Andreson looked at the wall and did not say anything.

"George thought I better come and tell you about it."

"There isn't anything I can do about it," Ole Andreson said.

"I'll tell you what they were like."

"I don't want to know what they were like," Ole Andreson said. He looked at the wall. "Thanks for coming to tell me about it."

"That's all right."

Nick looked at the big man lying on the bed.

"Don't you want me to go and see the police?"

"No," Ole Andreson said. "That wouldn't do any good."

"Isn't there something I could do?"

"No. There ain't anything to do."

"Maybe it was just a bluff."

"No. It ain't just a bluff."

Ole Andreson rolled over toward the wall.

"The only thing is," he said, talking toward the wall, "I just can't make up my mind to go out. I been in here all day."

"Couldn't you get out of town?"

"No," Ole Andreson said. "I'm through with all that running around."

He looked at the wall.

"There ain't anything to do now."

"Couldn't you fix it up some way?"

"No. I got in wrong." He talked in the same flat voice.

"There ain't anything to do. After a while I'll make up my mind to go out."

"I better go back and see George," Nick said.

"So long," said Ole Andreson. He did not look toward Nick. "Thanks for coming around."

Nick went out. As he shut the door he saw Ole Andreson with all his clothes on, lying on the bed looking at the wall.

"He's been in his room all day," the landlady said downstairs. "I guess he don't feel well. I said to him: 'Mr. Andreson, you ought to go out and take a walk on a nice fall day like this,' but he didn't feel like it."

"He doesn't want to go out."

"I'm sorry he don't feel well," the woman said. "He's an awfully nice man. He was in the ring, you know."

"I know it."

"You'd never know it except from the way his face is," the woman said. They stood talking just inside the street door. "He's just as gentle."

"Well, good night, Mrs. Hirsch," Nick said.

"I'm not Mrs. Hirsch," the woman said. "She owns the place. I just look after it for her. I'm Mrs. Bell."

"Well, good night, Mrs. Bell," Nick said.

"Good night," the woman said.

Nick walked up the dark street to the corner under the arc-light, and then along the car-tracks to Henry's eating-house. George was inside, back of the counter.

"Did you see Ole?"

"Yes," said Nick. "He's in his room and he won't go out."

The cook opened the door from the kitchen when he heard Nick's voice.

"I don't even listen to it," he said and shut the door.

"Did you tell him about it?" George asked.

"Sure I told him but he knows what it's all about."

"What's he going to do?"

"Nothing."

"They'll kill him."

"I guess they will."

"He must have got mixed up in something in Chicago."

"I guess so," said Nick.

"It's a hell of a thing."

"It's an awful thing," Nick said.

They did not say anything. George reached down for a towel and wiped the counter.

"I wonder what he did?" Nick said.

"Double-crossed somebody. That's what they kill them for."

"I'm going to get out of this town," Nick said.

"Yes," said George. "That's a good thing to do."

"I can't stand to think about him waiting in the room and knowing he's going to get it. It's too damned awful."

"Well," said George, "you better not think about it."

QUESTIONS

1. Hemingway has strongly influenced modern fiction with the kind of restraint and persistent understatement that marks "The Killers". Of this style of writing Hemingway has said, "If the writer of prose knows enough about what he is writing about, he may omit things that he knows, and the reader, if the writer is writing truly enough, will have a feeling of those things as strongly as though the writer had stated them." In the light of this statement by Hemingway, discuss either the scene in the lunchroom with the two killers, or the scene in Andreson's bedroom.

2. The story advances by four stages. Identify these stages.

3. The killers are described in some detail, the other three men in the lunchroom not at all. What is a possible reason for this visual focus?

4. (a) Hemingway emphasizes the size of the killers and the size of Ole Andreson. Why?
   (b) What is the significance of the killers being like twins in dress and size?
   (c) Hemingway does differentiate between the killers in their degree of inhumanity. How does he show this difference? Why is it important in the story?

5. One of the few similes in the story is filtered through the mind of George as he watches the departing killers pass under a street light: "In their tight coats and derby hats they looked like a vaudeville team." How else in the story is their comic aspect suggested? What purpose might Hemingway have in giving them this touch of absurdity?

6. How do the reactions of the three men differ in the incident after the killers have left, and in the final incident?

7. Nick says, "I'm going to get out of this town." Does his experience in the story represent a defeat or a victory for him in his development toward manhood? Justify your view.

8. Hemingway excludes any author's comment on the significance of the events that he relates; yet he has led the reader to make certain judgments. What are your conclusions regarding the society that is suggested by this story?

HUGH GARNER

b. 1913

One, two, three little Indians ✣ ✣ ✣

Like Orwell in his essay "Marrakech", Hugh Garner in this story comments on the fate of a dark-skinned people. And though he uses the more indirect techniques of fiction to make his comment, his writing carries a similar tone of restrained bitterness. This time, however, the bitterness is closer to us in time and place. The scene is not pre-war Africa but post-war Canada. In the midst of our continuing French-English squabbles "One, Two, Three Little Indians" reminds us of those other human beings who have suffered a deep wrong from both our "founding races". Hugh Garner is a free-lance Canadian writer whose experience has taken him into a great variety of places and jobs. During the 1930's he was, among other things, a harvest hand, a hobo, and a door-to-door salesman. In 1936 and 1937 his first writings appeared in *The Canadian Forum*. In 1937, like George Orwell, he fought for the Loyalist cause in the Spanish Civil War. After the Second World War, during which he served in the Royal Canadian Navy, he turned his wide experience to account in writing once more, and since then has published several novels: *Storm Below* (1944), *Cabbagetown* (1951), *Present Reckoning* (1951), *Waste No Tears* (1951), and *The Silence on the Shore* (1962). His other creative output includes several television plays and many essays, articles, and stories.

AFTER THEY HAD EATEN, Big Tom pushed the cracked and dirty supper things to the back of the table and took the baby from its high chair, carefully, so as not to spill the flotsam of bread crumbs and boiled potatoes from the chair to the floor.

He undressed the youngster, talking to it in the old dialect, trying to awaken its interest. All evening it had been listless and fretful by turns, but now it seemed to be soothed by the story of Po-chee-ah and the Lynx, although it was too young to understand him as his voice slid awkwardly through the ageless folktale of his people.

For long minutes after the baby was asleep he talked on, letting the victorious words fill the small cabin so that they shut out the sounds of the Northern Ontario night; the buzz of mosquitoes, the far-off bark of a dog, the noise of the cars and transport trucks passing on the gravelled road.

The melodious hum of his voice was like a strong soporific, lulling him with the return of half-forgotten memories, strengthening him with the knowledge that once his people had been strong and brave, men with a nation of their own, encompassing a million miles of teeming forest, lake, and tamarack swamp.

When he halted his monologue to place the baby in the big brass bed in the corner, the sudden silence was loud in his ears, and he cringed a bit as the present suddenly caught up with the past.

He covered the baby with a corner of the church-donated patchwork quilt, and lit the kerosene lamp that stood on the mirrorless dressing table beside the stove. Taking a broom from the corner he swept the mealtime debris across the door-sill.

This done, he stood and watched the headlights of the cars run along the trees bordering the road, like a small boy's stick along a picket fence. From the direction of the trailer camp a hundred yards away came the sound of a car engine being gunned, and the halting note-tumbles of a clarinet from a tourist's radio. The soft summer smell of spruce needles and wood smoke blended with the evening dampness of the earth and felt good in his nostrils, so that he filled his worn lungs until he began to cough. He spat the resinous phlegm into the weed-filled yard.

It had been this summer smell, and the feeling of freedom

it gave, that had brought him back to the woods after three years in the mines during the war. But only a part of him had come back, for the mining towns and the big money had done more than etch his lungs with silica. They had also brought him pain and distrust, and a wife who had learned to live in imitation of the gaudy boomtown life.

When his coughing attack subsided he peered along the path, hoping to catch a glimpse of his wife Mary returning from her work at the trailer camp. He was becoming worried about the baby, and her presence, while it might not make the baby well, would mean there was someone else to share his fears. He could see nothing but the still blackness of the trees and their shadows interwoven in a sombre pattern across the mottled ground.

He re-entered the cabin and began washing the dishes, stopping once or twice to cover the moving form of the sleeping baby. He wondered if he could have transmitted his own wasting sickness to the lungs of his son. He stood for long minutes at the side of the bed, staring, trying to diagnose the child's restlessness into something other than what he feared.

His wife came in and placed some things on the table. He picked up a can of pork-and-beans she had bought and weighed it in the palm of his hand. "The baby seems pretty sick," he said.

She crossed the room and looked at the sleeping child. "I guess it's his teeth."

He placed the pork-and-beans on the table and walked over to his chair beside the empty stove. As he sat down he noticed for the first time that his wife was beginning to show her pregnancy. Her squat form had sunk lower so that it almost filled the shapeless dress she wore. Her brown ankles were puffed above the broken-down heels of the dirty silver dancing pumps she was wearing.

"Is the trailer camp full?" he asked.

"Nearly. Two more Americans came about half an hour ago."

"Was Billy Woodhen around?"

"I didn't see him – only Elsie," she answered. "A woman promised me a dress tomorrow if I scrub out her trailer."

"Yeah?" He saw the happiness rise over her like a colour when she mentioned this. She was much younger than he was – twenty-two years against his thirty-nine – and her dark face had a fullness that is common to many Indian women. She was no longer pretty, and as he watched her he thought that wherever they went the squalor of their existence seemed to follow.

"It's a silk dress," Mary said, as though the repeated mention of it brought it nearer.

"A silk dress is no damn good around here. You should get some overalls," he said, angered by her lack of shame in accepting the cast-off garments of the trailer women.

She seemed not to notice his anger. "It'll do for the dances next winter."

"A lot of dancing you'll do," he said, pointing to her swollen body. "You'd better learn to stay around and take care of the kid."

She busied herself over the stove, lighting it with newspapers and kindling. "I'm going to have some fun. You should have married a grandmother."

He filled the kettle with water from an open pail near the door. The baby began to cough, and the mother turned it to its side in the bed. "As soon as I draw my money from Cooper I'm going to get him some cough syrup from the store," she said.

"It won't do any good. We should take him up to the doctor in town tomorrow."

"I can't. I've got to stay here and work."

He knew the folly of trying to reason with her. She had her heart set on earning the silk dress the woman had promised.

After they had drunk their tea he blew out the light. They took off some of their clothes and climbed over the baby into the bed. Long after his wife had fallen asleep he lay in the darkness listening to a ground moth beating its futile wings against the glass of the window.

They were awakened in the morning by the twittering of a small colony of tree sparrows who were feeding on the kitchen sweepings of the night before. Mary got up and went outside, returning a few minutes later carrying a handful of birch and poplar stovewood.

He waited until the beans were in the pan before rising and pulling on his pants. He stood in the doorway scratching his head and absorbing the sunlight through his bare feet upon the step.

The baby awoke while they were eating their breakfast.

"He don't look good," Big Tom said as he dripped some brown gravy sauce from his plate with a hunk of bread.

"He'll be all right later," his wife insisted. She poured some crusted tinned milk from the can into a cup and mixed it with water from the kettle.

Big Tom splashed his hands and face with cold water and dried himself on a shirt that lay over the back of a chair. "When you going to the camp – this morning?"

"This afternoon," Mary answered.

"I'll be back by then."

He took up a small pile of woven baskets from a corner and hung the handles over his arm. From the warming shelf of the stove he pulled a bedraggled band of cloth into which a large goose feather had been sewn. Carrying this in his hand, he went outside and strode down the path towards the highway.

He ignored the chattering sauciness of a squirrel that hurtled up the green ladder of a tree beside him. Above the small noises of the woods could be heard the roar of a transport truck braking its way down the hill from the burnt-out sapling-covered ridge to the north. The truck passed him as he reached the road, and he waved a desultory greeting to the driver, who answered him with a short blare of the horn.

Placing the baskets in a pile on the shoulder of the road, he adjusted the corduroy band on his head, so that the feather stuck up at the rear. He knew that by doing so he became part of the local colour, "a real Indian with a feather'n everything", and also that it helped him sell his baskets. In the time he had been living along the highway he had learned to give them what they expected.

The trailer residents were not yet awake, so he sat down on the wooden walk leading to the shower room, his baskets resting on the ground in a half-circle behind him.

After a few minutes a small boy descended from the door of a trailer and stood staring at him. Then he pushed his head back inside and spoke, pointing in Big Tom's direction. In a moment a man's hand parted the heavy curtains on the window and a bed-mussed unshaven face stared out. The small boy climbed back inside.

A little later two women approached on the duckboard walk, one attired in a pair of buttock-pinching brown slacks, and the other wearing a blue chenille dressing gown. They circled him warily and entered the shower room. From inside came the buzz of whispered conversation and the louder noises of running water.

During the morning several people approached and stared at Big Tom and the baskets. He sold two small ones to an elderly woman. She seemed surprised when she asked him what tribe he belonged to, and he did not answer in a monosyllable but said, "I belong to the Algonquins, ma'am." He got rid of one of the big forty-five cent baskets to the mother of the small boy who had been the first one up earlier in the day.

A man took a series of photographs of him with an expensive-looking camera, pacing off the distance and being very careful in setting his lens opening and shutter speeds.

"I wish he'd look into the camera," the man said loudly to a couple standing nearby, as though he were talking of an animal in a cage.

"You can't get any good picshus around here. Harold tried to get one of the five Dionney kids, but they wouldn't let him. The way they keep them quints hid you'd think they was made of china or somep'n," the woman said. She glanced at her companion for confirmation.

"They want you to buy their picshus," the man said. "We

was disappointed in 'em. They used to look cute before, when they was small, but now they're just five plain-looking kids."

"Yeah. My Gawd, you'd never believe how homely they got, would you Harold? An' everything's pure robbery in Callander. You know, old man Dionney's minting money up there. Runs his own sooveneer stand."

After lunch Big Tom watched Cooper prepare for his trip to North Bay. "Is there anybody going fishing, Mr. Cooper?" he asked.

The man took the radiator cap off the old truck and peered inside.

"Mr. Cooper!"

"Hey?" Cooper turned and looked at the Indian standing there, hands in pockets, his manner shy and deferential. He seemed to feel a vague irritation, as though sensing the overtone of servility in the Indian's attitude.

"Anybody going fishing?" Big Tom asked again.

"Seems to me Mr. Staynor said he'd like to go," Cooper answered. His voice was kind, with the amused kindness of a man talking to a child.

The big Indian remained standing where he was, saying nothing. His old second-hand army trousers drooped around his lean loins, and his plaid shirt was open at the throat, showing a grey high-water mark of dirt where his face washings began and ended.

"What's the matter?" Cooper asked. "You seem pretty anxious to go today."

"My kid's sick. I want to make enough to take him to the doctor."

Cooper walked around the truck and opened one of the doors, rattling the handle in his hand as if it were stuck. "You should stay home with it. Make it some pine-sap syrup. No need to worry. It's as healthy as a bear cub."

Mrs. Cooper came out of the house and eased her bulk into the truck cab. "Where's Mary?" she asked.

"Up at the shack," Big Tom answered.

"Tell her to scrub the washrooms before she does anything else. Mrs. Anderson, in that trailer over there, wants her to do her floors." She pointed across the lot to a large blue-and-white trailer parked behind a Buick.

"I'll tell her," he answered.

The Coopers drove between the whitewashed stones marking the entrance to the camp, and swung up the highway, leaving behind them a small cloud of dust from the pulverized gravel of the road.

Big Tom fetched Mary and the baby from the shack. He gave her Mrs. Cooper's instructions, and she transferred the baby from her arms to his. The child was feverish, its breath noisy and fast.

"Keep him warm," she said. "He's been worse since we got up. I think he's got a touch of the flu."

Big Tom placed his hand inside the old blanket and felt the baby's cheek. It was dry and burning to his palm.

He adjusted the baby's small weight in his arms and walked across the camp and down the narrow path to the lakeside where the boats were moored.

A man sitting in the stern sheets of a new-painted skiff looked up and smiled at his approach. "You coming out with me, Tom?" he asked.

The Indian nodded.

"Are you bringing the papoose along?"

Big Tom winced at the word papoose, but he answered, "He won't bother us. The wife is working this afternoon."

"Okay. I thought maybe we'd go over to the other side of the lake today and try to get some of them big fellows at the creek mouth. Like to try?"

"Sure," the Indian answered. He placed the baby along the wide seat in the stern and unshipped the oars.

He rowed silently for the best part of an hour, the sun beating through his shirt and causing the sweat to trickle coldly down his back. At times his efforts at the oars caused a constriction in his chest, and he coughed and spat into the water.

When they reached the mouth of the creek across the lake he let the oars drag and leaned over to look at the baby. It was sleeping restlessly, its lips slightly blue, and its breath laboured and harsh. Mr. Staynor was busy with his lines and tackle in the bow of the boat.

Tom picked the child up and felt its little body for sweat. The baby's skin was bone dry. He picked up the baling can from the boat bottom and dipped it over the side. With the tips of his fingers he brushed some of the cold water across the baby's forehead. The child woke up, looked around at the strange surroundings, and smiled up at the man. He gave it a drink of water from the can. Feeling reassured now, he placed the baby on the seat and went forward to help the fisherman with his gear.

Mr. Staynor fished for half an hour or so, catching some small fish and a large black bass, which writhed in the bottom of the boat. Big Tom watched its gills gasping its death throes, and he noted the similarity between the struggles of the fish and those of the baby lying on the seat in the blanket.

He became frightened again after a time and he turned to the man in the bow and said, "We'll have to go pretty soon. I'm afraid my kid's pretty sick."

"Eh! We've hardly started," the man answered. "Don't worry, there's not much wrong with the papoose."

Big Tom lifted the child from the seat and cradled it in his arms. He opened the blanket, and shading the baby's face, allowed the warm sun to shine on its chest. If I could only get him to sweat, he thought, everything would be all right then.

He waited as long as he dared, noting the blueness creeping over the baby's lips, before he placed the child again on the seat and addressed the man in the bow. "I'm going back now. You'd better pull in your line."

The man turned and felt his way along the boat. He stood over the Indian and parted the folds of the blanket, looking at the baby. "My God, he is sick, Tom! You'd better get him to a doctor right away!" He stepped across the writhing fish to the bow and began pulling in the line. Then he busied himself with his tackle, stealing glances now and again at the Indian and the baby.

Big Tom turned the boat around and with long straight pulls on the oars headed back across the lake. The fisherman took the child in his arms and blew cooling drafts of air against its fevered face.

As soon as they reached the jetty below the tourist camp Tom tied the boat's painter to a stump, and took the child from the other man.

Mr. Staynor handed him the fee for a full afternoon's work. "I'm sorry the youngster is sick, Tom," he said. "Don't play around. Get him up to the doctor in town right away. We'll try her again tomorrow afternoon."

Big Tom thanked him. Carrying the baby and unmindful of the grasping hands of the undergrowth he climbed the path through the trees. On reaching the parked cars and trailers he headed in the direction of the large blue-and-white one where his wife would be working.

When he knocked, the door opened and a woman said, "Yes?" He recognized her as the one who had been standing by in the morning while his picture was being taken.

"Is my wife here?" he asked.

"Your wife? Oh, I know who you mean. No, she's gone. She went down the road in a car a few minutes ago."

The camp was almost empty, most of the tourists having gone to the small bathing beach farther down the lake. A car full of bathers was pulling away to go down to the beach. Big Tom hurried over and held up his hand until it stopped. "Could you drive me to the doctor?" he asked. "My baby seems pretty sick."

There was a turning of heads within the car. A woman began talking in the back seat. The driver said, "I'll see what I can do, Chief, after I take the girls to the beach."

Big Tom sat down at the side of the driveway to wait. After a precious half hour had gone by, and they did not return, he got to his feet and started up the highway in the direction of town.

His long legs pounded on the loose gravel of the road, his anger and terror giving strength to his stride. He noticed that the passengers in the few cars he met were pointing at him and laughing, and suddenly he realized that he was still wearing the feather in the band around his head. He reached up, pulled it off, and threw it in the ditch.

When a car or truck came up from behind him he would step off the road and raise his hand to beg for a ride. After the first ones passed without pausing he stopped his useless, time-wasting gesture and strode straight ahead, impervious to the noise of their horns as they approached.

Now and again he placed his hand on the baby's face as he walked, reassuring himself that it was still alive. It was hours since it had cried or shown any other signs of consciousness.

Once, he stepped off the road at a small bridge over a stream, and making a crude cup with his hands, tried to get the baby to drink. He succeeded only in making it cough, harshly, so that its tiny face became livid with its efforts to breathe.

It was impossible that the baby should die. Babies did not die like this in their father's arms on a highway that ran fifteen miles north to a small town with a doctor and all the life-saving devices to prevent their death . . .

The sun fell low behind the trees and the swarms of black flies and mosquitoes began their nightly forage. He waved his hand above the fevered face of the baby, keeping them off, at the same time trying to waft a little air into the child's tortured lungs.

Suddenly, with feelings as black as hell itself, he knew that the baby was dying. He had seen too much of it not to know, now, that the child was in an advanced state of pneumonia. He stumbled along, his eyes devouring the darkening face of his son, while the hot tears ran from the corners of his eyes.

With nightfall he knew it was too late. He looked up into

the sky, where the first stars were being drawn in silver on a burnished copper plate, and he cursed them, and cursed what made them possible.

To the north-west the clouds were piling up in preparation for a summer storm. Reluctantly he turned and headed back down the road in the direction he had come.

It was almost midnight before he felt his way along the path through the trees to the shack. It was hard to see anything in the teeming rain, and the water ran from his shoulders in a steady stream, unheeded, soaking the sodden bundle he still carried in his arms.

Reaching the shanty he opened the door and fell inside. He placed the body of his son on the bed in the corner. Then, groping along the newspaper-lined walls, he found some matches in his mackinaw and lit the lamp. With a glance around the room he realized that his wife had not yet returned, so he placed the lamp on the table under the window and headed out again into the rain.

At the trailer camp he sat down on the rail fence near the entrance to wait. Some light shone from the small windows of the trailers and from Cooper's house across the road. The illuminated sign said: COOPER'S TRAILER CAMP — Hot and Cold Running Water, Rest Rooms. FISHING AND BOATING — INDIAN GUIDES.

One by one, as he waited, the lights went out, until only the sign lit up a small area at the gate.

He saw the car's headlights first, about a hundred yards down the road. When it pulled to a stop he heard some giggling, and Mary and another Indian girl, Elsie Woodhen, staggered out into the rain.

A man's voice shouted through the car door, "See you again, sweetheart. Don't forget next Saturday night." The voice belonged to one of the French-Canadians who worked at a creosote camp across the lake.

Another male voice shouted, "Wahoo!"

The girls clung to each other, laughing drunkenly, as the car pulled away.

They were not aware of Big Tom's approach until he grasped his wife by the hair and pulled her backwards to the ground. Elsie Woodhen screamed and ran away in the direction of the Cooper house. Big Tom bent down as if he was going to strike at Mary's face with his fist. Then he changed his mind and let her go.

She stared into his eyes and saw what was there. Crawling to her feet and sobbing hysterically she limped along towards the shack, leaving one of her silver shoes in the mud.

Big Tom followed behind, all the anguish and frustration drained from him so that there was nothing left to carry him into another day. Heedless now of the coughing which tore his chest apart, he pushed along in the rain, hurrying to join his wife in the vigil over their dead.

QUESTIONS

1. Explain the irony in the title.

2. (a) What judgments about Canadian society does this story invite you to make?
   (b) Compare your response to this story with your response to "Marrakech". Which method of artistic expression seems to offer a better chance of arousing the reader's pity and anger — the essay or the story? Explain your view.

3. By the time you have finished reading the story you have a pretty detailed sketch of Tom's character. What are his main qualities?

4. The opening division of the story details the domestic life of Tom and Mary. Show that in this brief section Garner
   (a) characterizes Tom and Mary,
   (b) reveals their relationship,
   (c) sets the tone for the story.

5. Of what significance to the story is the moth described on p. 55 as "beating its futile wings against the glass of the window"?

6. Several incidents show Tom in the presence of white people. Describe one such incident, explaining what qualities of character are contrasted in it.

7. Mr. Staynor is not quite like the other white people. In what way is he different? What is his importance in developing the theme?

8. The following passage occurs on p. 62: "Babies did not die like this in their father's arms on a highway that ran fifteen miles north to a small town with a doctor and all the life-saving devices to prevent their death . . ."

(a) Is this Tom's thought, or is it the author's comment? Or is it a combination of the two? Justify your opinion.

(b) In what way is this technique of narration different from Hemingway's technique in "The Killers"?

9. (a) What incident forms the climax of the story?

(b) Refer to preceding incidents to show that Garner has prepared his reader for this climax.

10. Referring to incidents throughout the story show that Garner has repeatedly emphasized the degradation endured by Tom.

11. Compare Garner's technique of revealing character in this story with that of Hemingway in "The Killers".

12. Compare "The Rockpile" and "One, Two, Three Little Indians", considering

(a) the statement about life that is implied,

(b) the use of pathos,

(c) the importance of "local colour" (the details that make the reader aware of a specific place and period of history).

JAMES BALDWIN

b. 1924

The rockpile ✦ ✦ ✦

One of the most powerful and independent of contemporary American fiction writers, James Baldwin, a Negro born and bred in the slums of Harlem, has learned to look with blazing irony into the heart of the white man's darkness, into the sham and cruelty and corruption of a world the Negro never made. But Baldwin, at his best, is an artist whose imagination breaks through all racial and local limits into a vision of life of which the stuff is neither white nor black but deeply human. Here is a story of Harlem, the black ghetto at the northern end of Manhattan island where New York's Negroes (and, more recently, its Puerto Rican immigrants) crowd together in ugly tenements and sub-standard houses. The rockpile, a challenge and a temptation to the young ones, mysteriously represents awesome forces which beckon to them but which they cannot understand. The rockpile "could not be taken away because without it the subway cars underground would fly apart, killing all the people". Perhaps Baldwin is suggesting that the rockpile is like Harlem, an excrescence indeed, yet necessary to the predatory life of New York, a symbol of the city without which the city could not know itself and would not be. This is a story of a "redeemed" family. Note the references to the prayer meeting, the "Reverend", "Sister" McCandless. We learn that the mother, Elizabeth, had been "saved" after a life of sin and the birth of one illegitimate child, John. And it is John, the outsider, the stranger, the illegitimate, who stands in need of protection from the "insider", the father of the "redeemed" family. Note how subtly Baldwin suggests that the mother is, in the eyes of the father, two persons – the woman of sin *and* the helpmeet given by the Lord. The child John forever remains the outsider, "his dark head near the toe of his father's boot". The story is about the need of even the despised to despise.

The Rockpile stands as a symbol of this mysterious need and of the awful, inescapable, universal presence of human guilt. Mr. Baldwin's most notable novels have been *Go Tell It on the Mountain* (1953), *Giovanni's Room* (1956), *Another Country* (1962).

ACROSS THE STREET from their house, in an empty lot between two houses, stood the rockpile. It was a strange place to find a mass of natural rock jutting out of the ground; and someone, probably Aunt Florence, had once told them that the rock was there and could not be taken away because without it the subway cars underground would fly apart, killing all the people. This, touching on some natural mystery concerning the surface and the center of the earth, was far too intriguing an explanation to be challenged, and it invested the rockpile, moreover, with such mysterious importance that Roy felt it to be his right, not to say his duty, to play there.

Other boys were to be seen there each afternoon after school and all day Saturday and Sunday. They fought on the rockpile. Sure footed, dangerous, and reckless, they rushed each other and grappled on the heights, sometimes disappearing down the other side in a confusion of dust and screams and upended, flying feet. "It's a wonder they don't kill themselves," their mother said, watching sometimes from the fire escape. "You children stay away from there, you hear me?" Though she said "children", she was looking at Roy, where he sat beside John on the fire escape. "The good Lord knows," she continued, "I don't want you to come home bleeding like a hog every day the Lord sends." Roy shifted impatiently, and continued to stare at the street, as though in this gazing he might somehow acquire wings. John said nothing. He had not really been spoken to; he was afraid of the rockpile and of the boys who played there.

Each Saturday morning John and Roy sat on the fire escape and watched the forbidden street below. Sometimes their mother sat in the room behind them, sewing, or dressing their younger sister, or nursing the baby, Paul. The sun fell across them and across the fire escape with a high, benevolent indifference; below them men and women, and boys and girls, sinners all, loitered; sometimes one of the church-members passed and saw them and waved. Then, for the moment that they waved decorously back, they were intimidated. They watched the saint, man or woman, until he or she had disappeared from sight. The passage of one of the redeemed made them consider, however vacantly, the wickedness of the street, their own latent wickedness in sitting where they sat; and made them think of their father, who came home early on Saturdays and who would soon be turning the corner and entering the dark hall below them.

But until he came to end their freedom, they sat, watching and longing above the street. At the end of the street nearest their house was the bridge which spanned the Harlem River and led to a city called the Bronx; which was where Aunt Florence lived. Nevertheless, when they saw her coming, she did not come from the bridge, but from the opposite end of the street. This, weakly, to their minds, she explained by saying that she had taken the subway, not wishing to walk, and that, besides, she did not live in that section of the Bronx. Knowing that the Bronx was across the river, they did not believe this story ever, but, adopting toward her their father's attitude, assumed that she had just left some sinful place which she dared not name, as, for example, a movie palace.

In the summertime boys swam in the river, diving off the wooden dock, or wading in from the garbage-heavy bank. Once a boy, whose name was Richard, drowned in the river. His mother had not known where he was; she had even come to their house, to ask if he was there. Then, in the evening, at six o'clock, they had heard from the street a woman screaming and wailing; and they ran to the windows and looked out. Down the street came the woman, Richard's mother, screaming, her face raised to the sky and tears running down her face. A woman walked beside her, trying to make her quiet and trying to hold her up. Behind them walked a man, Richard's father, with Richard's body in his arms. There were two white policemen walking in the gutter, who did not seem to know what should be done. Richard's father and Richard were wet, and Richard's body lay across his father's arms like a cotton baby. The woman's screaming filled all the street; cars slowed down and the people in the cars stared; people opened their windows and looked out and came rushing out of doors to stand in the gutter, watching. Then the small procession disappeared within the house which stood beside the rockpile. Then, "Lord, Lord, Lord!" cried Elizabeth, their mother, and slammed the window down.

One Saturday, an hour before his father would be coming home, Roy was wounded on the rockpile and brought screaming upstairs. He and John had been sitting on the fire escape and their mother had gone into the kitchen to sip tea with Sister McCandless. By and by Roy became bored and sat beside John in restless silence; and John began drawing into his schoolbook a newspaper advertisement which featured a new electric locomotive. Some friends of Roy passed beneath the fire escape and called him. Roy began to fidget, yelling down to them through the bars. Then a silence fell. John looked up. Roy stood looking at him.

"I'm going downstairs," he said.

"You better stay where you is, boy. You know Mama don't want you going downstairs."

"I be right back. She won't even know I'm gone, less you run and tell her."

"I ain't got to tell her. What's going to stop her from coming in here and looking out the window?"

"She's talking," Roy said. He started into the house.

"But Daddy's going to be home soon!"

"I be back before that. What you all the time got to be so scared for?" He was already in the house and he now turned, leaning on the windowsill, to swear impatiently, "I be back in five minutes."

John watched him sourly as he carefully unlocked the door and disappeared. In a moment he saw him on the sidewalk with his friends. He did not dare to go and tell his mother that Roy had left the fire escape because he had practically promised not to. He started to shout, "Remember, you said five minutes!" but one of Roy's friends was looking up at the fire escape. John looked down at his schoolbook; he became engrossed again in the problem of the locomotive.

When he looked up again he did not know how much time had passed, but now there was a gang fight on the rockpile. Dozens of boys fought each other in the harsh sun, clambering up the rocks and battling hand to hand, scuffed shoes sliding on the slippery rock; filling the bright air with curses and jubilant cries. They filled the air, too, with flying weapons: stones, sticks, tin cans, garbage, whatever could be picked up and thrown. John watched in a kind of absent amazement – until he remembered that Roy was still downstairs, and that he was one of the boys on the rockpile. Then he was afraid; he could not see his brother among the figures in the sun; and he stood up, leaning over the fire-escape railing. Then Roy appeared from the other side of the rocks; John saw that his shirt was torn; he was laughing. He moved until he stood at the very top of the rockpile. Then something, an empty tin can, flew out of the air and hit him on the forehead, just above the eye. Immediately, one side of Roy's face ran with blood, he fell and rolled on his face down the rocks. Then for a moment there was no movement at all, no sound; the sun, arrested, lay on the street and the sidewalk and the arrested boys. Then someone screamed or shouted; boys began to run away, down the street, toward the bridge. The figure on the ground, having caught its breath and felt its own blood, began to shout. John cried, "Mama! Mama!" and ran inside.

"Don't fret, don't fret," panted Sister McCandless as they

rushed down the dark, narrow, swaying stairs, "don't fret. Ain't a boy been born don't get his knocks every now and again. Lord!" they hurried into the sun. A man had picked Roy up and now walked slowly toward them. One or two boys sat silent on their stoops; at either end of the street there was a group of boys watching. "He ain't hurt bad," the man said. "Wouldn't be making this kind of noise if he was hurt real bad."

Elizabeth, trembling, reached out to take Roy, but Sister McCandless, bigger, calmer, took him from the man and threw him over her shoulder as she once might have handled a sack of cotton. "God bless you," she said to the man, "God bless you, son." Roy was still screaming. Elizabeth stood behind Sister McCandless to stare at his bloody face.

"It's just a flesh wound," the man kept saying, "just broke the skin, that's all." They were moving across the sidewalk, toward the house. John, not now afraid of the staring boys, looked toward the corner to see if his father was yet in sight.

Upstairs, they hushed Roy's crying. They bathed the blood away, to find, just above the left eyebrow, the jagged, superficial scar. "Lord, have mercy," murmured Elizabeth, "another inch and it would've been his eye." And she looked with apprehension toward the clock. "Ain't it the truth," said Sister McCandless, busy with bandages and iodine.

"When did he go downstairs?" his mother asked at last.

Sister McCandless now sat fanning herself in the easy chair, at the head of the sofa where Roy lay, bound and silent. She paused for a moment to look sharply at John. John stood near the window, holding the newspaper advertisement and the drawing he had done.

"We was sitting on the fire escape," he said. "Some boys he knew called him."

"When?"

"He said he'd be back in five minutes."

"Why didn't you tell me he was downstairs?"

He looked at his hands, clasping his notebook, and did not answer.

"Boy," said Sister McCandless, "you hear your mother a-talking to you?"

He looked at his mother. He repeated:

"He said he'd be back in five minutes."

"He said he'd be back in five minutes," said Sister McCandless with scorn, "don't look to me like that's no right answer. You's the man of the house, you supposed to look after your baby brothers and sisters – you ain't supposed to let them run off and get half-killed. But I expect," she added, rising from the chair, dropping the cardboard fan, "your Daddy'll make you tell the truth. Your Ma's way too soft with you."

He did not look at her, but at the fan where it lay in the dark red, depressed seat where she had been. The fan advertised a pomade for the hair and showed a brown woman and her baby, both with glistening hair, smiling happily at each other.

"Honey," said Sister McCandless, "I got to be moving along. Maybe I drop in later tonight. I don't reckon you going to be at Tarry Service tonight?"

Tarry Service was the prayer meeting held every Saturday night at church to strengthen believers and prepare the church for the coming of the Holy Ghost on Sunday.

"I don't reckon," said Elizabeth. She stood up; she and Sister McCandless kissed each other on the cheek. "But you be sure to remember me in your prayers."

"I surely will do that." She paused, with her hand on the door knob, and looked down at Roy and laughed. "Poor little man," she said, "reckon he'll be content to sit on the fire escape now."

Elizabeth laughed with her. "It sure ought to be a lesson to him. You don't reckon," she said nervously, still smiling, "he going to keep that scar, do you?"

"Lord, no," said Sister McCandless, "Ain't nothing but a scratch. I declare, Sister Grimes, you worse than a child.

Another couple of weeks and you won't be able to see no scar. No, you go on about your housework, honey, and thank the Lord it weren't no worse." She opened the door; they heard the sound of feet on the stairs. "I expect that's the Reverend," said Sister McCandless, placidly, "I bet he going to raise cain."

"Maybe it's Florence," Elizabeth said. "Sometimes she get here about this time." They stood in the doorway, staring, while the steps reached the landing below and began again climbing to their floor. "No," said Elizabeth then, "that ain't her walk. That's Gabriel."

"Well, I'll just go on," said Sister McCandless, "and kind of prepare his mind." She pressed Elizabeth's hand as she spoke and started into the hall, leaving the door behind her slightly ajar. Elizabeth turned slowly back into the room. Roy did not open his eyes, or move; but she knew that he was not sleeping; he wished to delay until the last possible moment any contact with his father. John put his newspaper and his notebook on the table and stood, leaning on the table, staring at her.

"It wasn't my fault," he said. "I couldn't stop him from going downstairs."

"No," she said, "you ain't got nothing to worry about. You just tell your Daddy the truth."

He looked directly at her, and she turned to the window, staring into the street. What was Sister McCandless saying? Then from her bedroom she heard Delilah's thin wail and she turned, frowning, looking toward the bedroom and toward the still open door. She knew that John was watching her. Delilah continued to wail; she thought, angrily, Now that girl's getting too big for that, but she feared that Delilah would awaken Paul and she hurried into the bedroom. She tried to soothe Delilah back to sleep. Then she heard the front door open and close — too loud. Delilah raised her voice, with an exasperated sigh Elizabeth picked the child up. Her child and Gabriel's, her children and Gabriel's: Roy, Delilah, Paul. Only John was nameless and a stranger, living, unalterable testimony to his mother's days in sin.

"What happened?" Gabriel demanded. He stood, enormous, in the center of the room, his black lunchbox dangling from his hand, staring at the sofa where Roy lay. John stood just before him, it seemed to her astonished vision just below him, beneath his fist, his heavy shoe. The child stared at the man in fascination and terror – when a girl down home she had seen rabbits stand so paralyzed before the barking dog. She hurried past Gabriel to the sofa, feeling the weight of Delilah in her arms like the weight of a shield, and stood over Roy, saying:

"Now, ain't a thing to get upset about, Gabriel. This boy sneaked downstairs while I had my back turned and got hisself hurt a little. He's alright now."

Roy, as though in confirmation, now opened his eyes and looked gravely at his father. Gabriel dropped his lunchbox with a clatter and knelt by the sofa.

"How do you feel, son? Tell your Daddy what happened."

Roy opened his mouth to speak and then, relapsing into panic, began to cry. His father held him by the shoulder.

"You don't want to cry. You's Daddy's little man. Tell your Daddy what happened."

"He went downstairs," said Elizabeth, "where he didn't have no business to be, and got to fighting with them bad boys playing on that rockpile. That's what happened and it's a mercy it weren't nothing worse."

He looked up at her. "Can't you let this boy answer me for hisself?"

Ignoring this, she went on, more gently: "He got cut on the forehead, but it ain't nothing to worry about."

"You call a doctor? How you know it ain't nothing to worry about?"

"Is you got money to be throwing away on doctors? No, I ain't called no doctor. Ain't nothing wrong with my eyes that I can't tell whether he's hurt bad or not. He got a fright more'n anything else, and you ought to pray God it teaches him a lesson."

"You got a lot to say now," he said, "but I'll have me something to say in a minute. I'll be wanting to know when all this happened, what you was doing with your eyes then." He turned back to Roy, who had lain quietly sobbing, eyes wide open and body held rigid; and who now, at his father's touch, remembered the height, the sharp, sliding rock beneath his feet, the sun, the explosion of the sun, his plunge into darkness and his salty blood; and recoiled, beginning to scream, as his father said, "Hold still. Don't cry. Daddy ain't going to hurt you, he just wants to see this bandage, see what they've done to his little man." But Roy continued to scream and would not be still and Gabriel dared not lift the bandage for fear of hurting him more. And he looked at Elizabeth in fury: "Can't you put that child down and help me with this boy? John, take your baby sister from your mother – don't look like neither of you got good sense."

John took Delilah and sat down with her in the easy chair. His mother bent over Roy, and held him still, while his father, carefully – but still Roy screamed – lifted the bandage and stared at the wound. Roy's sobs began to lessen. Gabriel readjusted the bandage. "You see," said Elizabeth, finally, "he ain't nowhere near dead."

"It sure ain't your fault that he ain't dead." He and Elizabeth considered each other for a moment in silence. "He came mighty close to losing an eye. Course, his eyes ain't as big as your'n, so I reckon you don't think it matters so much." At this her face hardened; he smiled. "Lord, have mercy," he said, "you think you ever going to learn to do right? Where was you when all this happened? Who let him go downstairs?"

"Ain't nobody let him go downstairs, he just went. He got a head just like his father, it got to be broken before it'll bow. I was in the kitchen."

"Where was Johnnie?"

"He was in here."

"Where?"

"He was on the fire escape."

"Didn't he know Roy was downstairs?"

"I reckon."

"What you mean, you reckon? He ain't got your big eyes for nothing, does he?" He looked over at John. "Boy, you see your brother go downstairs?"

"Gabriel, ain't no sense in trying to blame Johnnie. You know right well if you have trouble making Roy behave, he ain't going to listen to his brother. He don't hardly listen to me."

"How come you didn't tell your mother Roy was downstairs?"

John said nothing, staring at the blanket which covered Delilah.

"Boy, you hear me? You want me to take a strap to you?"

"No, you ain't," she said. "You ain't going to take no strap to this boy, not today you ain't. Ain't a soul to blame for Roy's lying up there now but you – you because you done spoiled him so that he thinks he can do just anything and get away with it. I'm here to tell you that ain't no way to raise no child. You don't pray to the Lord to help you do better than you been doing, you going to live to shed bitter tears that the Lord didn't take his soul today." And she was trembling. She moved, unseeing, toward John and took Delilah from his arms. She looked back at Gabriel, who had risen, who stood near the sofa, staring at her. And she found in his face not fury alone, which would not have surprised her; but hatred so deep as to become insupportable in its lack of personality. His eyes were struck alive, unmoving, blind with malevolence – she felt, like the pull of the earth at her feet, his longing to witness her perdition. Again as though it might be propitiation, she moved the child in her arms. And at this his eyes changed, he looked at Elizabeth, the mother of his children, the helpmeet given by the Lord. Then her eyes clouded; she moved to leave the room; her foot struck the lunchbox lying on the floor.

"John," she said, "pick up your father's lunchbox like a good boy."

She heard, behind her, his scrambling movement as he left the easy chair, the scrape and jangle of the lunchbox as he picked it up, bending his dark head near the toe of his father's heavy shoe.

QUESTIONS

1. Describe the neighbourhood in which the story is set.
2. Locate all the references to religion and religious attitudes and practices in the story.
3. Why is John, unlike the others, afraid of the rockpile?
4. What is the importance for the story of the drowning of Richard?
5. Distinguish between the parts played in the story by John and Roy, Gabriel and Elizabeth.
6. Explain the look of hatred on Gabriel's face as the mother moves towards John.
7. What is the significance of the last two sentences for the story as a whole?

ALAN PATON

b. 1903

Ha'penny ✥ ✥ ✥

A novelist with a deep feeling for the segregated black and coloured people of his native South Africa, Alan Paton has been an active crusader in the cause of racial equality and human dignity. While he continues to struggle politically against the racist policies of the South African government, his broad social concerns have never smothered his human and artistic sense of the plight of the individual. In this short story he enters the mind and heart of a homeless waif who lives pathetically in a world of his imagination and dies of the shame of the truth. "Ha'penny" is a moving realization of the impossible pain of loneliness and of the universal human craving for dignity and for love. And it stands, too, as a valid symbol of the agony and awfulness of being *set apart*. For this story, through the little boy, plumbs the agony of a race, of a whole people. Alan Paton's best known novel is *Cry the Beloved Country* (1948).

OF THE SIX HUNDRED BOYS at the reformatory, about one hundred were from ten to fourteen years of age. My Department had from time to time expressed the intention of taking them away, and of establishing a special institution for them, more like an industrial school than a reformatory. This would have been a good thing, for their offences were very trivial, and they would have been better by themselves. Had such a school been established, I should have liked to have been Principal of it myself, for it would have been an easier job; small boys turn instinctively towards affection, and one controls them by it, naturally and easily.

Some of them, if I came near them, either on parade or in

school or at football, would observe me watchfully, not directly or fully, but obliquely and secretly; sometimes I would surprise them at it, and make some small sign of recognition, which would satisfy them so that they would cease to observe me, and would give their full attention to the event of the moment. But I knew that my authority was thus confirmed and strengthened.

These secret relations with them were a source of continuous pleasure to me. Had they been my own children I would no doubt have given a greater expression to it. But often I would move through the silent and orderly parade, and stand by one of them. He would look straight in front of him with a little frown of concentration that expressed both childish awareness of and manly indifference to my nearness. Sometime I would tweak his ear, and he would give me a brief smile of acknowledgment, or frown with still greater concentration. It was natural I suppose to confine these outward expressions to the very smallest, but they were taken as symbolic, and some older boys would observe them and take themselves to be included. It was a relief, when the reformatory was passing through times of turbulence and trouble, and when there was danger of estrangement between authority and boys, to make these simple and natural gestures, which were reassurances both to me and them that nothing important had changed.

On Sunday afternoons when I was on duty, I would take my car to the reformatory and watch the free boys being signed out at the gate. This simple operation was also watched by many boys not free, who would tell each other "in so many weeks I'll be signed out myself." Amongst the watchers were always some of the small boys, and these I would take by turns in the car. We would go out to the Potchefstroom Road with its ceaseless stream of traffic, and to the Baragwanath crossroads, and come back by the Van Wyksrus Road to the reformatory. I would talk to them about their families, their parents, their sisters and brothers, and I would pretend to know nothing of Durban, Port Elizabeth,

Potchefstroom, and Clocolan, and ask them if these places were bigger than Johannesburg.

One of the small boys was Ha'penny, and he was about twelve years old. He came from Bloemfontein and was the biggest talker of them all. His mother worked in a white person's house, and he had two brothers and two sisters. His brothers were Richard and Dickie and his sisters Anna and Mina.

"Richard and Dickie?" I asked.

"Yes, *meneer*."

"In English," I said, "Richard and Dickie are the same name."

When we returned to the reformatory, I sent for Ha'penny's papers; there it was plainly set down, Ha'penny was a waif, with no relatives at all. He had been taken in from one home to another, but he was naughty and uncontrollable, and eventually had taken to pilfering at the market.

I then sent for the Letter Book, and found that Ha'penny wrote regularly, or rather that others wrote for him till he could write himself, to Mrs. Betty Maarman, of 48 Vlak Street, Bloemfontein. But Mrs. Maarman had never once replied to him. When questioned, he had said, perhaps she is sick. I sat down and wrote at once to the Social Welfare Officer at Bloemfontein, asking him to investigate.

The next time I had Ha'penny out in the car, I questioned him again about his family. And he told me the same as before, his mother, Richard and Dickie, Anna and Mina. But he softened the "D" of "Dickie", so that it sounded now like Tickie.

"I thought you said Dickie," I said.

"I said Tickie," he said.

He watched me with concealed apprehension, and I came to the conclusion that this waif of Bloemfontein was a clever boy, who had told me a story that was all imagination, and had changed one single letter of it to make it safe from any question. And I thought I understood it all too, that he was ashamed of being without a family, and had invented them all, so that no one might discover that he was fatherless and motherless, and that no one in the world cared whether he was alive or dead. This gave me a strong feeling for him, and I went out of my way to manifest towards him the fatherly care that the State, though not in those words, had enjoined upon me by giving me this job.

Then the letter came from the Social Welfare Officer in Bloemfontein, saying that Mrs. Betty Maarman of 48 Vlak Street was a real person, and that she had four children, Richard and Dickie, Anna and Mina, but that Ha'penny was no child of hers, and she knew him only as a derelict of the streets. She had never answered his letters, because he wrote to her as *mother,* and she was no mother of his, nor did she wish to play any such role. She was a decent woman, a faithful member of the church, and she had no thought of corrupting her family by letting them have anything to do with such a child.

But Ha'penny seemed to me anything but the usual delinquent, his desire to have a family was so strong, and his reformatory record was so blameless, and his anxiety to please and obey so great, that I began to feel a great duty towards him. Therefore I asked him about his "mother".

He could not speak enough of her, nor with too high praise. She was loving, honest, and strict. Her home was clean. She had affection for all her children. It was clear that the homeless child, even as he had attached himself to me, would have attached himself to her; he had observed her even as he had observed me, but did not know the secret of how to open her heart, so that she would take him in, and save him from the lonely life that he led.

"Why did you steal when you had such a mother?" I asked.

He could not answer that; not all his brains nor his courage could find an answer to such a question, for he knew that with such a mother he would not have stolen at all.

"The boy's name is Dickie," I said, "not Tickie."

And then he knew the deception was revealed. Another

boy might have said, "I told you it was Dickie," but he was too intelligent for that; he knew that if I had established that the boy's name was *Dickie,* I must have established other things too. I was shocked by the immediate and visible effect of my action. His whole brave assurance died within him, and he stood there exposed, not as a liar, but as a homeless child who had surrounded himself with mother, brothers, and sisters, who did not exist. I had shattered the very foundations of his pride, and his sense of human significance.

He fell sick at once, and the doctor said it was tuberculosis. I wrote at once to Mrs. Maarman, telling her the whole story, of how this small boy had observed her, and had decided that she was the person he desired for his mother. But she wrote back saying that she could take no responsibility for him. For one thing, Ha'penny was a Mosuto, and she was a coloured woman; for another, she had never had a child in trouble, and how could she take such a boy?

Tuberculosis is a strange thing; sometimes it manifests itself suddenly in the most unlikely host, and swiftly sweeps to the end. Ha'penny withdrew himself from the world, from all Principals and mothers, and the doctor said there was little hope. In desperation I sent money for Mrs. Maarman to come.

She was a decent homely woman, and seeing that the situation was serious, she, without fuss or embarrassment, adopted Ha'penny for her own. The whole reformatory accepted her as his mother. She sat the whole day with him, and talked to him of Richard and Dickie, Anna and Mina, and how they were all waiting for him to come home. She poured out her affection on him, and had no fear of his sickness, nor did she allow it to prevent her from satisfying his hunger to be owned. She talked to him of what they would do when he came back, and how he would go to the school, and what they would buy for Guy Fawkes night.

He in his turn gave his whole attention to her, and when I visited him he was grateful, but I had passed out of his world. I felt judged in that I had sensed only the existence and not the measure of his desire. I wished I had done something sooner, more wise, more prodigal.

We buried him on the reformatory farm, and Mrs. Maarman said to me, "When you put up the cross, put he was my son."

"I'm ashamed," she said, "that I wouldn't take him."

"The sickness," I said, "the sickness would have come."

"No," she said, shaking her head with certainty. "It wouldn't have come. And if it had come at home. it would have been different."

So she left for Bloemfontein, after her strange visit to a reformatory. And I was left too, with the resolve to be more prodigal in the task that the State, though not in so many words, had enjoined on me.

QUESTIONS

1. By what means does the author suggest the character and attitude of the narrator?

2. What impression is given of the boys themselves? What do you learn of them by their response to the narrator?

3. Why does Ha'penny change the name "Dickie" to "Tickie"?

4. Was the narrator's statement "The boy's name is Dickie" deliberate – or a slip?

5. Explain Mrs. Maarman's reluctance to accept Ha'penny.

6. Why does the narrator feel "judged"?

7. Do you find any relief from the pain of the story in the narrator's final resolution? With what kind of feeling does the story leave you?

PART TWO
THE OUTSIDERS

JAMES THURBER

1894-1961

The Macbeth murder mystery

During his lifetime, Thurber earned an international reputation as the American humourist who satirized in cartoon and story the perpetual battle of the sexes. He brought into the healthy arena of laughter the recurring American nightmare in which helpless man has the life drained from him by militant woman. In the story that follows we have a typical Thurber situation – a domineering female imposes her ideas on an ineffectual male. Under her influence, the narrator applies to Shakespeare the who-dunit reader's method of story analysis. Together they produce theories on *Macbeth* that put them outside even the lunatic fringe of literary criticism. Among Thurber's humorous books are *Is Sex Necessary?* in collaboration with E. B. White (1929), *My Life and Hard Times* (1933), *My World and Welcome to It* (1937), *The Male Animal,* a play in collaboration with Elliott Nugent (1940), and *Thurber Country* (1952).

"IT WAS A STUPID MISTAKE to make," said the American woman I had met at my hotel in the English lake country, "but it was on the counter with the other Penguin books – the little sixpenny ones, you know, with the paper covers – and I supposed of course it was a detective story. All the others were detective stories. I'd read all the others, so I bought this one without really looking at it carefully. You can imagine how mad I was when I found it was Shakespeare." I murmured something sympathetically. "I don't see why the Penguin-books people had to get out Shakespeare's plays in the same size and everything as the detective stories," went on my companion. "I think they have different-colored jackets," I said. "Well, I didn't notice that," she said. "Anyway, I got real comfy in bed that night and all ready to read a good mystery story and here I had 'The Tragedy of Macbeth' — a book for high-school students. Like 'Ivanhoe'." "Or 'Lorna Doone'." I said. "Exactly," said the American lady. "And I was just crazy for a good Agatha Christie, or something. Hercule Poirot is my favourite detective." "Is he the rabbity one?" I asked. "Oh, no," said my crime-fiction expert. "He's the Belgian one. You're thinking of Mr. Pinkerton, the one that helps Inspector Bull. He's good, too."

Over her second cup of tea my companion began to tell the plot of a detective story that had fooled her completely — it seems it was the old family doctor all the time. But I cut in on her. "Tell me," I said. "Did you read 'Macbeth'?" "I *had* to read it," she said. "There wasn't a scrap of anything else to read in the whole room." "Did you like it?" I asked. "No, I did not," she said, decisively. "In the first place, I don't think for a moment that Macbeth did it." I looked at her blankly. "Did what?" I asked. "I don't think for a moment that he killed the King," she said. "I don't think the Macbeth woman was mixed up in it, either. You suspect them the most, of course, but those are the ones that are never guilty — or shouldn't be, anyway." "I'm afraid," I began, "that I—" "But don't you see?" said the American lady. "It would spoil everything if you could figure out right away who did it. Shakespeare was too smart for that. I've read that people never *have* figured out 'Hamlet', so it isn't likely Shakespeare would have made 'Macbeth' as simple as it seems." I thought this over while I filled my pipe. "Who do you suspect?" I asked, suddenly. "Macduff," she said, promptly. "Good God!" I whispered, softly.

"Oh, Macduff did it, all right," said the murder specialist. "Hercule Poirot would have got him easily." "How did you figure it out?" I demanded. "Well," she said, "I didn't right away. At first I suspected Banquo. And then, of course, he was the second person killed. That was good right in there, that part. The person you suspect of the first murder should always be the second victim." "Is that so?" I murmured. "Oh, yes," said my informant. "They have to keep surprising you. Well, after the second murder I didn't know *who* the killer was for a while." "How about Malcolm and Donalbain, the King's sons?" I asked. "As I remember it, they fled right after the first murder. That looks suspicious." "Too suspicious," said the American lady. "Much too suspicious. When they flee, they're never guilty. You can count on that." "I believe," I said, "I'll have a brandy," and I summoned the waiter. My companion leaned toward me, her eyes bright, her teacup quivering. "Do you know who discovered Duncan's body?" she demanded. I said I was sorry, but I had forgotten. "Macduff discovers it," she said, slipping into the historical present. "Then he comes running downstairs and shouts, 'Confusion has broke open the Lord's anointed temple' and 'Sacrilegious murder has made his masterpiece' and on and on like that." The good lady tapped me on the knee. "All that stuff was *rehearsed,*" she said. "You wouldn't say a lot of stuff like that, offhand, would you – if you had found a body?" She fixed me with a glittering eye. "I –" I began. "You're right!" she said. "You wouldn't! Unless you had practised it in advance. 'My God, there's a body in here!' is what an innocent man would say." She sat back with a confident glare.

I thought for a while. "But what do you make of the Third Murderer?" I asked. "You know, the Third Murderer has puzzled 'Macbeth' scholars for three hundred years." "That's because they never thought of Macduff," said the American lady. "It was Macduff, I'm certain. You couldn't have one of the victims murdered by two ordinary thugs – the murderer always has to be somebody important." "But what about the banquet scene?" I asked, after a moment. "How do you account for Macbeth's guilty actions there, when Banquo's ghost came in and sat in his chair?" The lady leaned forward and tapped me on the knee again. "There wasn't any ghost," she said. "A big, strong man like that doesn't go around seeing ghosts – especially in a brightly lighted banquet hall with dozens of people around. Macbeth was *shielding somebody*!" "Who was he shielding?" I asked. "Mrs. Macbeth, of course," she said. "He thought she did it and he was going to take the rap himself. The husband always does that when the wife is suspected." "But what," I demanded, "about the sleepwalking scene, then?" "The same thing, only the other way around," said my companion. "That time *she* was shielding *him*. She wasn't asleep at all. Do you remember where it says, 'Enter Lady Macbeth with a taper'?" "Yes," I said. "Well, people who walk in their sleep *never carry lights*!" said my fellow-traveler. "They have a second sight. Did you ever hear of a sleepwalker carrying a light?" "No," I said, "I never did." "Well, then, she wasn't asleep. She was acting guilty to shield Macbeth." "I think," I said, "I'll have another brandy," and I called the waiter. When he brought it, I drank it rapidly and rose to go. "I believe," I said, "that you have got hold of something. Would you lend me that 'Macbeth'? I'd like to look it over tonight. I don't feel, somehow, as if I'd ever really read it." "I'll get it for you," she said. "But you'll find that I am right."

I read the play over carefully that night, and the next morning, after breakfast, I sought out the American woman. She was on the putting green, and I came up behind her silently and took her arm. She gave an exclamation. "Could I see you alone?" I asked, in a low voice. She nodded cautiously and followed me to a secluded spot. "You've found out something?" she breathed. "I've found out," I said, triumphantly, "the name of the murderer!" "You mean it wasn't Macduff?" she said. "Macduff is as innocent of those murders," I said, "as Macbeth and the Macbeth woman." I opened the copy of the play, which I had with me, and turned to Act II, Scene 2. "Here," I said, "you will see where Lady Macbeth says, 'I laid their daggers ready. He could not miss 'em. Had he not resembled my father as he slept, I had done it.' Do you see?" "No," said the American woman, bluntly, "I don't." "But it's simple!" I exclaimed. "I wonder I didn't see it years ago. The reason Duncan resembled Lady Macbeth's father as he slept is that *it actually was her father*!" "Good God!" breathed my companion, softly. "Lady Macbeth's father killed the King," I said, "and, hearing someone coming, thrust the body under the bed and crawled into the bed himself." "But," said the lady, "you can't have a murderer who only appears in the story once. You can't have that." "I know that," I said, and I turned to Act II, Scene 4. "It says here, 'Enter Ross with an old Man.' Now, that old man is never identified and it is my contention he was old Mr. Macbeth, whose ambition it was to make his daughter Queen. There you have your motive." "But even then," cried the American lady, "he's still a minor character!" "Not," I said, gleefully, "when you realize that he was also *one of the weird sisters in disguise!*" "You mean one of the three witches?" "Precisely," I said. "Listen to this speech of the old man's. 'On Tuesday last, a falcon towering in her pride of place, was by a mousing owl hawk'd at and kill'd.' Who does that sound like?" "It sounds like the way the three witches talk," said my companion, reluctantly. "Precisely!" I said again. "Well," said the American woman, "maybe you're right, but —" "I'm sure I am," I said. "And do you know what I'm going to do now?" "No," she said. "What?" "Buy a copy of 'Hamlet'," I said, "and solve *that*!" My companion's eyes brightened. "Then," she said, "you don't think Hamlet did it?" "I am," I said, "absolutely positive he didn't." "But who," she demanded, "do you suspect?" I looked at her cryptically. "Everybody," I said, and disappeared into a small grove of trees as silently as I had come.

QUESTIONS

1. Are the deductions of these two literary detectives completely wild, or is there a sort of insane consistency to them? If their theories have some consistency, what provides it?

2. At the beginning of the story how does Thurber establish the leader-follower relationship between the woman and the man?

3. The female of the story is identified only as "the American woman", never by a name. What might be Thurber's purpose in leaving her nameless?

4. What evidence in the story suggests that Thurber is poking fun not only at shallow, aggressive women, but also at over-refined literary critics of Shakespeare?

5. It is possible that the character narrating the story never really accepted the woman's theories, but merely led her further into absurdity as a way of asserting his superiority over her. What in the story leads you to accept or reject this possibility?

FRANK O'CONNOR

b. 1903

My Oedipus complex ✥ ✥ ✥

Frank O'Connor (the pen-name of Michael O'Donovon) is an Irish writer who has published plays, critical works, and poetry; but it is in the short story that he has been most prolific and has won the greatest acclaim. Among his collections of stories are *The Stories of Frank O'Connor* (1952), *More Stories by Frank O'Connor* (1954), and *Domestic Relations* (1957). For many years O'Connor has lived in the United States, but his fiction goes back to the turbulent Ireland of his childhood and adolescence. The account of this period in his autobiography, *An Only Child* (1961), makes it clear that the factual details were harsher than those depicted in "My Oedipus Complex"; still, Larry's jealous love for his mother and his furious rivalry with his father are very close to O'Connor's own pre-school conflicts. It is worth noticing how the narrator blends his amused, adult perspective with the perplexity and anguish of the little boy that he once was. The story thus has two points of view simultaneously. A good deal of the pleasure in reading "My Oedipus Complex" comes from witnessing events close up as Larry experiences them, and at the same time from the serene distance of the grown man's understanding.

FATHER WAS in the army all through the war — the first war, I mean — so, up to the age of five, I never saw much of him, and what I saw did not worry me. Sometimes I woke and there was a big figure in khaki peering down at me in the candlelight. Sometimes in the early morning I heard the slamming of the front door and the clatter of nailed boots down the cobbles of the lane. These were Father's entrances and exits. Like Santa Claus he came and went mysteriously.

In fact, I rather liked his visits, though it was an uncomfortable squeeze between Mother and him when I got into the big bed in the early morning. He smoked, which gave him a pleasant musty smell, and shaved, an operation of astounding interest. Each time he left a trail of souvenirs – model tanks and Gurkha knives with handles made of bullet cases, and German helmets and cap badges and button-sticks, and all sorts of military equipment – carefully stowed away in a long box on top of the wardrobe, in case they ever came in handy. There was a bit of the magpie about Father; he expected everything to come in handy. When his back was turned, Mother let me get a chair and rummage through his treasures. She didn't seem to think so highly of them as he did.

The war was the most peaceful period of my life. The window of my attic faced southeast. My mother had curtained it, but that had small effect. I always woke with the first light and, with all the responsibilities of the previous day melted, feeling myself rather like the sun, ready to illumine and rejoice. Life never seemed so simple and clear and full of possibilities as then. I put my feet out from under the clothes – I called them Mrs. Left and Mrs. Right – and invented dramatic situations for them in which they discussed the problems of the day. At least Mrs. Right did; she was very demonstrative, but I hadn't the same control of Mrs. Left, so she mostly contented herself with nodding agreement.

They discussed what Mother and I should do during the day, what Santa Claus should give a fellow for Christmas, and what steps should be taken to brighten the home. There was that little matter of the baby, for instance. Mother and I could never agree about that. Ours was the only house in the terrace without a new baby, and Mother said we couldn't afford one till Father came back from the war because they cost seventeen and six. That showed how simple she was. The Geneys up the road had a baby, and everyone knew they couldn't afford seventeen and six. It was probably a cheap baby, and Mother wanted something really good, but I felt she was too exclusive. The Geneys' baby would have done us fine.

Having settled my plans for the day, I got up, put a chair under the attic window, and lifted the frame high enough to stick out my head. The window overlooked the front gardens of the terrace behind ours, and beyond these it looked over a deep valley to the tall, red-brick houses terraced up the opposite hillside, which were all still in shadow, while those at our side of the valley were all lit up, though with long strange shadows that made them seem unfamiliar; rigid and painted.

After that I went into Mother's room and climbed into the big bed. She woke and I began to tell her of my schemes. By this time, though I never seem to have noticed it, I was petrified in my nightshirt, and I thawed as I talked until, the last frost melted, I fell asleep beside her and woke again only when I heard her below in the kitchen, making the breakfast.

After breakfast we went into town; heard Mass at St. Augustine's and said a prayer for Father, and did the shopping. If the afternoon was fine we either went for a walk in the country or a visit to Mother's great friend in the convent, Mother St. Dominic. Mother had them all praying for Father, and every night, going to bed, I asked God to send him back safe from the war to us. Little, indeed, did I know what I was praying for!

One morning, I got into the big bed, and there, sure enough, was Father in his usual Santa Claus manner, but later, instead of uniform, he put on his best blue suit, and Mother was as pleased as anything. I saw nothing to be pleased about, because, out of uniform, Father was altogether less interesting, but she only beamed, and explained that our prayers had been answered, and off we went to Mass to thank God for having brought Father safely home.

The irony of it! That very day when he came in to dinner he took off his boots and put on his slippers, donned the dirty old cap he wore about the house to save him from colds, crossed his legs, and began to talk gravely to Mother, who looked anxious. Naturally, I disliked her looking anxious, because it destroyed her good looks, so I interrupted him.

"Just a moment, Larry!" she said gently.

This was only what she said when we had boring visitors, so I attached no importance to it and went on talking.

"Do be quiet, Larry!" she said impatiently. "Don't you hear me talking to Daddy?"

This was the first time I had heard those ominous words, "talking to Daddy," and I couldn't help feeling that if this was how God answered prayers, he couldn't listen to them very attentively.

"Why are you talking to Daddy?" I asked with as great a show of indifference as I could muster.

"Because Daddy and I have business to discuss. Now, don't interrupt again!"

In the afternoon, at Mother's request, Father took me for a walk. This time we went into town instead of out to the country, and I thought at first, in my usual optimistic way, that it might be an improvement. It was nothing of the sort. Father and I had quite different notions of a walk in town. He had no proper interest in trams, ships, and horses, and the only thing that seemed to divert him was talking to fellows as old as himself. When I wanted to stop he simply went on, dragging me behind him by the hand; when he wanted to stop I had no alternative but to do the same. I noticed that it seemed to be a sign that he wanted to stop for a long time whenever he leaned against a wall. The second time I saw him do it I got wild. He seemed to be settling himself forever. I pulled him by the coat and trousers, but, unlike Mother who, if you were too persistent, got into a wax and said: "Larry, if you don't behave yourself, I'll give you a good slap," Father had an extraordinary capacity for amiable inattention. I sized him up and wondered would I cry, but he seemed to be too remote to be annoyed even by that. Really, it was like going for a walk with a mountain! He either ignored the wrenching and pummelling entirely, or else glanced down with a grin of amusement from his peak. I had never met anyone so absorbed in himself as he seemed.

At teatime, "talking to Daddy" began again, complicated this time by the fact that he had an evening paper, and every few minutes he put it down and told Mother something new out of it. I felt this was foul play. Man for man, I was prepared to compete with him any time for Mother's attention, but when he had it all made up for him by other people it left me no chance. Several times I tried to change the subject without success.

"You must be quiet while Daddy is reading, Larry," Mother said impatiently.

It was clear that she either genuinely liked talking to Father better than talking to me, or else that he had some terrible hold on her which made her afraid to admit the truth.

"Mummy," I said that night when she was tucking me up, "do you think if I prayed hard God would send Daddy back to the war?"

She seemed to think about that for a moment.

"No, dear," she said with a smile. "I don't think he would."

"Why wouldn't he, Mummy?"

"Because there isn't a war any longer, dear."

"But, Mummy, couldn't God make another war, if he liked?"

"He wouldn't like to, dear. It's not God who makes wars, but bad people."

"Oh!" I said.

I was disappointed about that. I began to think that God wasn't quite what he was cracked up to be.

Next morning I woke at my usual hour, feeling like a bottle of champagne. I put out my feet and invented a long conversation in which Mrs. Right talked of the trouble she had with her own father till she put him in the Home. I didn't quite know what the Home was but it sounded the right place for Father. Then I got my chair and stuck my head out of the attic window. Dawn was just breaking, with a guilty air that made me feel I had caught it in the act. My head bursting with stories and schemes, I stumbled in next door, and in the half-darkness scrambled into the big bed. There was no room at Mother's side so I had to get between her and Father. For the time being I had forgotten about him, and for several minutes I sat bolt upright, racking my brains to know what I could do with him. He was taking up more than his fair share of the bed, and I couldn't get comfortable, so I gave him several kicks that made him grunt and stretch. He made room all right, though. Mother waked and felt for me. I settled back comfortably in the warmth of the bed with my thumb in my mouth.

"Mummy!" I hummed, loudly and contentedly.

"Sssh! dear," she whispered. "Don't wake Daddy!"

This was a new development, which threatened to be even more serious than "talking to Daddy". Life without my early-morning conferences was unthinkable.

"Why?" I asked severely.

"Because poor Daddy is tired."

This seemed to me a quite inadequate reason, and I was sickened by the sentimentality of her "poor Daddy". I never liked that sort of gush; it always struck me as insincere.

"Oh!" I said lightly. Then in my most winning tone: "Do you know where I want to go with you today, Mummy?"

"No, dear," she sighed.

"I want to go down the Glen and fish for thornybacks with my new net, and then I want to go out to the Fox and Hounds, and —"

"Don't-wake-Daddy!" she hissed angrily, clapping her hand across my mouth.

But it was too late. He was awake, or nearly so. He grunted and reached for the matches. Then he stared incredulously at his watch.

"Like a cup of tea, dear?" asked Mother in a meek, hushed voice I had never heard her use before. It sounded almost as though she were afraid.

"Tea?" he exclaimed indignantly. "Do you know what the time is?"

"And after that I want to go up the Rathcooney Road," I said loudly, afraid I'd forget something in all those interruptions.

"Go to sleep at once, Larry!" she said sharply.

I began to snivel. I couldn't concentrate, the way that pair went on, and smothering my early-morning schemes was like burying a family from the cradle.

Father said nothing, but lit his pipe and sucked it, looking out into the shadows without minding Mother or me. I knew he was mad. Every time I made a remark Mother hushed me irritably. I was mortified. I felt it wasn't fair; there was even something sinister in it. Every time I had pointed out to her the waste of making two beds when we could both sleep in one, she had told me it was healthier like that, and now here was this man, this stranger, sleeping with her without the least regard for her health!

He got up early and made tea, but though he brought Mother a cup he brought none for me.

"Mummy," I shouted, "I want a cup of tea, too."

"Yes, dear," she said patiently. "You can drink from Mummy's saucer."

That settled it. Either Father or I would have to leave the house. I didn't want to drink from Mother's saucer; I wanted to be treated as an equal in my own home, so, just to spite her, I drank it all and left none for her. She took that quietly, too.

But that night when she was putting me to bed she said gently:

"Larry, I want you to promise me something."

"What is it?" I asked.

"Not to come in and disturb poor Daddy in the morning. Promise?"

"Poor Daddy" again! I was becoming suspicious of everything involving that quite impossible man.

"Why?" I asked.

"Because poor Daddy is worried and tired and he doesn't sleep well."

"Why doesn't he, Mummy?"

"Well, you know, don't you, that while he was at the war Mummy got the pennies from the Post Office?"

"From Miss MacCarthy?"

"That's right. But now, you see, Miss MacCarthy hasn't any more pennies, so Daddy must go out and find us some. You know what would happen if he couldn't?"

"No," I said, "tell us."

"Well, I think we might have to go out and beg for them like the poor old woman on Fridays. We wouldn't like that, would we?"

"No," I agreed. "We wouldn't."

"So you'll promise not to come in and wake him?"

"Promise."

Mind you, I meant that. I knew pennies were a serious matter, and I was all against having to go out and beg like the old woman on Fridays. Mother laid out all my toys in a complete ring round the bed so that, whatever way I got out, I was bound to fall over one of them.

When I woke I remembered by promise all right. I got up and sat on the floor and played — for hours, it seemed to me. Then I got my chair and looked out the attic window for more hours. I wished it was time for Father to wake; I wished someone would make me a cup of tea. I didn't feel in the least like the sun; instead, I was bored and so very, very cold! I simply longed for the warmth and depth of the big featherbed.

At last I could stand it no longer. I went into the next room. As there was still no room at Mother's side I climbed over her and she woke with a start.

"Larry," she whispered, gripping my arm very tightly, "what did you promise?"

"But I did, Mummy," I wailed, caught in the very act. "I was quiet for ever so long."

"Oh, dear, and you're perished!" she said sadly, feeling

me all over. "Now, if I let you stay will you promise not to talk?"

"But I want to talk, Mummy," I wailed.

"That has nothing to do with it," she said with a firmness that was new to me. "Daddy wants to sleep. Now, do you understand that?"

I understood it only too well. I wanted to talk, he wanted to sleep – whose house was it, anyway?

"Mummy," I said with equal firmness, "I think it would be healthier for Daddy to sleep in his own bed."

That seemed to stagger her, because she said nothing for a while.

"Now, once for all," she went on, "you're to be perfectly quiet or go back to your own bed. Which is it to be?"

The injustice of it got me down. I had convicted her out of her own mouth of inconsistency and unreasonableness, and she hadn't even attempted to reply. Full of spite, I gave Father a kick, which she didn't notice but which made him grunt and open his eyes in alarm.

"What time is it?" he asked in a panic-stricken voice, not looking at Mother but the door, as if he saw someone there.

"It's early yet," she replied soothingly. "It's only the child. Go to sleep again. . . . Now, Larry," she added, getting out of bed, "you've wakened Daddy and you must go back."

This time, for all her quiet air, I knew she meant it, and knew that my principal rights and privileges were as good as lost unless I asserted them at once. As she lifted me, I gave a screech, enough to wake the dead, not to mind Father. He groaned.

"That damn child! Doesn't he ever sleep?"

"It's only a habit, dear," she said quietly, though I could see she was vexed.

"Well, it's time he got out of it," shouted Father, beginning to heave in the bed. He suddenly gathered all the bedclothes about him, turned to the wall, and then looked back over his shoulder with nothing showing only two small, spiteful, dark eyes. The man looked very wicked.

To open the bedroom door, Mother had to let me down, and I broke free and dashed for the farthest corner, screeching. Father sat bolt upright in bed.

"Shut up, you little puppy!" he said in a choking voice.

I was so astonished that I stopped screeching. Never, never had anyone spoken to me in that tone before. I looked at him incredulously and saw his face convulsed with rage. It was only then that I fully realized how God had codded me, listening to my prayers for the safe return of this monster.

"Shut up, you!" I bawled, beside myself.

"What's that you said?" shouted Father, making a wild leap out of bed.

"Mick, Mick!" cried Mother. "Don't you see the child isn't used to you?"

"I see he's better fed than taught," snarled Father, waving his arms wildly. "He wants his bottom smacked."

All his previous shouting was as nothing to these obscene words referring to my person. They really made my blood boil.

"Smack your own!" I screamed hysterically. "Smack your own! Shut up! Shut up!"

At this he lost his patience and let fly at me. He did it with the lack of conviction you'd expect of a man under Mother's horrified eyes, and it ended up as a mere tap, but the sheer indignity of being struck at all by a stranger, a total stranger who had cajoled his way back from the war into our big bed as a result of my innocent intercession, made me completely dotty. I shrieked and shrieked, and danced in my bare feet, and Father, looking awkward and hairy in nothing but a short grey army shirt, glared down at me like a mountain out for murder. I think it must have been then that I realized he was jealous too. And there stood Mother in her night-dress, looking as if her heart was broken between us. I hoped she felt as she looked. It seemed to me that she deserved it all.

From that morning out my life was a hell. Father and I were enemies, open and avowed. We conducted a series of skirmishes against one another, he trying to steal my time with Mother and I his. When she was sitting on my bed, telling me a story, he took to looking for some pair of old boots which he alleged he had left behind him at the beginning of the war. While he talked to Mother I played loudly with my toys to show my total lack of concern. He created a terrible scene one evening when he came in from work and found me at his box, playing with his regimental badges, Gurkha knives, and button-sticks. Mother got up and took the box from me.

"You mustn't play with Daddy's toys unless he lets you, Larry," she said severely. "Daddy doesn't play with yours."

For some reason Father looked at her as if she had struck him and then turned away with a scowl.

"Those are not toys," he growled, taking down the box again to see had I lifted anything. "Some of those curios are very rare and valuable."

But as time went on I saw more and more how he managed to alienate Mother and me. What made it worse was that I couldn't grasp his method or see what attraction he had for Mother. In every possible way he was less winning than I. He had a common accent and made noises at his tea. I thought for a while that it might be the newspapers she was interested in, so I made up bits of news of my own to read to her. Then I thought it might be the smoking, which I personally thought attractive, and took his pipes and went round the house dribbling into them till he caught me. I even made noises at my tea, but Mother only told me I was disgusting. It all seemed to hinge round that unhealthy habit of sleeping together, so I made a point of dropping into their bedroom and nosing round, talking to myself, so that they wouldn't know I was watching them, but they were never up to anything that I could see. In the end it beat me. It seemed to depend on being grown-up and giving people rings, and I realized I'd have to wait.

But at the same time I wanted him to see that I was only waiting, not giving up the fight. One evening when he was being particularly obnoxious, chattering away well above my head, I let him have it.

"Mummy," I said, "do you know what I'm going to do when I grow up?"

"No, dear," she replied. "What?"

"I'm going to marry you," I said quietly.

Father gave a great guffaw out of him, but he didn't take me in. I knew it must only be pretence. And Mother, in spite of everything, was pleased. I felt she was probably relieved to know that one day Father's hold on her would be broken.

"Won't that be nice?" she said with a smile.

"It'll be very nice," I said confidently. "Because we're going to have lots and lots of babies."

"That's right, dear," she said placidly. "I think we'll have one soon, and then you'll have plenty of company."

I was no end pleased about that because it showed that in spite of the way she gave in to Father she still considered my wishes. Besides, it would put the Geneys in their place.

It didn't turn out like that, though. To begin with, she was very preoccupied – I supposed about where she would get the seventeen and six – and though Father took to staying out late in the evenings it did me no particular good. She stopped taking me for walks, became as touchy as blazes, and smacked me for nothing at all. Sometimes I wished I'd never mentioned the confounded baby – I seemed to have a genius for bringing calamity on myself.

And calamity it was! Sonny arrived in the most appalling hullabaloo – even that much he couldn't do without a fuss – and from the first moment I disliked him. He was a difficult child – so far as I was concerned he was always difficult – and demanded far too much attention. Mother was simply silly about him, and couldn't see when he was only showing off. As company he was worse than useless. He slept all day, and I had to go round the house on tiptoe to avoid waking him. It wasn't any longer a question of not waking Father. The slogan now was "Don't wake Sonny!" I couldn't understand why the child wouldn't sleep at the proper time, so whenever Mother's back was turned I woke him. Sometimes to keep him awake I pinched him as well. Mother caught me at it one day and gave me a most unmerciful flaking.

One evening, when Father was coming in from work, I was playing trains in the front garden. I let on not to notice him; instead, I pretended to be talking to myself, and said in a loud voice: "If another bloody baby comes into this house, I'm going out."

Father stopped dead and looked at me over his shoulder.

"What's that you said?" he asked sternly.

"I was only talking to myself," I replied, trying to conceal my panic. "It's private."

He turned and went in without a word. Mind you, I intended it as a solemn warning, but its effect was quite different. Father started being quite nice to me. I could understand that, of course. Mother was quite sickening about Sonny. Even at mealtimes she'd get up and gawk at him in the cradle with an idiotic smile, and tell Father to do the same. He was always polite about it, but he looked so puzzled you could see he didn't know what she was talking about. He complained of the way Sonny cried at night, but she only got cross and said that Sonny never cried except when there was something up with him — which was a flaming lie, because Sonny never had anything up with him, and only cried for attention. It was really painful to see how simple-minded she was. Father wasn't attractive, but he had a fine intelligence. He saw through Sonny, and now he knew that I saw through him as well.

One night I woke with a start. There was someone beside me in the bed. For one wild moment I felt sure it must be Mother, having come to her senses and left Father for good, but then I heard Sonny in convulsions in the next room, and Mother saying: "There! There! There!" and I knew it wasn't she. It was Father. He was lying beside me, wide awake, breathing hard and apparently as mad as hell.

After a while it came to me what he was mad about. It

was his turn now. After turning me out of the big bed, he had been turned out himself. Mother had no consideration now for anyone but that poisonous pup, Sonny. I couldn't help feeling sorry for Father. I had been through it all myself, and even at that age I was magnanimous. I began to stroke him down and say: "There! There!" He wasn't exactly responsive.

"Aren't you asleep either?" he snarled.

"Ah, come on and put your arm around us, can't you?" I said, and he did, in a sort of way. Gingerly, I suppose, is how you'd describe it. He was very bony but better than nothing.

At Christmas he went out of his way to buy me a really nice model railway.

QUESTIONS

1. The author's attitude towards his characters is all-important in this story. How does he communicate this attitude to the reader?

2. A main technical problem in the story for O'Connor was to blend the narrator's sophisticated viewpoint with the innocent outlook of the five-year-old. Do you think he has succeeded, or do the two viewpoints jar against each other? Choose a passage of at least several lines and refer to it to illustrate your opinion.

3. (a) The opening section of the story introduces Larry's wish for a baby in the house and his prayer for his father's safe return. Explain the irony of these two wishes.
   (b) Examples of irony abound in "My Oedipus Complex" (the title, for instance). Pick out three other examples of irony from the story and explain what effect on the reader you think each example is intended to have.

4. (a) How does O'Connor reveal that the father is not the sinister monster of Larry's imagining, but really a somewhat immature and comic figure?
   (b) In what ways does the mother form a contrast to the father?

5. Show that the antagonism between child and father is developed by three stages, the third one forming a climax of comic violence.

6. How does O'Connor avoid sentimentality in the father-Larry reconciliation incidents that follow Sonny's arrival?

7. Compare "My Oedipus Complex" and "Charles", considering
   (a) the point of view from which the story is narrated,
   (b) the element of surprise,
   (c) the importance of dialogue,
   (d) the sources of humour.

SHIRLEY JACKSON

b. 1919

Charles ✦ ✦ ✦

Shirley Jackson is best known for her tales of the abnormal and the supernatural, as in her collection of short stories *The Lottery* (1949) and in such novels as *Hangsaman* (1951), *The Bird's Nest* (1954), *The Sundial* (1958), and *The Haunting of Hill House* (1959). However, her treatment of the outsider, the abnormal one who chafes against the bonds of the socially acceptable, can also be humorous. That "Charles" has a strong element of autobiography is hinted at in the name of its hero, Laurie. Shirley Jackson's first-born son, who was about five when this story was written, is named Laurence. And her two collections of personal essays that deal with her life as a suburban mother and wife are entitled *Life Among the Savages* (1953) and *Raising Demons* (1957). We may hope that, like some other outsiders (James Thurber, for instance), Laurie turned out well in later life. At least he would never be dull. As you read, try to listen to the dialogue. To write the speech of a five-year-old so that it sounds believable is a difficult feat for a writer to bring off. Does Shirley Jackson succeed here?

THE DAY MY SON LAURIE started kindergarten he renounced corduroy overalls with bibs and began wearing blue jeans with a belt; I watched him go off the first morning with the older girl next door, seeing clearly that an era of my life was ended, my sweet-voiced nursery-school tot replaced by a long-trousered, swaggering character who forgot to stop at the corner and wave good-bye to me.

He came home the same way, the front door slamming open, his cap on the floor, and the voice suddenly become raucous shouting, "Isn't anybody *here*?"

At lunch he spoke insolently to his father, spilled his baby sister's milk, and remarked that his teacher said we were not to take the name of the Lord in vain.

"How *was* school today?" I asked, elaborately casual.

"All right," he said.

"Did you learn anything?" his father asked.

Laurie regarded his father coldly. "I didn't learn nothing," he said.

"Anything," I said. "Didn't learn anything."

"The teacher spanked a boy, though," Laurie said, addressing his bread and butter. "For being fresh," he added, with his mouth full.

"What did he do?" I asked. "Who was it?"

Laurie thought. "It was Charles," he said. "He was fresh. The teacher spanked him and made him stand in a corner. He was awfully fresh."

"What did he do?" I asked again, but Laurie slid off his chair, took a cookie, and left, while his father was still saying, "See here, young man."

The next day Laurie remarked at lunch, as soon as he sat down, "Well, Charles was bad again today." He grinned enormously and said, "Today Charles hit the teacher."

"Good heavens," I said, mindful of the Lord's name, "I suppose he got spanked again?"

"He sure did," Laurie said. "Look up," he said to his father.

"What?" his father said, looking up.

"Look down," Laurie said. "Look at my thumb. Gee, you're dumb." He began to laugh insanely.

"Why did Charles hit the teacher?" I asked quickly.

"Because she tried to make him color with red crayons," Laurie said. "Charles wanted to color with green crayons so he hit the teacher and she spanked him and said nobody play with Charles but everybody did."

The third day – it was Wednesday of the first week – Charles bounced a see-saw on to the head of a little girl and made her bleed, and the teacher made him stay inside all during recess. Thursday Charles had to stand in a corner during story-time because he kept pounding his feet on the floor. Friday Charles was deprived of blackboard privileges because he threw chalk.

On Saturday I remarked to my husband, "Do you think kindergarten is too unsettling for Laurie? All this toughness, and bad grammar, and this Charles boy sounds like such a bad influence."

"It'll be all right," my husband said reassuringly. "Bound to be people like Charles in the world. Might as well meet them now as later."

On Monday Laurie came home late, full of news. "Charles," he shouted as he came up the hill; I was waiting anxiously on the front steps. "Charles," Laurie yelled all the way up the hill, "Charles was bad again."

"Come right in," I said, as soon as he came close enough. "Lunch is waiting."

"You know what Charles did?" he demanded, following me through the door. "Charles yelled so in school they sent a boy in from first grade to tell the teacher she had to make Charles keep quiet, and so Charles had to stay after school. And so all the children stayed to watch him."

"What did he do?" I asked.

"He just sat there," Laurie said, climbing into his chair at the table. "Hi, Pop, y'old dust mop."

"Charles had to stay after school today," I told my husband. "Everyone stayed with him."

"What does this Charles look like?" my husband asked Laurie. "What's his other name?"

"He's bigger than me," Laurie said. "And he doesn't have any rubbers and he doesn't ever wear a jacket."

Monday night was the first Parent-Teachers meeting, and only the fact that the baby had a cold kept me from going; I wanted passionately to meet Charles's mother. On Tuesday Laurie remarked suddenly, "Our teacher had a friend come to see her in school today."

"Charles's mother?" my husband and I asked simultaneously.

"Naaah," Laurie said scornfully. "It was a man who came and made us do exercises, we had to touch our toes. Look." He climbed down from his chair and squatted down and touched his toes. "Like this," he said. He got solemnly back into his chair and said, picking up his fork, "Charles didn't even *do* exercises."

"That's fine," I said heartily. "Didn't Charles want to do exercises?"

"Naaah," Laurie said. "Charles was so fresh to the teacher's friend he wasn't *let* do exercises."

"Fresh again?" I said.

"He kicked the teacher's friend," Laurie said. "The teacher's friend told Charles to touch his toes like I just did and Charles kicked him."

"What are they going to do about Charles, do you suppose?" Laurie's father asked him.

Laurie shrugged elaborately. "Throw him out of school, I guess," he said.

Wednesday and Thursday were routine; Charles yelled during story hour and hit a boy in the stomach and made him cry. On Friday Charles stayed after school again and so did all the other children.

With the third week of kindergarten Charles was an institution in our family; the baby was being a Charles when she cried all afternoon; Laurie did a Charles when he filled his wagon full of mud and pulled it through the kitchen; even my husband, when he caught his elbow in the telephone cord and pulled telephone, ashtray, and a bowl of flowers off the table, said, after the first minute, "Looks like Charles."

During the third and fourth weeks it looked like a reformation in Charles; Laurie reported grimly at lunch on Thursday of the third week, "Charles was so good today the teacher gave him an apple."

"What?" I said, and my husband added warily, "You mean Charles?"

"Charles," Laurie said. "He gave the crayons around and he picked up the books afterward and the teacher said he was her helper."

"What happened?" I asked incredulously.

"He was her helper, that's all," Laurie said, and shrugged.

"Can this be true, about Charles?" I asked my husband that night. "Can something like this happen?"

"Wait and see," my husband said cynically. "When you've got a Charles to deal with, this may mean he's only plotting."

He seemed to be wrong. For over a week Charles was the teacher's helper; each day he handed things out and he picked things up; no one had to stay after school.

"The P.T.A. meeting's next week again," I told my husband one evening. "I'm going to find Charles's mother there."

"Ask her what happened to Charles," my husband said. "I'd like to know."

"I'd like to know myself," I said.

On Friday of that week things were back to normal. "You know what Charles did today?" Laurie demanded at the lunch table, in a voice slightly awed. "He told a little girl to say a word and she said it and the teacher washed her mouth out with soap and Charles laughed."

"What word?" his father asked unwisely, and Laurie said, "I'll have to whisper it to you, it's so bad." He got down off his chair and went around to his father. His father bent his head down and Laurie whispered joyfully. His father's eyes widened.

"Did Charles tell the little girl to say *that*?" he asked respectfully.

"She said it *twice*," Laurie said. "Charles told her to say it *twice*."

"What happened to Charles?" my husband asked.

"Nothing," Laurie said. "He was passing out the crayons."

Monday morning Charles abandoned the little girl and

said the evil word himself three or four times, getting his mouth washed out with soap each time. He also threw chalk.

My husband came to the door with me that evening as I set out for the P.T.A. meeting. "Invite her over for a cup of tea after the meeting," he said. "I want to get a look at her."

"If only she's there," I said prayerfully.

"She'll be there," my husband said. "I don't see how they could hold a P.T.A. meeting without Charles's mother."

At the meeting I sat restlessly, scanning each comfortable matronly face, trying to determine which one hid the secret of Charles. None of them looked to me haggard enough. No one stood up in the meeting and apologized for the way her son had been acting. No one mentioned Charles.

After the meeting I identified and sought out Laurie's kindergarten teacher. She had a plate with a cup of tea and a piece of chocolate cake; I had a plate with a cup of tea and a piece of marshmallow cake. We manoeuvred up to one another cautiously, and smiled.

"I've been so anxious to meet you," I said. "I'm Laurie's mother."

"We're all so interested in Laurie," she said.

"Well, he certainly likes kindergarten," I said. "He talks about it all the time."

"We had a little trouble adjusting, the first week or so," she said primly, "but now he's a fine little helper. With occasional lapses, of course."

"Laurie usually adjusts very quickly," I said. "I suppose this time it's Charles's influence."

"Charles?"

"Yes," I said, laughing, "you must have your hands full in that kindergarten, with Charles."

"Charles?" she said. "We don't have any Charles in the kindergarten."

QUESTIONS

1. The clash between belief and reality is often a source of humour. How does this clash occur in "Charles"?

2. (a) What effect does the author gain by relying mostly on dialogue and excluding descriptions of physical appearance?
(b) What is the purpose of the one reference to dress at the beginning of the story?

3. What characteristics does the author assign to the mother and father? Show how the dialogue brings out these qualities.

4. Some of the dialogue suggests that Laurie is experiencing an especial hostility towards his father. What speeches indicate this feeling?

5. (a) If the story works as Shirley Jackson hoped it would, the concluding sentence has the effect of a comic explosion. Does the story work? Explain why you think it does, or does not.
(b) What clues has she inserted along the way to prepare her reader for the final revelation?

6. Do you find Laurie's behaviour believable? Explain your opinion.

7. Compare Shirley Jackson's use of irony in "Charles" with Frank O'Connor's use of it in "My Oedipus Complex".

STEPHEN LEACOCK

1869-1944

My discovery of England

Stephen Leacock depends for much of his humorous effect on the art of caricature. With an eye that is deadly sharp he catches an oddity, an eccentricity, a contradiction in human or social behaviour, and proceeds to enlarge on what he has noticed, high-lighting the oddity, exaggerating the discrepancy. Here he creates his caricature of the tourist who becomes an authority on a foreign land after a quick whirlwind visit. The strategy is to turn the tables on the English visitor to North America by making himself a quick whirlwind tour of England. The genius of the piece is in its double thrust – at the tourist mind (whether it be English or American) and at blind spots in the mentality of both Englishmen and North Americans. You will find it amusing as well as instructive to read side by side with the Leacock piece the excerpts from T. H. White's "America at Last", the impressions of an English writer and lecturer during a quick whirlwind tour of the United States. Stephen Leacock, one of the most justly celebrated and widely read of Canadian writers, is best known for such volumes of humorous sketches as *Sunshine Sketches of a Little Town* (1912), *Arcadian Adventures with the Idle Rich* (1914), *Frenzied Fiction* (1918), *My Discovery of England* (1922), *My Remarkable Uncle* (1942).

FOR SOME YEARS PAST a rising tide of lecturers and literary men from England has washed upon the shores of this continent. They come over to us traveling in great simplicity, and they return in the ducal suite of the *Aquitania*. They carry away with them their impressions of America, and when they reach England they sell them. This irregular and one-sided traffic has now assumed such great proportions that we are compelled to ask whether it is right to allow these people to carry away from us impressions of the very highest commercial value without giving us any pecuniary compensation whatever. English lecturers have been known to land in New York, pass the customs, drive uptown in a closed taxi, and then forward to England *from the closed taxi itself* ten dollars' worth of impressions of American national character. I have myself seen an English literary man sitting in the corridor of a fashionable New York hotel and looking gloomily into his hat, and then *from his very hat* produce an estimate of the genius of America at twenty cents a word. The nice question as to whose twenty cents that was never seems to have occurred to him.

I am not writing in the faintest spirit of jealousy. I quite admit the extraordinary ability that is involved in this peculiar susceptibility to impressions. But I do feel that somehow these impressions are inadequate and fail to depict us as we really are.

Let me illustrate what I mean. Here are some of the impressions of New York, gathered from various visitors' discoveries of America, and reproduced, not, perhaps, word for word, but as closely as I can remember them. "New York," writes one, "nestling at the foot of the Hudson, gave me an impression of coziness, of tiny graciousness; in short, of weeness." But compare this: "New York," according to another discoverer of America, "gave me an impression of size, of vastness; there seemed to me a bigness about it not found in smaller places." A third visitor writes, "New York struck me as hard, cruel, almost inhuman." This, I think, was because his taxi driver had charged him three dollars.

Nor is it only the impressions of the metropolis that seem to fall short of reality. Let me quote a few others taken at random here and there over the continent.

"I took from Pittsburgh," says an English visitor, "an impression of something that I could hardly define — an atmosphere rather than an idea."

All very well. But, after all, had he the right to take it? Granted that Pittsburgh has an atmosphere rather than an idea, the attempt to carry away this atmosphere surely borders on rapacity. . . .

"Chicago," according to another book of discovery, "struck me as a large city. Situated as it is and where it is, it seems destined to be a place of great importance."

Or here, again, is a form of "impression" that recurs again and again, "At Cleveland I felt a distinct note of optimism in the air."

This same note of optimism is found also at Toledo, at Toronto – in short, I believe it indicates nothing more than that somebody gave the visitor a cigar. . . .

In the course of time a considerable public feeling was aroused in the United States and Canada over this state of affairs. The lack of reciprocity in it seemed unfair. It was felt (or at least I felt) that the time had come when someone ought to go over and take some impressions off England. The choice of such a person (my choice) fell upon myself. By an arrangement with the Geographical Society of America, acting in conjunction with the Royal Geographic Society of England (to both of which I communicated my project), I went at my own expense. . . .

I pass over the details of my pleasant voyage from New York to Liverpool. During the last fifty years so many travelers have made the voyage across the Atlantic that it is now impossible to obtain from the ocean any impressions of the slightest commercial value. . . . I will content myself with chronicling the fact that during the voyage we passed two dolphins, one whale, and one iceberg (none of them moving very fast at the time). . . .

I pass over also the incidents of my landing at Liverpool, except, perhaps, to comment upon the extraordinary behavior of the English customs officials. Without wishing in any way to disturb international relations, one cannot help commenting on the brutal and inquisitorial methods of the English customs men as compared with the gentle and affectionate ways of the American officials at New York. The two trunks which I brought with me were dragged brutally into an open shed; the strap of one of them was rudely unbuckled, while the lid of the other was actually lifted at least four inches. The trunks were then roughly scrawled with chalk, the lids slammed to, and that was all. Not one of the officials seemed to care to look at my things or to have the politeness to pretend to want to. I had arranged my dress suit and my pajamas so as to make as effective a display as possible; a New York customs officer would have been delighted with it. Here they simply passed it over.

"Do open this trunk," I asked one of the officials, "and see my pajamas."

"I don't think it is necessary, sir," the man answered.

There was a coldness about it that cut me to the quick.

But bad as is the conduct of the English customs men, the immigration officials are even worse. I could not help also being struck by the dreadful carelessness with which people are admitted into England. There is, it is true, a group of officials said to be in charge of immigration, but they know nothing of the discriminating care exercised on the other side of the Atlantic.

"Do you want to know," I asked of one of them, "whether I am a polygamist?"

"No, sir," he said, very quietly.

"Would you like me to tell you whether I am fundamentally opposed to any and every system of government?"

The man seemed mystified. "No, sir," he said, "I don't know that I would."

"Don't you care?" I asked.

"Well, not particularly, sir," he answered.

I was determined to arouse him from his lethargy.

"Let me tell you, then," I said, "that I am an anarchistic polygamist, that I am opposed to all forms of government, that I object to any kind of revealed religion, that I regard the state and property and marriage as the mere tyranny of the bourgeoisie, and that I want to see class hatred carried to the point where it forces everyone into brotherly love. Now do I get in?"

The official looked puzzled for a minute. "You are not Irish, are you, sir?" he said.

"No."

"Then I think you can come in all right," he answered.

The journey from Liverpool to London is like all other English journeys, in short. This is due to the fact that England is a small country; it contains only 50,000 square miles, whereas the United States, as everyone knows, contains three and a half billion. I mentioned this fact to an English fellow passenger on the train, together with a provisional estimate of the American corn crop for 1922; but he only drew his rug about his knees, took a sip of brandy from his traveling flask, and sank into a state resembling death. I contented myself with jotting down an impression of incivility and lack of generosity as two phases of English character, and paid no further attention to my fellow traveler other than to read the labels on his luggage and to peruse the headings of his newspaper by peeping over his shoulder.

It was my first experience of traveling with a fellow passenger in a compartment of an English train, and I admit now that I was as yet ignorant of the proper method of conduct. Later on I became fully conversant with the rules of travel as understood in England. I should have known, of course, that I must on no account speak to the man. But I should have let down the window a little bit and in such a way as to make a strong draught on his ear. Had this failed to break down his reserve, I should have placed a heavy valise in the rack over his head, so balanced that it might fall on him at any moment. Failing this again, I could have blown rings of smoke at him or stepped on his feet under a pretense of looking out of the window. Under the English rule, as long as he bears this in silence you are not supposed to know him. In fact, he is not supposed to be there. You and he each presume the other to be a mere piece of empty space. But let him once be driven to say: "Oh, I beg your pardon! I wonder if you would mind my closing the window," and he is lost. After that you are entitled to tell him anything about the corn crop that you care to.

But in the present case I knew nothing of this, and after three hours of charming silence I found myself in London.

London, the name of which is already known to millions of readers of this magazine, is beautifully situated on the river Thames, which here sweeps in a wide curve and has much the same breadth and majesty as the St. Jo River at South Bend, Indiana. London, like South Bend itself, is a city of clean streets and admirable sidewalks, and has an excellent water supply. One is at once struck by the number of excellent and well-appointed motor cars that one sees on every hand, the neatness of the shops, and the cleanliness and cheerfulness of the faces of the people. In short, as an English visitor said of Peterborough, Ontario, there is a distinct note of optimism in the air.

These, however, are but superficial pictures of London, gathered by the eye of the tourist. A far deeper meaning is found in the examination of the great historic monuments of the city. The principal ones of these are the Tower of London (just mentioned), the British Museum, and Westminster Abbey. No visitor to London should fail to see these. Indeed, he ought to feel that his visit to England is wasted unless he has seen them. I speak strongly on the point because I feel strongly on it. To my mind there is something about the grim fascination of the historic Tower, the cloistered quiet of the Museum, and the majesty of the ancient Abbey, which will make it the regret of my life that I didn't see any one of the three. I fully meant to, but I failed; and I can only hope that the circumstances of my failure may be helpful to other visitors.

The Tower of London I most certainly intended to inspect. Each day, after the fashion of every tourist, I wrote for myself a little list of things to do, and I always put the Tower of London on it. No doubt the reader knows the kind of little list that I mean. It runs:

1. Go to bank.
2. Buy a shirt.
3. National Picture Gallery.
4. Razor blades.
5. Tower of London.
6. Soap.

The itinerary, I regret to say, was never carried out in full. I was able at times both to go to the bank and to buy a shirt in a single morning; at other times I was able to buy razor blades and almost to find the National Picture Gallery. Meantime I was urged on all sides by my London acquaintances not to fail to see the Tower. "There's a grim fascination about the place," they said; "you mustn't miss it." I am quite certain that in due course of time I should have made my way to the Tower but for the fact that I made a fatal discovery. I found out that the London people who urged me to go and see the Tower had never seen it themselves. It appears they never go near it. One night at a dinner a man next to me said:

"Have you seen the Tower? You really ought to. There's a grim fascination about it."

I looked him in the face. "Have you seen it yourself?" I asked.

"Oh, yes," he answered, "I've seen it."

"When?" I asked.

The man hesitated. "When I was just a boy," he said. "My father took me there."

"How long ago is that?" I inquired.

"About forty years ago," he answered. "I always mean to go again, but I don't somehow seem to get the time."

After this I got to understand that when a Londoner says, "Have you seen the Tower of London?" the answer is, "No, and neither have you."

Take the parallel case of the British Museum. Here is a place that is a veritable treasure house, a repository of some of the most priceless historical relics to be found upon the earth. It contains, for instance, the famous Papyrus Manuscript of Thotmes II of the first Egyptian dynasty — a thing known to scholars all over the world as the oldest extant specimen of what can be called writing. . . . The first time I went by it in a taxi I felt quite a thrill. "Inside those walls," I thought to myself, "is the Manuscript of Thotmes II." The next time I actually stopped the taxi.

"Is that the British Museum?" I asked the driver.

"I think it is something of the sort, sir," he said.

I hesitated. "Drive me," I said, "to where I can buy safety-razor blades."

After that I was able to drive past the Museum with the quiet assurance of a Londoner, and to take part in dinner-table discussions as to whether the British Museum or the Louvre contains the greater treasures. . . .

The Abbey, I admit, is indeed majestic. I did not intend to miss going into it. But I felt, as so many tourists have, that I wanted to enter it in the proper frame of mind. I never got into the frame of mind; at least not when near the Abbey itself. I have been in exactly that frame of mind when on State Street, Chicago, or on King Street, Toronto, or anywhere three thousand miles away from the Abbey. But by bad luck I never struck both the frame of mind and the Abbey at the same time. . . .

But for the ordinary visitor to London the greatest interest of all attaches to the spacious and magnificent Parliament Buildings. The House of Commons is commodiously situated beside the river Thames. The principal features of the House are the large lunch room on the western side and the tea room on the terrace on the eastern. A series of smaller luncheon rooms extends (apparently) all round about the premises, while a commodious bar offers a ready access to the members at all hours of the day. While any members are in the bar a light is kept burning in the tall Clock Tower at one corner of the building, but when the bar is closed the light is turned off by whichever of the Scotch members leaves last. There is a handsome legislative chamber attached to the premises from which — so the antiquarians tell us — the

House of Commons took its name. But it is not usual now for the members to sit in the legislative chamber, as the legislation is now all done outside. . . . The House, however, is called together at very frequent intervals to give it an opportunity of hearing the latest legislation and allowing the members to indulge in cheers, groans, sighs, votes, and other expressions of vitality. After having cheered as much as is good for them they go back again to the lunch rooms and go on eating till they are needed again.

The Parliament Buildings are so vast that it is not possible to state with certainty what they do, or do not, contain. But it is generally said that somewhere in the building is the House of Lords. When they meet they are said to come together very quietly shortly before the dinner hour, take a glass of dry sherry and a biscuit (they are all abstemious men), reject whatever bills may be before them at the moment, take another dry sherry, and then adjourn for two years. . . .

No description of London would be complete without a reference, however brief, to the singular salubrity and charm of the London climate. This is seen at its best during the autumn and winter months. The climate of London, and indeed of England generally, is due to the influence of the Gulf Stream. The way it works is this: The Gulf Stream, as it nears the shores of the British Isles and feels the propinquity of Ireland, rises into the air, turns into soup, and comes down on London. At times this soup is thin and is in fact little more than a mist; at other times it has the consistency of a thick *potage St.-Germain*. London people flatter their atmosphere by calling it a fog; but it is not; it is soup.

But the notion that no sunlight ever gets through and that in the London winter people never see the sun, is a ridiculous error, circulated, no doubt, by the jealousy of foreign nations. I have myself seen the sun plainly visible in London, without the aid of glasses, on a November day in broad daylight; and again one night about four o'clock in the afternoon, I saw the sun distinctly appear through the clouds.

The whole subject of daylight in the London winter is, however, one which belongs rather to the technic of astronomy than to a paper of description. In practice daylight is but little used. Electric lights are burned all the time in all private houses, buildings, railway stations, and clubs. This practice, which is now universally observed, is called daylight saving.

But the distinction between day and night during the London winter is still quite obvious to anyone of an observant mind. It is indicated by various signs such as the striking of clocks, the tolling of bells, the closing of the saloons, and the raising of the taxi rates. Expert Londoners are able to tell the difference between day and night almost as easily as we do, and speak of "this evening" and "tomorrow morning" with the greatest accuracy.

It is, however, much less easy to distinguish the technical approach of night in the other cities of England that lie outside the confines, physical and intellectual, of London and live in a continuous gloom. In such places as the great manufacturing cities of Bugginham-under-Smoke or Gloomsburg-on-Ooze night may be said to be perpetual. But of these places I propose to speak in a later paper.

QUESTIONS

1. Point out effects of caricature in Leacock's account of the "discovery" of America by visiting Englishmen.

2. What other humorous devices or effects do you find in this account?

3. Who is being satirized in the episode of the English customs and immigration officials? In the episode of the English train?

4. What is the effect of the comparison between London and South Bend, Indiana?

5. How does he manage to poke fun at both visitor and visited in the British Museum episode? In the description of Parliament?

6. What is the humorous aim and effect of his comments on the "singular salubrity and charm of the English climate"? Is the thrust of the humour here double or, for once, single?

T. H. WHITE

b. 1906

America at last ✦ ✦ ✦

This journal of an American visit is unashamedly impressionistic. T. H. White was in America at the time of the Kennedy assassination and at a moment when the race question and the problem of black-white integration was entering the consciousness of most Americans. The author gives us a series of snapshots of high and low life, of a constantly changing landscape of places, people, and ideas. Do Leacock's complaints about the "impressionism" of the travelling English lecturer apply to T. H. White's "American Journal"? Or is it possible that an eye, sharpened by a sense of difference, can see at a glance realities that are sometimes blurred by over-familiarity? White's Arthurian novel *The Once and Future King* appeared in parts from 1939 to 1958.

I WENT TO AMERICA once before, and that was to stay with Julie Andrews when she was acting in *Camelot,* the musical. I was there two or three months and adored everybody, from Julie and Richard Burton to the affable stagehands, and I thought New York was stunning — not terrible, as expected. The result was that people liked me back.

The two things that appealed most to me about New York were the Queensborough Bridge and the comicality of the skyscrapers. The bridge, with its traffic as ceaseless as hell, was the sort of Colossus which Gustave Doré might have imagined — London Bridge in a way, but with elephantiasis, an enormity of grandeur, of sheer size that could not fail to be impressive. You expected to see King Kong swinging about among the girders.

The skyscrapers (I suffer from the horror of height called acrophobia) were more than huge building blocks to overhang and terrify you. They had taken pains to be cheerful or individual or artistic and, what is more, their owners had been willing to spend money on the decoration. The only part of the skyscraper that can afford to be different from its neighbours is its top. The rest has to be utilitarian. So the tops have a gaiety of their own. I can't help thinking that it is a good thing when even businessmen are ready to acknowledge beauty, whatever their idea of it may be, by ornamenting their structures with gargoyles that must weigh hundreds of tons and cost thousands of dollars. "Look at me," says one skyscraper, "pretending to be something to do with Santa Sofia." "Or me," says another, "I am Gothic, as you can see by my sort of perpendicular arches." In a way it is a funny charade, like a lot of huge square ladies trying on Paris hats. My favourite one — and you do get to have favourites — had an airy gilt crown (can it have been gilded, or has my memory deceived me?) which she illuminated at night, coquettishly.

And, of course, the night-lit cliffs of Manhattan, those sky-filling hugenesses of bright windows for troglodytes, were a wonder of the world — as was the sinister landscape of Central Park as you looked down on it after sunset. In it, I privately believed, there emerged during the hours of darkness prehistoric tribes of Cherokees, hidden underground during the daytime, to mingle with the bums, ponces, and queers.

What I didn't like about the American trip was the Boeing 707's. In these horrifying monsters I flew at incalculable altitudes with Julie's husband, Tony Walton, both of us with streaming colds, aching ears, pocketfuls of pills, and a gradually disintegrating cardboard model of one of Tony's stage sets, unwrapped.

So this time we are going by sea in the Queen Elizabeth.

It is for a lecture tour which will cover the continent and probably destroy us with exhaustion — it is practically a matter of one-night stands. Julie's eighteen-year-old sister-in-law Carol is coming as my secretary, but really as a protectress. We are quarrelling already about tickets, visas, and lecture notes ("This is beginning to get me down," says Carol, when I point out that the notes won't be ready, which they won't – she then proceeds to invite a girl friend to tea) but this is a healthy attitude, and a safety-valve, and we can't permanently annoy each other after being friends for four years.

Our good relations, which are bound to be strained by three months of strenuous tour, depend on me. Carol I know to be an adorable member of an adorable family – not one bad one in the whole boiling – so anything which goes wrong will be my fault. I am a testy, opinionated old gentleman and in moments of stress I had better read this paragraph, preferably in private and on my knees.

It is best to face the fact, from the start, that we shan't make any money to bring back. For one thing we are going first class, and for another I have hotel bills and air fares to pay and Carol's wages – well worth it, in exchange for sanity and protection.

I am making the trip to distract the private unhappiness of old age, rather like knocking your head against a wall when you have toothache.

But today, coming down from London by train after a tussle with the American Embassy about visas, I suddenly realized that I might enjoy it – that we both might.

So why not write a book as we go? It would keep us observant, not be too much trouble for a short entry every day, and at least it could do no harm. Also, it would be a distraction in all those hundreds and thousands of miles by terrifying airplanes.

Query: Does it do harm to write needless books? "Of the making of books there is no end." Why write if you have nothing to write about? Is one trip round America sufficient excuse? Millions do it.

I suppose it is excusable, if you keep your eyes wide open. . . .

23.10.63

The sun rises on L.A. and there, outside the windows of our very luxurious motel – which has a coffee-making machine in each bedroom – are the palm trees of the subtropics, looking like a lot of untidy mops standing upside down. Also, very typical of every part of America, there is a garage ornamented with hundreds of small triangular pennants.

10 p.m. If I don't get this written now, the diary will fall behind and never never catch up with itself in the killing weeks that are to come.

This is a brief picture of our day. We got up at 8 a.m. I was interviewed at 9 a.m. by a newspaper. At 9:30 I recorded a broadcast by telephone, a broadcast I never did get around to hearing and so far as I know nor did anybody else. At 10 we took a taxi with a coloured driver who drove us the long distance to Watts Towers. At 12:30 we lunched at a diner on the way back. At 1:30 we were picked up by Professor Arnold and motored to the University buildings where I lectured to a smallish and slightly sticky audience at 1:30. (University of S. California. N.B. This Pleasures of Learning lecture is getting stale. I must develop it and not complain about sticky audiences.) At 3 o'clock Professor Arnold – a most charming, interesting, and obliging gentleman – drove us up to his rich home in Beverly Hills, where we met his clever ex-actress wife, had a cup of coffee and were taken on a tour through those heights and back through Hollywood. At 7 p.m. (somehow I seem to have changed into a tuxedo en route) we dined with the Friends of the Library, about 70, and after dinner I spoke to them till 9:30. This talk was extempore and was a success. Now I am back in the motel, tired and writing this.

We had a long conversation with the Negro cabdriver. His most interesting contribution to the integration argument was this: It is useless, said he, to put white and coloured children together at high school level. It must be done long before the age of puberty, at kindergarten level in fact, so that they may grow up getting used to each other. He himself (one of a family of 10) was interested in music, had broken off his formal education halfway through high school and joined the Army to serve abroad. He was willing to be friendly and ended by trusting us. He said to me very simply when we parted, God bless you. I said, Thank you. We passed a Negro high school on our way, which seemed clean, spacious, and full of happy children in the big playing fields. There was one white boy among them. . . .

30.10.63

Today we leave the endless spread of L.A. whose seven million people have four million cars and whose adolescents can get driving licenses at sixteen. I am not sorry, in spite of the kind people who live there and like all Americans are proud of their city, to get away from the flat, garish plain where everywhere is too far from everywhere else. Its symbol is the smog which it creates for itself, a layer which hurts the eyes and lies above the plain of motor fumes that make it.

We left its oil derricks and the pumps like praying mantises and the NO SMOKING signs which you find even out of doors in areas liable to forest fires. We left its industries and Standard Oil.

From L.A. to Portland, Oregon, it was 879 miles in a 720 jet of Western Airlines at 35,000 feet. I peered before we set out into the mysterious fans of its jet engines and admired in the first-class interior the vase of artificial flowers which adorned it.

Will artificial flowers eventually replace real ones? They don't take time and soil to grow and can be thrown away when dusty. If the imitation becomes perfect, the laws of economy will tell in their favour. Presumably they can be scented. Imitation is the sincerest form of flattery. They would be typical of Los Angeles.

I suppose we must have flown up the San Joaquin and

Sacramento valleys, leaving many miles away on our starboard wing the height of Mt. Whitney (14,496 ft.) and Yosemite Park and Lake Tahoe and Carson City and Reno where you go to be divorced (about the same size as Las Vegas where you go to gamble) and the Crater Lake. We were following the spine of the Sierra Nevada and the Cascades, an endless corrugation of crumpled paper or cardboard, desolate, terrific, lunar, deserted. Carson "was one of the legendary figures of the West who fully deserved his fame. He began as a trapper, a mountain man, in the Rockies when trappers were the only white men there, and later he guided Frémont on two epic expeditions to find a passable trail through the Rockies and the Sierra Nevada to California. Between adventures Kit Carson lived in Taos with his New Mexican wife. He was loved and trusted by everyone who knew him, whether Spanish-American, Anglo-American or Indian. His later military expeditions against the Navajos may appear ruthless in retrospect, but even there he was only doing what seemed right and proper at the time, and doing it as decently as possible."

I will never see a "Western" again on TV or movie without feeling differently about its Hollywood nonsense, after flying across these parched, Arabian, Persian Gulf desolations and grandeurs. It was lovely to get out of the urbanness, you can't say urbanity, of Los Angeles into the empty, forbidding sierras and the Oregon pines.

Yawn as you descend in a jet, and the massive thunder of its engines re-creates itself in your ears. At the real moment of descent it rumbles. . . .

5.11.63

The rest of yesterday evening was a fine lazy time in the luxurious Hilton bedroom, watching hootnannies (singsongs), etc. on the TV. I learned that the impetuous Mme. Nhu — her husband and brother-in-law assassinated — was holed up in the hotel where we had dinner with Julie. I also learned of *tab-opening cans*. You can now open a beer can, and, it is to be hoped, you will soon be able to open any other can, without a tin opener. Watching a Western movie, I reflected how important it was to know what sort of West? The West stretches from the snowy mountains where we are now to the Mojave desert where we were so recently, and no "cowboy" film can be authentic unless it is rigidly true to its own environment. I also pondered the following facts: 1) Nobody in a "Western" does any work. 2) The scenery is generally beautiful. 3) There seem to be lots of people about. (In real life, the bearded old characters slaved at their labour in frightful heat or cold, in desert landscapes which were practically unpopulated.) 4) Everybody is "on his honour" – in reality the law was the gun. 5) Everybody is rather well dressed with particularly well-tailored buttocks – in fact, most forty-niners must have been in tatters. 6) The well-fed blood horses of the movie world must really have been skin and bone.

Will anybody ever make a film about the real grandeur and toil and suffering and dauntless persistence of the pioneers who managed to survive? . . .

26.11.63

It was interesting to lie in half a coma watching America adjust itself to the assassination. The first reaction was blank, like a jigsaw puzzler who holds a piece which won't fit in anywhere. Presidents had been assassinated, they knew, but that was history and somehow not here and now. It was Lady Macbeth's reaction. "What, in *our* house?" The second was the random suspicions and rumours. Everybody in the South said that the President had been warned repeatedly not to go to Texas, to wear a bulletproof vest, etc. There was a strong faction who thought his assassin (Oswald) had had to be silenced by the second man (Ruby) because it was a "gangland" murder, or a political one (Communist, Cuban?). There was even a prevalent rumour that Ruby had hanged himself in his cell. (It gradually became plain to my own mind that Oswald had been a crazy megalomaniac with persecution mania, operating on his own, and Ruby a psychopathic lover of policemen also on his own — a random association of two loonies. It is lunatics who are the real menace to crowned heads.) The next reaction was touching. Everybody in Texas, where the murder took place, everybody in New Orleans, where the murderer was born, began to feel personally guilty. A good deal of hatred toward Kennedy had been developing in the South, a) because he came from the North and the Civil War has never been forgotten, b) because he was antisegregation, and perhaps c) because it was felt that he had bungled the Cuban situation. The consciousness of this hatred, though it had never been even near the level of assassination, made the Southerners blush with shame. Everybody felt, especially when the second killing took place, that the watching world would think ill of Americans. It was like a schoolboy's innocent guilt, very affecting.

Americans are a people who, like the Irish, have not had the benefit of spending a couple of hundred years under the discipline of the Lex and Pax Romana — the education of S.P.Q.R. They are not English, but then they are not French or Italian or Mexican or Negro either. They are all these, in the intensely important process of fusion, and the future, if there is a future, is certain to come from them. This is at present the most exciting place on earth.

Americans have a streak of lawlessness. In 1961, one murder happened every hour — this in a population of about 190 million. Somebody said on the radio yesterday, "There is a strain of violence in U.S. nature." It is to be expected. In the first place, they are bred from parents who had enough individualism, anarchy, guts, or whatever you like to call it, to emigrate. They are not bred from stay-at-homes. They are bred from the rebels who burst out. In the second place, in spreading over the relentless continent and winning the West, they have had to establish law as they pushed forward their boundaries by the individual law of the gun. In the third place, as I have been telling my audiences for two months, they are living in an actual Renaissance, a new birth of culture. People who live in Renaissances are apt to live with violence – like Marlowe or Webster or Ford. Here and now, with the cops and the gangsters and the outrages which suddenly explode, we are among the Borgias again and know the Duchess of Malfi.

Americans are young, inexperienced, idealistic, sentimental, longing for culture, confiding, lovable, wanting to be loved. They are as sweet in this way as boys at puberty, as touching, as protectable. They long to be grown-up, "correct".

After killing their President, they looked upon me uncertainly, blushing, guilty, fearing *and hoping* that I would scold them for doing wrong.

It was a deep shock to them. The people of Dallas are going about saying doubtfully, We are not really wicked?

This voluntary acceptance of blame, this innocent ambition to be an adult civilization, moved me very much.

Fortunately, in the sunlight of the late fall, it was a perfect funeral. There were no visible journalists, no crowding, no need for policemen, no vulgarity, no hysteria. Thousands upon thousands of people conducted themselves with silent dignity, sorrow and reflection in a wonderful, daylong purgation of emotion which brought the act of horror under control again.

Kennedy's death will probably do more good for the cause of integration than his life.

I watched the four-day serial on a beat-up TV set in the hospital. It was odd to see the dead President's demagogic cares being shifted from his simple and restful grave to the shoulders of his successor.

Well, death may be what life is for.

27.11.63

Adolescent America. Of course I am writing of the average, not of the intellectual – who is as international as anybody else. The average person is simple, religious, modest if not Puritan about sex, proud of his nation and particularly of his own birthplace, uncultured but respectful to culture, anxious as any other adolescent to be admired for being right, essentially good, benevolent, sentimental, prone like the young to outbursts, not very intelligent, dedicated to the herd, obtuse about variants, vigorous, in short like most other average schoolboys. He has a hard side of obstinate intolerance which comes out in witch hunts — most adolescents want to "belong" to clubs or societies — Ku Klux Klans — and he is uncertain about the difference between right and wrong, uncertain whether he is being "correct". The American dreams of ancestry and pedigree, as schoolboys dream of having been the sons of kings. His charm is that he *wants* to be good — surely it is better to be a do-gooder than a do-badder — and that he is trying with the truthful idealism of a nice teenager to become a great man.

He most certainly will, and I love him. . . .

QUESTIONS

1. Do you think a native New Yorker could have noticed, in this way, the "tops" of skyscrapers or the "sinister" landscape of Central Park?

2. Would Leacock approve of White's "excuse" for writing this book?

3. What does White imply about the problem of integration in his chat with the Negro cabdriver? What does the quick glimpse of the Negro high school and the "one white boy" add to the impression he intends to convey?

4. Comment on the artificial flowers as a symbol of Los Angeles — and Hollywood.

5. Why has no one made a real "Western" — a film about the "grandeur and toil and suffering and dauntless persistence of the pioneers who managed to survive"?

6. How does White explain American guilt feelings over the Kennedy assassination?

7. Do you agree that "Kennedy's death will probably do more good for the cause of integration than his life"?

8. Is White's comment on "adolescent" America just? prejudiced? patronizing?

PART THREE
MEN AND WOMEN

JOHN CIARDI
b. 1916

The unfading beauty: a well-filled mind ❖ ❖ ❖

The college degree in our Society is often thought of and sought after as a union card or a status symbol. How often is it dinned into us that the college man has all the best chances at all the best jobs? How many are there (their number is legion) whose academic goal is nothing more than a college-bred husband and membership in the University Women's Club? John Ciardi is not disputing the economic or social rewards of a college education. Such rewards are, at best, by-products, he implies, of a pursuit of knowledge and value whose true end is "some sense of the dimensions of a meaningful life". In this essay, the author is addressing himself to young women. But what he has to say here about the function of the imagination and the life-giving power of art is worth pondering by the young man, too – whether he is to be a teacher, a stock-broker, a medical man, an engineer, *or* an artist. John Ciardi is an editor of *Saturday Review,* a poet in his own right, and a champion of the modern idiom in American poetry. He has taught at Michigan, Harvard, and Rutgers.

ANATOLE FRANCE once observed of his countrymen that they raised their daughters in convents and then married them to pirates. Most of today's college girls will find themselves married not long after graduation, and whether or not they later think of their college days as having been passed in a convent, few of them will find themselves married to anything quite as dramatic as a real pirate, or quite as revolting as a late-nineteenth-century French pirate of finance. The present-day standard model husband is more likely to come out as a serious suburban gardener who flies his week-end flag from the patio of a split-level, and who does his daily cruising in a car pool or on the 7:45 local in the morning and on the 4:40 in the afternoon. The girls are headed for a well-advertised and basically well-padded way of life, but the gist of Anatole France's observation may still apply: it may still be that what the girls do in school is no real preparation for what they will be doing after graduation.

What a liberal arts college is supposed to do in theory is certainly clear enough and can be summarized in the single phrase: "To see life steadily and see it whole." The college exists to teach some sense of the dimensions of a meaningful life. Were our college infallibly fulfilling that purpose, there would be nothing to say to college girls, today's or yesterday's, except to congratulate, to admire them, and to envy them happily.

World as it is, however, being in college is no occasion for unreserved congratulation. Hundreds of Bachelor's degrees are being conferred annually by American colleges, and not one of them serves as any real evidence in itself that a reasonably adequate education has taken place, or that the holder of the degree has some viable sense of the whole dimension of the life that starts next.

True, it is still possible for an able and willing student to get something like an education in almost any college in the land, but the fact seems to be that no college any longer insists upon it. The educational insistence of a college is defined by its minimum standards, and the minimum standards of American colleges are everywhere too low. Even Harvard, proud as it is of its scholarly tradition, will grant a Bachelor's degree on a four-year scholastic average of three C's and a D. "Three C's and a D and keep your name out of the papers," the rule runs: practical sounding, certainly, but a bit smaller in scale than "To see life steadily and see it whole."

The colleges, for their part, can educate only up to the level permitted by society, and our society has been reluctant as a general thing to support "egghead institutions" that think Aristotle is more important than a well-rounded social life that somehow develops a quality called "leadership", a quality that seems to be best developed by doing exactly the same thing everyone else does.

I do not know by what confusion of the national mores we are so insistent on this idea of leadership, but I have received hundreds of application forms in the last year or two, and there is hardly a one that does not contain a dotted line labeled "Leadership?" Certainly as things are, no man need be an intellectual explorer to do well in American business. The chances are, in fact, that he will go further on a little common sense and a lot of social manner than he will on an enthusiasm for Chaucer. No salesman who has made the mistake of acquiring a Phi Beta Kappa key can afford to make the mistake of wearing it when he goes to call on a customer.

Nor is it likely that the affable young man with his destiny in an attaché-case is going to scour the *summa cum laude* list when he starts looking for a wife. He wants her pretty, easy to get along with, a good mixer, a good dancer, and without any freakishly high-brow ideas. Besides, there really isn't room for more than a small decorative bookcase in the rumpus-room of a split-level — not once you have put in the bar, the TV set, the TV chairs, and the card table.

The girls know all this very well, and to the extent that they know it, they have before them no such transition as Anatole France saw from the convent to the pirate's bed. They know the advertised standard and most of them will slip into it eagerly and without a hitch. The chance they must take, however, is that the dreary gist of that advertised standard will eventually trap them into dullness. A few years ago one of our largest corporations prepared for distribution in the Ivy League colleges a pamphlet advising the boys how to behave as undergraduates if they wanted a corporation career after graduation. One sentence from that pamphlet could not be improved as a summary of the necessary intellectual tone. "Personal opinions," it read, "can cause a lot of trouble." The student editor of the Princeton newspaper assaulted the pamphlet and especially that sentence as a desecration of the free mind, and the corporation sent down as trouble-shooters the man who had written the pamphlet and a vice-president in charge of public relations. As I have the story, the pamphlet writer could not see what there was to argue. Personal opinions *can* cause a lot of trouble; everyone knows that. The vice-president, on the other hand, granted the student's point and the pamphlet was withdrawn and later rewritten. Victory for the free mind, perhaps, but there still remains one speculation: did the vice-president really see that a great principle was involved, or was he simply acting as a good public-relations man soothing a possibly troublesome crackpot?

Wherever the speculation comes out, the girls are reasonably well aware of what is required of a successful corporate wife, and while they have enough public-relations sense on their own to get along with the fuddy-duddy faculty, they are certainly not going to ruin their chances by getting themselves reputations as bookworm intellectuals.

So it happens that our colleges are divided into two cultural groups whose values tend to meet only in the most tangential ways. The faculty group is made up of men and women not particularly distinguished as smooth dancers but, rather, dedicated to books; so dedicated, in fact, that they are willing to live on academic salaries in return for the freedom of having their reading interfered with by students, most of whom are only taking the course because they have to. The student group does share the same campus with the faculty group, but tends to center around the jukebox in the snack bar rather than around the library. Professor Jones is eager to explain the Greek aorist and to show its connection with the Latin ablative absolute, but what the girls really want out of Greek Week is a good date for the dance. Let the faculty praise great minds; the girls are there to get married, most of them as per the advertised standard.

And were that advertised standard a sufficient and a lasting truth, the colleges would be more than justified in becoming finishing schools of the minor social graces. And may the graces flourish: the least thing the world needs is ungainly and ungracious women. The trouble with the advertised standard is that it simply is not true enough. It does to lounge in; it cannot do to live by. Its plot starts well, but the later chapters have an alarming tendency to fall to pieces.

It is those later chapters the girls generally fail to foresee, and it is that failure that still gives point to Anatole France's observation. For it may well be argued that we are raising our daughters in some sort of illusory heaven and then turning them loose to be mortal. Americans have always tended to be a bit surprised at their own deaths; it all seems so unprogressive. It almost seems that the Constitution, or at least General Motors, should have taken care of that.

But why should the girls be thinking of mortality? They have better things to foresee, glorious things. They see the excitement of the wedding, of the honeymoon, of setting up housekeeping, of the children arriving, and of the busy happy years of raising a family. It seems a paradise, and it is. It seems an eternity, and it is not. But who needs Plato among the nursery babble? As Yeats put it, beginning with what might very reasonably be taken as a reference to the faculty:

> That is no country for old men. The young
> In one another's arms, birds in the trees
> – Those dying generations – at their song,
> The salmon-falls, the mackerel-crowded seas,
> Fish, flesh, or fowl, commend all summer long
> Whatever is begotten, born, and dies.
> Caught in that sensual music, all neglect
> Monuments of unaging intellect.

The faculty has no place in paradise. Their monuments of unaging intellect are meaningless to those caught up in that sensual music. The monuments have point only in the silence that follows the music.

And that silence comes. By the time today's college girl has reached thirty-five and forty, having spent fifteen or twenty years busily and happily rearing a family that has needed her, she will find that the children have grown free. There will come a morning after the last of them has moved out to his own life. She will get up at 7:30 for a strangely silent breakfast with her husband who eight years ago was promoted from the 7:45 local to the 8:50. She would like to talk to him, but through her busy years she will have lost touch with his business affairs. And he, doggedly working away at his thrombosis, has his own thoughts to think.

By 8:30 he will have left, and there is the day stretching ahead. Dawdle as she will, the breakfast dishes are in the dishwasher by 9:00. The cleaning woman will be in tomorrow to do the house, which is immaculate anyhow. And the ironing woman will be in the day after to do the clothes. She could write that letter to Mary, but 10:00 o'clock is still a long way off. And 11:00. And is lunch worth bothering with just for herself? Well, maybe a really fancy dinner. But that is hours ahead and the pushbutton oven will do most of that anyhow. And what is there to do? Today, tomorrow, and the next day? What will there ever be to do?

She will have entered the First Loneliness. Statistically, too, she will have entered the circle of possible widowhood. The years that follow are those in which her husband is more and more likely to achieve the final thrombosis of his success. American women outlive their husbands by an average of six years. Six years is perhaps not an alarming figure, but to begin with it is a bit higher among the wives of professional men. And if the average for all is six years, it must follow that the average for half will be more nearly twelve, and that for a quarter of them it will be more nearly twenty-four. May it be later rather than sooner, but there can be no doubt that the unadvertised years also lie ahead.

And what will today's college girls take into those long,

well-padded, and lonely years? There is touring, of course. And there is bridge. And there is TV. And there are community projects, and gardening, and gay little shopping trips with the other girls. But is it enough? Ernest Hemingway once said to Marlene Dietrich, "Daughter, never confuse motion with action." Our better suburbs – and by this time most of the girls will have graduated from the split-level to the custom-built house – are full of little organizations devoted to making motions for the girls to go through. But there still remains that force at the core of the unstultified psyche that cries for a more meaningful and more human thing to do, that cries for action rather than motion.

Many such women make sudden awkward gestures of turning to the arts again. They used to play the piano rather well. Or they used to write for the college magazine. Now that they no longer have the P.T.A. on their hands, why not start again?

Many of them turn to poetry; and because a poet is easily taken as some sort of summonable clergyman, many have sent their poems to me, as if I had no more to do than to spend a day reading and criticizing them. At that, one would somehow make the time if the poems were not so hopeless. For invariably it is too late. There is that about an art form that will not survive being held in abeyance for a decade or two. They should have had enough devotion to have kept it alive. If only in a stolen hour of the day. If only at the expense of sleep. It can be done. As Salvador Dali once declared: "One always has time to do what he really wants to do." One may have to pay a price for it, but one does pay the price for his true hungers. It is not easy, but to quote Yeats once again:

> To be born woman is to know,
> Though it's not taught to us at school,
> That we must labor to be beautiful.

No, it is not easy. It is something better than easy: it is joyous. It is, as Frost put it, "The pleasure of taking pains." That gracious lady, distinguished biographer, and my good friend,

Catherine Drinker Bowen, raised her family and managed her household for years while turning out a series of meticulously researched biographies, stealing one piece of every day at whatever cost, putting herself through the routine busyness of her day in the excitement of anticipating that hour at her own particular work. She had, in fact, had two books selected by the Book of the Month Club before she dared label her income-tax form "author" rather than "housewife".

A human being is finally defined by what he does with his attention. It is difficult to keep one's attention in order; difficult and demanding. How much easier it is to let one's mind into a lawn chair of the advertised life and to tune it there to Hollywood scenarios, or to let it drift into what Aldous Huxley called "the endless idiot gibberish of the reverie". It is easier to be inane; but the price is boredom, emptiness, and finally the inability to communicate meaningfully with any human being. How many mothers are there in America today who have begotten sons of their own body and pain and are now unable to speak to them except in the stereotype of "Mom" and "Dicky-boy", rather than as human being to human being, open to both joys and distresses but bound together by a love that includes understanding. It was a better thing than stereotypes that Adam and Eve began, and whoever allows that better thing to be lessened in himself lessens the possibility of the race.

It is what one does with his attention that defines him, and because art is the best ordering we have of human attention, there can be no truly meaningful life without the dimension of art. The arts – and I take them to include religion, philosophy, and history at those points where they are least dogmatic and most speculative – teach us not only ideas but the very dimension of possibility in idea. There is a resonance in a great line of poetry without which the mind cannot truly tune itself. Listen to your own mind. Think the best thing you know. Then measure it against such a line as Wallace Stevens' "The major abstraction is the idea of man." Who can permit himself to think that what was in his mind before he read that line was as good as what was in his mind as he read it? Or listen to John Donne: "And now goodmorrow to our waking souls/Which watch not one another out of fear." Those lines may take a bit of mental focusing, but what a concept of love they speak! Whatever mental effort they require is indistinguishable from joy, and what the effort leaves behind it is a better human being.

Art is the resonance of inseeing joy, but that resonance is only the beginning. Every work of art is a piece of life one may have for the taking. It is not a thing said about an experience, it is the experience itself, not only re-enacted but given form, and therefore, value. Art is the best memory of the race. Art stores up in everlasting form the most meaningful experiences of the most perceptive minds of the past, and because there is such a thing as vicarious experience any man is free to relive those experiences, which is to say, he is free to take those lives into his life. May heaven defend those people who live no lives but their own. Imagine being only Susie Jones when one could also be Penelope, and Cleopatra, and Ophelia, and Madame Du Barry, and Emma Bovary, and Anna Karenina. And may heaven defend the man married to the woman who has not tried all those other necessary lives into herself. Nothing will defend monogamy sooner than a wife who — this side of schizophrenia, to be sure — contains her pluralities. "Age cannot wither her, nor custom stale/Her infinite variety."

And that finally is what any good book is about. A good book offers the reader a life he has no time for on the clock-as-it-ticks, and a world he may enter *as if* in actual fact. A great book is distinguished from a good book only by the size of the life and the world it offers, but no novel or book of poems is worth reading unless it has that basic fact of experience to offer.

Art cannot fend loss and loneliness from any life. Loss and loneliness will fall as they must, and for many people they fall inevitably. But let the meaningful woman look at the statistical probability of that loss and loneliness that lies before her, and let her ask what she will take into those years. Can a mind with Mozart in it ever be as lost as a mind with nothing in it? If girls now in college, just out of college, or even several years away from it do no more than set themselves a twenty-year program of reading meaningfully and carrying alive in their minds one passage a day from the English poets, can they fail to see that they will be more valuable to their families as mothers, and more valuable to themselves as widows?

One of Hemingway's characters in "Winner Take Nothing" is told that so-and-so is a coward and he answers, "He didn't invent it." The line is underplayed but a great understanding and a great mercy shine through it. One could do worse than to store a bit of that understanding and mercy for himself. So stored, one may learn in time that whatever happens to him is not his own invention. He may learn to see then that there is such a thing as the experience of the race on this planet, and learning that he will learn that one who takes that experience into himself has joined himself to the ever-uncertain but ever-hopeful and sometimes glorious continuum of man-and-woman born of man-and-woman.

It is that one must say to today's college girls. That they are beautiful, and ignorant, and illusory. And that only as they learn to shape their attention to the long memory we call the humanities, can they be beautiful after the bloom is off, and understandingly compassionate as time furrows them, and real to the lives they labor to make shapely.

QUESTIONS

1. What does the author believe to be the central purpose of the liberal arts college? What is your own principal reason for "going to college"?

2. Does the author believe that the colleges are successful in doing what in theory they are supposed to be doing?

3. To what extent does the author believe Society to be responsible for the shortcomings of the colleges? How do the attitudes and expectations of modern Society affect the standards and values of the colleges and of the students themselves?

4. Explain what the author means by saying that "our colleges are divided into two cultural groups"? What is the importance for his argument of the fact of this division, this great gulf fixed between faculty and students? Do you know of any recent efforts to change this situation?

5. In relation to the argument of the essay, what is meant by Hemingway's advice: "never confuse motion with action"?

6. What does the author mean by "the arts"? To what extent, in his view, can the arts overcome the "First Loneliness" and turn motion into action?

7. Explain the importance for the argument here of the quotation from Hemingway's "Winner Take Nothing".

8. What, in effect, is the author's advice to a student about to begin his studies at a university or college?

D. H. LAWRENCE

1885-1930

Odour of chrysanthemums ✦ ✦

"Odour of Chrysanthemums" was one of Lawrence's earliest stories. When the editor of the *English Review* read it, he accepted it for publication in his magazine immediately, regarding it as a work of genius. Lawrence was then twenty-six years old. Lawrence's stories and novels often expressed the theme first announced here – that men and women can seldom satisfy their profound need for love, and most of the time live in desperate isolation. Some of his novels that develop this conviction are *Sons and Lovers* (1913), *The Rainbow* (1915), *Women in Love* (1920), and *Lady Chatterley's Lover* (1928). His stories are collected in a volume entitled *Tales of D. H. Lawrence* (1934). The gifted son of a coal-miner, Lawrence grew up in the coal-mining district of Nottinghamshire. Through scholarships he was able to attend university, and for several years taught school. His mother, a strong-willed former teacher who despised her husband, encouraged her son in his studies and tried to find consolation for her unhappy marriage in his artistic development. "Odour of Chrysanthemums" is strongly influenced by Lawrence's memory of her and of his troubled childhood. In 1912 he wrote to an acquaintance, "It is a story full of my childhood's atmosphere." His attempt to re-create this atmosphere is clear from the opening paragraphs.

THE SMALL locomotive engine, Number 4, came clanking, stumbling down from Selston with seven full wagons. It appeared round the corner with loud threats of speed, but the colt that it startled from among the gorse, which still flickered indistinctly in the raw afternoon, out-distanced it at a canter. A woman, walking up the railway line to Underwood, drew back into the hedge, held her basket aside, and watched the footplate of the engine advancing. The trucks thumped heavily past, one by one, with slow inevitable movement, as she stood insignificantly trapped between the jolting black wagons and the hedge; then they curved away towards the coppice where the withered oak leaves dropped noiselessly, while the birds, pulling at the scarlet hips beside the track, made off into the dusk that had already crept into the spinney. In the open, the smoke from the engine sank and cleaved to the rough grass. The fields were dreary and forsaken, and in the marshy strip that led to the whimsey, a reedy pit-pond, the fowls had already abandoned their run among the alders, to roost in the tarred fowl-house. The pit-bank loomed up beyond the pond, flames like red sores licking its ashy sides, in the afternoon's stagnant light. Just beyond rose the tapering chimneys and the clumsy black headstocks of Brinsley Colliery. The two wheels were spinning fast up against the sky, and the winding engine rapped out its little spasms. The miners were being turned up.

The engine whistled as it came into the wide bay of railway lines beside the colliery, where rows of trucks stood in harbour.

Miners, single, trailing and in groups, passed like shadows diverging home. At the edge of the ribbed level of sidings squat a low cottage, three steps down from the cinder track. A large bony vine clutched at the house, as if to claw down the tiled roof. Round the bricked yard grew a few wintry primroses. Beyond, the long garden sloped down to a bush-covered brook course. There were some twiggy apple trees, winter-crack trees, and ragged cabbages. Beside the path hung dishevelled pink chrysanthemums, like pink cloths hung on bushes. A woman came stooping out of the felt-covered fowl-house, half-way down the garden. She closed and padlocked the door, then drew herself erect, having brushed some bits from her white apron.

She was a tall woman of imperious mien, handsome, with definite black eyebrows. Her smooth black hair was parted exactly. For a few moments she stood steadily watching the miners as they passed along the railway: then she turned towards the brook course. Her face was calm and set, her mouth was closed with disillusionment. After a moment she called:

"John!" There was no answer. She waited, and then said distinctly:

"Where are you?"

"Here!" replied a child's sulky voice from among the bushes. The woman looked piercingly through the dusk.

"Are you at that brook?" she asked sternly.

For answer the child showed himself before the raspberry-canes that rose like whips. He was a small, sturdy boy of five. He stood quite still, defiantly.

"Oh!" said the mother, conciliated. "I thought you were down at that wet brook – and you remember what I told you——"

The boy did not move or answer.

"Come, come on in," she said more gently, "it's getting dark. There's your grandfather's engine coming down the line!"

The lad advanced slowly, with resentful taciturn movement. He was dressed in trousers and waistcoat of cloth that was too thick and hard for the size of the garments. They were evidently cut down from a man's clothes.

As they went slowly towards the house he tore at the ragged wisps of chrysanthemums and dropped the petals in handfuls among the path.

"Don't do that – it does look nasty," said his mother. He refrained, and she, suddenly pitiful, broke off a twig with three or four wan flowers and held them against her face. When mother and son reached the yard her hand hesitated, and instead of laying the flower aside, she pushed it in her apron-band. The mother and son stood at the foot of the three steps looking across the bay of lines at the passing home of the miners. The trundle of the small train was imminent. Suddenly the engine loomed past the house and came to a stop opposite the gate.

The engine-driver, a short man with round grey beard, leaned out of the cab high above the woman.

"Have you got a cup of tea?" he said in a cheery, hearty fashion.

It was her father. She went in, saying she would mash. Directly, she returned.

"I didn't come to see you on Sunday," began the little grey-bearded man.

"I didn't expect you," said his daughter.

The engine-driver winced; then, reassuming his cheery, airy manner, he said:

"Oh, have you heard then? Well, and what do you think——?"

"I think it is soon enough," she replied.

At her brief censure the little man made an impatient gesture, and said coaxingly, yet with dangerous coldness:

"Well, what's a man to do? It's no sort of life for a man of my years, to sit at my own hearth like a stranger. And if I'm going to marry again it may as well be soon as late – what does it matter to anybody?"

The woman did not reply, but turned and went into the house. The man in the engine-cab stood assertive till she returned with a cup of tea and a piece of bread and butter on a plate. She went up the steps and stood near the foot-plate of the hissing engine.

"You needn't 'a' brought me bread an' butter," said her father. "But a cup of tea" – he sipped appreciatively – "it's very nice." He sipped for a moment or two, then: "I heard as Walter's got another bout on," he said.

"When hasn't he?" said the woman bitterly.

"I heerd tell of him in the 'Lord Nelson' braggin' as he was going to spend that b——afore he went: half a sovereign that was."

"When?" asked the woman.

"A' Sat'day night – I know that's true."

"Very likely," she laughed bitterly. "He gives me twenty-three shillings."

"Aye, it's a nice thing, when a man can do nothing with his money but make a beast of himself!" said the grey-whiskered man. The woman turned her head away. Her father swallowed the last of his tea and handed her the cup.

"Aye," he sighed, wiping his mouth. "It's a settler, it is——"

He put his hand on the lever. The little engine strained and groaned, and the train rumbled towards the crossing. The woman again looked across the metals. Darkness was settling over the spaces of the railway and trucks: the miners, in grey sombre groups, were still passing home. The winding engine pulsed hurriedly, with brief pauses. Elizabeth Bates looked at the dreary flow of men, then she went indoors. Her husband did not come.

The kitchen was small and full of firelight; red coals piled glowing up the chimney mouth. All the life of the room seemed in the white, warm hearth and the steel fender reflecting the red fire. The cloth was laid for tea; cups glinted in the shadows. At the back, where the lowest stairs protruded into the room, the boy sat struggling with a knife and a piece of white wood. He was almost hidden in the shadow. It was half-past four. They had but to await the father's coming to begin tea. As the mother watched her son's sullen little struggle with the wood, she saw herself in his silence and pertinacity; she saw the father in her child's indifference to all but himself. She seemed to be occupied by her husband. He had probably gone past his home, slunk past his own door, to drink before he came in, while his dinner spoiled and wasted in waiting. She glanced at the clock, then took the potatoes to strain them in the yard. The garden and fields beyond the brook were closed in uncertain darkness. When she rose with the saucepan, leaving the drain steaming into the night behind her, she saw the yellow lamps were lit along the high road that went up the hill away beyond the space of the railway lines and the field.

Then again she watched the men trooping home, fewer now and fewer.

Indoors the fire was sinking and the room was dark red. The woman put her saucepan on the hob, and set a batter-pudding near the mouth of the oven. Then she stood unmoving. Directly, gratefully, came quick young steps to the door. Someone hung on the latch a moment, then a little girl entered and began pulling off her outdoor things, dragging a mass of curls, just ripening from gold to brown, over her eyes with her hat.

Her mother chid her for coming late from school, and said she would have to keep her at home the dark winter days.

"Why, mother, it's hardly a bit dark yet. The lamp's not lighted, and my father's not home."

"No, he isn't. But it's a quarter to five! Did you see anything of him?"

The child became serious. She looked at her mother with large, wistful blue eyes.

"No, mother, I've never seen him. Why? Has he come up an' gone past, to Old Brinsley? He hasn't, mother, 'cos I never saw him."

"He'd watch that," said the mother bitterly, "he'd take care as you didn't see him. But you may depend upon it, he's seated in the 'Prince o' Wales'. He wouldn't be this late."

The girl looked at her mother piteously.

"Let's have our teas, mother, should we?" said she.

The mother called John to table. She opened the door once more and looked out across the darkness of the lines. All was deserted: she could not hear the winding engines.

"Perhaps," she said to herself, "he's stopped to get some ripping done."

They sat down to tea. John, at the end of the table near the door, was almost lost in the darkness. Their faces were hidden from each other. The girl crouched against the fender slowly moving a thick piece of bread before the fire. The lad, his face a dusky mark on the shadow, sat watching her who was transfigured in the red glow.

"I do think it's beautiful to look in the fire," said the child.

"Do you?" said her mother. "Why?"

"It's so red, and full of little caves – and it feels so nice, and you can fair smell it."

"It'll want mending directly," replied her mother, "and then if your father comes he'll carry on and say there never is a fire when a man comes home sweating from the pit. A public-house is always warm enough."

There was silence till the boy said complainingly: "Make haste, our Annie."

"Well, I am doing! I can't make the fire do it no faster, can I?"

"She keeps wafflin' it about so's to make 'er slow," grumbled the boy.

"Don't have such an evil imagination, child," replied the mother.

Soon the room was busy in the darkness with the crisp sound of crunching. The mother ate very little. She drank her tea determinedly, and sat thinking. When she rose her anger was evident in the stern unbending of her head. She looked at the pudding in the fender, and broke out:

"It is a scandalous thing as a man can't even come home to his dinner! If it's crozzled up to a cinder I don't see why I should care. Past his very door he goes to get to a public-house, and here I sit with his dinner waiting for him——"

She went out. As she dropped piece after piece of coal on the red fire, the shadows fell on the walls, till the room was almost in total darkness.

"I canna see," grumbled the invisible John. In spite of herself, the mother laughed.

"You know the way to your mouth," she said. She set the dust-pan outside the door. When she came again like a shadow on the hearth, the lad repeated, complainingly, sulkily:

"I canna see."

"Good gracious!" cried the mother irritably, "you're as bad as your father if it's a bit dusk!"

Nevertheless, she took a paper spill from a sheaf on the mantelpiece and proceeded to light the lamp that hung from the ceiling in the middle of the room. As she reached up, her figure displayed itself just rounding with maternity.

"Oh, mother——!" exclaimed the girl.

"What?" said the woman, suspended in the act of putting the lamp-glass over the flame. The copper reflector shone handsomely on her, as she stood with uplifted arm, turning to face her daughter.

"You've got a flower in your apron!" said the child, in a little rapture at this unusual event.

"Goodness me!" exclaimed the woman, relieved. "One would think the house was afire." She replaced the glass and waited a moment before turning up the wick. A pale shadow was seen floating vaguely on the floor.

"Let me smell!" said the child, still rapturously, coming forward and putting her face to her mother's waist.

"Go along, silly!" said the mother, turning up the lamp. The light revealed their suspense so that the woman felt it almost unbearable. Annie was still bending at her waist. Irritably, the mother took the flowers out from her apron band.

"Oh, mother – don't take them out!" Annie cried, catching her hand and trying to replace the sprig.

"Such nonsense!" said the mother, turning away. The child put the pale chrysanthemums to her lips, murmuring:

"Don't they smell beautiful!"

Her mother gave a short laugh.

"No," she said, "not to me. It was chrysanthemums when I married him, and chrysanthemums when you were born, and the first time they ever brought him home drunk, he'd got brown chrysanthemums in his button-hole."

She looked at the children. Their eyes and their parted lips were wondering. The mother sat rocking in silence for some time. Then she looked at the clock.

"Twenty minutes to six!" In a tone of fine bitter carelessness she continued: "Eh, he'll not come now till they bring him. There he'll stick! But he needn't come rolling in here in his pit-dirt, for *I* won't wash him. He can lie on the floor – Eh, what a fool I've been, what a fool! And this is what I came here for, to this dirty hole, rats and all, for him to slink past his very door. Twice last week – he's begun now——"

She silenced herself, and rose to clear the table.

While for an hour or more the children played, subduedly intent, fertile of imagination, united in fear of the mother's wrath, and in dread of their father's home-coming, Mrs. Bates sat in her rocking-chair making a 'singlet' of thick cream-coloured flannel, which gave a dull wounded sound as she tore off the grey edge. She worked at her sewing with energy, listening to the children, and her anger wearied itself, lay down to rest, opening its eyes from time to time and steadily watching, its ears raised to listen. Sometimes even her anger quailed and shrank, and the mother suspended her sewing, tracing the footsteps that thudded along the sleepers outside; she would lift her head sharply to bid the children "hush", but she recovered herself in time, and the footsteps went past the gate, and the children were not flung out of their play-world.

But at last Annie sighed, and gave in. She glanced at her wagon of slippers, and loathed the game. She turned plaintively to her mother.

"Mother!" – but she was inarticulate.

John crept out like a frog from under the sofa. His mother glanced up.

"Yes," she said, "just look at those shirt-sleeves!"

The boy held them out to survey them, saying nothing. Then somebody called in a hoarse voice away down the line, and suspense bristled in the room, till two people had gone by outside, talking.

"It is time for bed," said the mother.

"My father hasn't come," wailed Annie plaintively. But her mother was primed with courage.

"Never mind. They'll bring him when he does come — like a log." She meant there would be no scene. "And he may sleep on the floor till he wakes himself. I know he'll not go to work tomorrow after this!"

The children had their hands and faces wiped with a flannel. They were very quiet. When they had put on their nightdresses, they said their prayers, the boy mumbling. The mother looked down at them, at the brown silken bush of intertwining curls in the nape of the girl's neck, at the little black head of the lad, and her heart burst with anger at their father, who caused all three such distress. The children hid their faces in her skirts for comfort.

When Mrs. Bates came down, the room was strangely empty, with a tension of expectancy. She took up her sewing and stitched for some time without raising her head. Meantime her anger was tinged with fear.

II

The clock struck eight and she rose suddenly dropping her sewing on her chair. She went to the stair-foot door, opened it listening. Then she went out, locking the door behind her.

Something scuffled in the yard, and she started, though she knew it was only the rats with which the place was overrun. The night was very dark. In the great bay of railway lines, bulked with trucks, there was no trace of light, only away back she could see a few yellow lamps at the pit-top, and the red smear of the burning pit-bank on the night. She hurried along the edge of the track, then, crossing the converging lines, came to the stile by the white gates, whence she emerged on the road. Then the fear which had led her shrank. People were walking up to New Brinsley; she saw the lights in the houses; twenty yards farther on were the broad windows of the 'Prince of Wales', very warm and bright, and the loud voices of men could be heard distinctly. What a fool she had been to imagine that anything had happened to him! He was merely drinking over there at the

'Prince of Wales'. She faltered. She had never yet been to fetch him, and she never would go. So she continued her walk towards the long straggling line of houses, standing back on the highway. She entered a passage between the dwellings.

"Mr. Rigley? – Yes! Did you want him? No, he's not in at this minute."

The raw-boned woman leaned forward from her dark scullery and peered at the other, upon whom fell a dim light through the blind of the kitchen window.

"Is it Mrs. Bates?" she asked in a tone tinged with respect.

"Yes. I wondered if your Master was at home. Mine hasn't come yet."

" 'Asn't 'e! Oh, Jack's been 'ome an' 'ad 'is dinner an' gone out. 'E's just gone for 'alf an hour afore bed-time. Did you call at the 'Prince of Wales'?"

"No——"

"No, you didn't like——! It's not very nice." The other woman was indulgent. There was an awkward pause. "Jack never said nothink about – about your Master," she said.

"No! – I expect he's stuck in there!"

Elizabeth Bates said this bitterly, and with recklessness. She knew that the woman across the yard was standing at her door listening, but she did not care. As she turned:

"Stop a minute! I'll just go an' ask Jack if 'e knows anythink," said Mrs. Rigley.

"Oh no – I wouldn't like to put——!"

"Yes, I will, if you'll just step inside an' see as th' childer doesn't come downstairs and set theirselves afire."

Elizabeth Bates, murmuring a remonstrance, stepped inside. The other woman apologized for the state of the room.

The kitchen needed apology. There were little frocks and trousers and childish undergarments on the squab and on the floor, and a litter of playthings everywhere. On the black American cloth of the table were pieces of bread and cake, crusts, slops, and a teapot with cold tea.

"Eh, ours is just as bad," said Elizabeth Bates, looking at

the woman, not at the house. Mrs. Rigley put a shawl over her head and hurried out, saying:

"I shanna be a minute."

The other sat, noting with faint disapproval the general untidiness of the room. Then she fell to counting the shoes of various sizes scattered over the floor. There were twelve. She sighed and said to herself: "No wonder!" – glancing at the litter. There came the scratching of two pairs of feet on the yard, and the Rigleys entered. Elizabeth Bates rose. Rigley was a big man, with very large bones. His head looked particularly bony. Across his temple was a blue scar, caused by a wound got in the pit, a wound in which the coal-dust remained blue like tattooing.

" 'Asna 'e come whoam yit?" asked the man, without any form of greeting, but with deference and sympathy. "I couldna say wheer he is – 'e's non ower theer!" – he jerked his head to signify the 'Prince of Wales'.

" 'E's 'appen gone up to th' 'Yew'," said Mrs. Rigley.

There was another pause. Rigley had evidently something to get off his mind:

"Ah left 'im finishin' a stint," he began. "Loose-all 'ad bin gone about ten minutes when we com'n away, an' I shouted: 'Are ter comin', Walt?' an' 'e said: 'Go on, Ah shanna be but a'ef a minnit,' so we com'n ter th' bottom, me an' Bowers, thinkin' as 'e wor just behint, an' 'ud come up i' th' next bantle——"

He stood perplexed, as if answering a charge of deserting his mate. Elizabeth Bates, now again certain of disaster, hastened to reassure him:

"I expect 'e's gone up to th' 'Yew Tree', as you say. It's not the first time. I've fretted myself into a fever before now. He'll come home when they carry him."

"Ay, isn't it too bad!" deplored the other woman.

"I'll just step up to Dick's an' see if 'e *is* theer," offered the man, afraid of appearing alarmed, afraid of taking liberties.

"Oh, I wouldn't think of bothering you that far," said

Elizabeth Bates, with emphasis, but he knew she was glad of his offer.

As they stumbled up the entry, Elizabeth Bates heard Rigley's wife run across the yard and open her neighbour's door. At this, suddenly all the blood in her body seemed to switch away from her heart.

"Mind!" warned Rigley. "Ah've said many a time as Ah'd fill up them ruts in this entry, sumb'dy 'ill be breakin' their legs yit."

She recovered herself and walked quickly along with the miner.

"I don't like leaving the children in bed, and nobody in the house," she said.

"No, you dunna!" he replied courteously. They were soon at the gate of the cottage.

"Well, I shanna be many minnits. Dunna you be frettin' now 'e'll be all right," said the butty.

"Thank you very much, Mr. Rigley," she replied.

"You're welcome!" he stammered, moving away. "I shanna be many minnits."

The house was quiet. Elizabeth Bates took off her hat and shawl, and rolled back the rug. When she had finished, she sat down. It was a few minutes past nine. She was startled by the rapid chuff of the winding engine at the pit, and the sharp whirr of the brakes on the rope as it descended. Again she felt the painful sweep of her blood, and she put her hand to her side, saying aloud: "Good gracious! – it's only the nine o'clock deputy going down," rebuking herself.

She sat still, listening. Half an hour of this, and she was wearied out.

"What am I working myself up like this for?" she said pitiably to herself, "I s'll only be doing myself some damage."

She took out her sewing again.

At a quarter to ten there were footsteps. One person! She watched for the door to open. It was an elderly woman, in a black bonnet and a black woollen shawl – his mother. She was about sixty years old, pale, with blue eyes, and her face all wrinkled and lamentable. She shut the door and turned to her daughter-in-law peevishly.

"Eh, Lizzie, whatever shall we do, whatever shall we do!" she cried.

Elizabeth drew back a little sharply.

"What is it, mother?" she said.

The elder woman seated herself on the sofa.

"I don't know, child, I can't tell you!" – she shook her head slowly. Elizabeth sat watching her, anxious and vexed.

"I don't know," replied the grandmother sighing very deeply. "There's no end to my troubles, there isn't. The things I've gone through, I'm sure it's enough——!" She wept without wiping her eyes, the tears running.

"But, mother," interrupted Elizabeth, "what do you mean? What is it?"

The grandmother slowly wiped her eyes. The fountains of her tears were stopped by Elizabeth's directness. She wiped her eyes slowly.

"Poor child! Eh, you poor thing!" she moaned. "I don't know what we're going to do, I don't – and you as you are – it's a thing, it is indeed!"

Elizabeth waited.

"Is he dead?" she asked, and at the words her heart swung violently, though she felt a slight flush of shame at the ultimate extravagance of the question. Her words sufficiently frightened the old lady, almost brought her to herself.

"Don't say so, Elizabeth! We'll hope it's not as bad as that; no, may the Lord spare us that, Elizabeth. Jack Rigley came just as I was sittin' down to a glass afore going to bed, an' 'e said: ''Appen you'll go down th' line, Mrs. Bates. Walt's had an accident. 'Appen you'll go an' sit wi' 'er till we can get him home.' I hadn't time to ask him a word afore he was gone. An' I put my bonnet on an' come straight down Lizzie. I thought to myself: 'Eh, that poor blessed child, if anybody should come an' tell her of a sudden, there's no knowin' what'll 'appen to 'er.' You mustn't let it upset you, Lizzie – or you know what to expect. How long is it, six months — or is it five, Lizzie? Ay!" — the old woman shook her head — "time slips on, it slips on! Ay!"

Elizabeth's thoughts were busy elsewhere. If he was killed — would she be able to manage on the little pension and what she could earn? — she counted up rapidly. If he was hurt — they wouldn't take him to the hospital — how tiresome he would be to nurse! — but perhaps she'd be able to get him away from the drink and his hateful ways. She would — while he was ill. The tears offered to come to her eyes at the picture. But what sentimental luxury was this she was beginning? She turned to consider the children. At any rate she was absolutely necessary for them. They were her business.

"Ay!" repeated the old woman, "it seems but a week or two since he brought me his first wages. Ay — he was a good lad, Elizabeth, he was, in his way. I don't know why he got to be such a trouble, I don't. He was a happy lad at home, only full of spirits. But there's no mistake he's been a handful of trouble, he has! I hope the Lord'll spare him to mend his ways. I hope so, I hope so. You've had a sight o' trouble with him, Elizabeth, you have indeed. But he was a jolly enough lad wi' me, he was, I can assure you. I don't know how it is. . . ."

The old woman continued to muse aloud, a monotonous, irritating sound, while Elizabeth thought concentratedly, startled once, when she heard the winding-engine chuff quickly, and the brakes skirr with a shriek. Then she heard the engine more slowly, and the brakes made no sound. The old woman did not notice. Elizabeth waited in suspense. The mother-in-law talked, with lapses into silence.

"But he wasn't your son, Lizzie, an' it makes a difference. Whatever he was, I remember him when he was little, an' I learned to understand him and to make allowances. You've got to make allowances for them——"

It was half-past ten, and the old woman was saying: "But it's trouble from beginning to end; you're never too old for trouble, never too old for that——" when the gate banged back, and there were heavy feet on the steps.

"I'll go, Lizzie, let me go," cried the old woman, rising. But Elizabeth was at the door. It was a man in pit clothes.

"They're bringin' 'im, Missis," he said. Elizabeth's heart halted a moment. Then it surged on again, almost suffocating her.

"Is he – is it bad?" she asked.

The man turned away, looking at the darkness.

"The doctor says 'e'd been dead hours. 'E saw 'im i' th' lamp-cabin."

The old woman, who stood just behind Elizabeth, dropped into a chair, and folded her hands, crying: "Oh, my boy, my boy!"

"Hush!" said Elizabeth, with a sharp twitch of a frown. "Be still, mother, don't waken th' children: I wouldn't have them down for anything!"

The old woman moaned softly, rocking herself. The man was drawing away. Elizabeth took a step forward.

"How was it?" she asked.

"Well, I couldn't say for sure," the man replied, very ill at ease. " 'E wor finishin' a stint an' th' butties 'ad gone, an' a lot o' stuff come down atop 'n 'im."

"And crushed him?" cried the widow, with a shudder.

"No," said the man, "it fell at th' back of 'im. 'E wor under th' face, an' it niver touch 'im. It shut 'im in. It seems 'e wor smothered."

Elizabeth shrank back. She heard the old woman behind her cry:

"What? – what did 'e say it was?"

The man replied, more loudly: " 'E wor smothered!"

Then the old woman wailed aloud, and this relieved Elizabeth.

"Oh, mother," she said, putting her hand on the old woman, "don't waken th' children, don't waken th' children."

She wept a little, unknowing, while the old mother rocked

herself and moaned. Elizabeth remembered that they were bringing him home, and she must be ready. "They'll lay him in the parlour," she said to herself, standing a moment pale and perplexed.

Then she lighted a candle and went into the tiny room. The air was cold and damp, but she could not make a fire, there was no fireplace. She set down the candle and looked round. The candle-light glittered on the lustre-glasses, on the two vases that held some of the pink chrysanthemums, and on the dark mahogany. There was a cold, deathly smell of chrysanthemums in the room. Elizabeth stood looking at the flowers. She turned away, and calculated whether there would be room to lay him on the floor, between the couch and the chiffonier. She pushed the chairs aside. There would be room to lay him down and to step round him. Then she fetched the old red table-cloth, and another old cloth, spreading them down to save her bit of carpet. She shivered on leaving the parlour; so, from the dresser drawer she took a clean shirt and put it at the fire to air. All the time her mother-in-law was rocking herself in the chair and moaning.

"You'll have to move from there, mother," said Elizabeth. "They'll be bringing him in. Come in the rocker."

The old mother rose mechanically, and seated herself by the fire, continuing to lament. Elizabeth went into the pantry for another candle, and there, in the little pent-house under the naked tiles, she heard them coming. She stood still in the pantry doorway, listening. She heard them pass the end of the house, and come awkwardly down the three steps, a jumble of shuffling footsteps and muttering voices. The old woman was silent. The men were in the yard.

Then Elizabeth heard Matthews, the manager of the pit, say: "You go in first, Jim. Mind!"

The door came open, and the two women saw a collier backing into the room, holding one end of a stretcher, on which they could see the nailed pit-boots of the dead man. The two carriers halted, the man at the head stooping to the lintel of the door.

"Wheer will you have him?" asked the manager, a short, white-bearded man.

Elizabeth roused herself and came from the pantry carrying the unlighted candle.

"In the parlour," she said.

"In there, Jim!" pointed the manager, and the carriers backed round into the tiny room. The coat with which they had covered the body fell off as they awkwardly turned through the two doorways, and the women saw their man, naked to the waist, lying stripped for work. The old woman began to moan in a low voice of horror.

"Lay th' stretcher at th' side," snapped the manager, "an' put 'im on th' cloths. Mind now, mind! Look you now——!"

One of the men had knocked off a vase of chrysanthemums. He stared awkwardly, then they set down the stretcher. Elizabeth did not look at her husband. As soon as she could get in the room, she went and picked up the broken vase and the flowers.

"Wait a minute!" she said.

The three men waited in silence while she mopped up the water with a duster.

"Eh, what a job, what a job, to be sure!" the manager was saying, rubbing his brow with trouble and perplexity. "Never knew such a thing in my life, never! He'd no business to ha' been left. I never knew such a thing in my life! Fell over him clean as a whistle, an' shut him in. Not four foot of space, there wasn't – yet it scarce bruised him."

He looked down at the dead man, lying prone, half naked, all grimed with coal-dust.

" ' 'Sphyxiated', the doctor said. It *is* the most terrible job I've ever known. Seems as if it was done o' purpose. Clean over him, an' shut 'im in, like a mouse-trap" – he made a sharp, descending gesture with his hand.

The colliers standing by jerked aside their heads in hopeless comment.

The horror of the thing bristled upon them all.

Then they heard the girl's voice upstairs calling shrilly:

"Mother, mother – who is it? Mother, who is it?"

Elizabeth hurried to the foot of the stairs and opened the door:

"Go to sleep!" she commanded sharply. "What are you shouting about? Go to sleep at once – there's nothing——"

Then she began to mount the stairs. They could hear her on the boards, and on the plaster floor of the little bedroom. They could hear her distinctly:

"What's the matter now? – what's the matter with you, silly thing?" – her voice was much agitated, with an unreal gentleness.

"I thought it was some men come," said the plaintive voice of the child. "Has he come?"

"Yes, they've brought him. There's nothing to make a fuss about. Go to sleep now, like a good child."

They could hear her voice in the bedroom, they waited whilst she covered the children under the bedclothes.

"Is he drunk?" asked the girl, timidly, faintly.

"No! No – he's not! He – he's asleep."

"Is he asleep downstairs?"

"Yes – and don't make a noise."

There was silence for a moment, then the men heard the frightened child again:

"What's that noise?"

"It's nothing, I tell you, what are you bothering for?"

The noise was the grandmother moaning. She was oblivious of everything, sitting on her chair rocking and moaning. The manager put his hand on her arm and bade her "Sh – sh!!"

The old woman opened her eyes and looked at him. She was shocked by this interruption, and seemed to wonder.

"What time is it?" the plaintive thin voice of the child, sinking back unhappily into sleep, asked this last question.

"Ten o'clock," answered the mother more softly. Then she must have bent down and kissed the children.

Matthews beckoned to the men to come away. They put on their caps and took up the stretcher. Stepping over the body, they tiptoed out of the house. None of them spoke till they were far from the wakeful children.

When Elizabeth came down she found his mother alone on the parlour floor, leaning over the dead man, the tears dropping on him.

"We must lay him out," the wife said. She put on the kettle, then returning knelt at the feet, and began to unfasten the knotted leather laces. The room was clammy and dim with only one candle, so that she had to bend her face almost to the floor. At last she got off the heavy boots and put them away.

"You must help me now," she whispered to the old woman. Together they stripped the man.

When they arose, saw him lying in the naïve dignity of death, the women stood arrested in fear and respect. For a few moments they remained still, looking down, the old mother whimpering. Elizabeth felt countermanded. She saw him, how utterly inviolable he lay in himself. She had nothing to do with him. She could not accept it. Stooping, she laid her hand on him, in claim. He was still warm, for the mine was hot where he had died. His mother had his face between her hands, and was murmuring incoherently. The old tears fell in succession as drops from wet leaves; the mother was not weeping, merely her tears flowed. Elizabeth embraced the body of her husband, with cheek and lips. She seemed to be listening, inquiring, trying to get some connection. But she could not. She was driven away. He was impregnable.

She rose, went into the kitchen, where she poured warm water into a bowl, brought soap and flannel and a soft towel.

"I must wash him," she said.

Then the old mother rose stiffly, and watched Elizabeth as she carefully washed his face, carefully brushing the big blond moustache from his mouth with the flannel. She was afraid with a bottomless fear, so she ministered to him. The old woman, jealous, said:

"Let me wipe him!" – and she kneeled on the other side drying slowly as Elizabeth washed, her big black bonnet sometimes brushing the dark head of her daughter-in-law. They worked thus in silence for a long time. They never forgot it was death, and the touch of the man's dead body gave them strange emotions, different in each of the women; a great dread possessed them both, the mother felt the lie was given to her womb, she was denied; the wife felt the utter isolation of the human soul, the child within her was a weight apart from her.

At last it was finished. He was a man of handsome body, and his face showed no traces of drink. He was blond, full-fleshed, with fine limbs. But he was dead.

"Bless him," whispered his mother, looking always at his face, and speaking out of sheer terror. "Dear lad – bless him!" She spoke in a faint, sibilant ecstasy of fear and mother love.

Elizabeth sank down again to the floor, and put her face against his neck, and trembled and shuddered. But she had to draw away again. He was dead, and her living flesh had no place against his. A great dread and weariness held her: she was so unavailing. Her life was gone like this.

"White as milk he is, clear as a twelve-month baby, bless him, the darling!" the old woman murmured to herself. "Not a mark on him, clear and clean and white, beautiful as ever a child was made," she murmured with pride. Elizabeth kept her face hidden.

"He went peaceful, Lizzie – peaceful as sleep. Isn't he beautiful, the lamb? Ay – he must ha' made his peace, Lizzie. 'Appen he made it all right, Lizzie, shut in there. He'd have time. He wouldn't look like this if he hadn't made his peace. The lamb, the dear lamb. Eh, but he had a hearty laugh. I loved to hear it. He had the heartiest laugh, Lizzie, as a lad –"

Elizabeth looked up. The man's mouth was fallen back, slightly open under the cover of the moustache. The eyes, half shut, did not show glazed in the obscurity. Life with its smoky burning gone from him, had left him apart and utterly alien to her. And she knew what a stranger he was to her. In her womb was ice of fear, because of this separate stranger with whom she had been living as one flesh. Was this what it all meant — utter, intact separateness, obscured by heat of living? In dread she turned her face away. The fact was too deadly. There had been nothing between them, and yet they had come together, exchanging their nakedness repeatedly. Each time he had taken her, they had been two isolated beings, far apart as now. He was no more responsible than she. The child was like ice in her womb. For as she looked at the dead man, her mind, cold and detached, said clearly: "Who am I? What have I been doing? I have been fighting a husband who did not exist. *He* existed all the time. What wrong have I done? What was that I have been living with? There lies the reality, this man." And her soul died in her for fear: she knew she had never seen him, he had never seen her, they had met in the dark and had fought in the dark, not knowing whom they met nor whom they fought. And now she saw, and turned silent in seeing. For she had been wrong. She had said he was something he was not; she had felt familiar with him. Whereas he was apart all the while, living as she never lived, feeling as she never felt.

In fear and shame she looked at his naked body, that she had known falsely. And he was the father of her children. Her soul was torn from her body and stood apart. She looked at his naked body and was ashamed, as if she had denied it. After all, it was itself. It seemed awful to her. She looked at his face, and she turned her own face to the wall. For his look was other than hers, his way was not her way. She had denied him what he was — she saw it now. She had refused him as himself. And this had been her life, and his life. She was grateful to death, which restored the truth. And she knew she was not dead.

And all the while her heart was bursting with grief and pity for him. What had he suffered? What stretch of horror for this helpless man! She was rigid with agony. She had not been able to help him. He had been cruelly injured, this naked man, this other being, and she could make no reparation. There were the children — but the children belonged to life. This dead man had nothing to do with them. He and she were only channels through which life had flowed to issue in the children. She was a mother — but how awful she knew it now to have been a wife. And he, dead now, how awful he must have felt it to be a husband. She felt that in the next world he would be a stranger to her. If they met there, in the beyond, they would only be ashamed of what had been before. The children had come, for some mysterious reason, out of both of them. But the children did not unite them. Now he was dead, she knew how eternally he was apart from her, how eternally he had nothing more to do with her. She saw this episode of her life closed. They had denied each other in life. Now he had withdrawn. An anguish came over her. It was finished then: it had become hopeless between them long before he died. Yet he had been her husband. But how little!

"Have you got his shirt, 'Lizabeth?"

Elizabeth turned without answering, though she strove to weep and behave as her mother-in-law expected. But she could not, she was silenced. She went into the kitchen and returned with the garment.

"It is aired," she said, grasping the cotton shirt here and there to try. She was almost ashamed to handle him; what right had she or anyone to lay hands on him; but her touch was humble on his body. It was hard work to clothe him. He was so heavy and inert. A terrible dread gripped her all the while: that he could be so heavy and utterly inert, unresponsive, apart. The horror of the distance between them was almost too much for her — it was so infinite a gap she must look across.

At last it was finished. They covered him with a sheet and left him lying, with his face bound. And she fastened the door of the little parlour, lest the children should see what was lying there. Then, with peace sunk heavy on her heart, she went about making tidy the kitchen. She knew she submitted to life, which was her immediate master. But from death, her ultimate master, she winced with fear and shame.

QUESTIONS

1. How would you describe the atmosphere in this story, which Lawrence felt was so like the atmosphere of his own childhood?

2. (a) What dominant mood is established in the opening paragraph?
   (b) What words or phrases in this paragraph indicate the writer's attitude towards the scene that he describes?

3. What character traits in the woman are revealed through the incidents with her son and her father?

4. At what point does Lawrence begin to take us into the woman's mind so that we may observe her unspoken thoughts and emotions? Why is this shift to her viewpoint necessary? In what ways would this be a different story if it were told from the boy's viewpoint?

5. Although Walter Bates does not appear directly in the first section, his relationship with his wife is vividly suggested. Describe this relationship and show how it is brought out in the first section of the story.

6. Towards the end of section I, how does Lawrence foreshadow Bates' death?

7. (a) What details of Elizabeth Bates' visit to the Rigley cottage emphasize her humiliation?
   (b) What purpose is served by the description of Mrs. Rigley's kitchen?

8. Instead of the Nottingham manner of speech common to the other characters, Elizabeth almost always uses standard English. What is the significance of this difference?

9. What is the function in the story of the old woman, Bates' mother?

10. How is our understanding of Elizabeth modified by her thoughts and behaviour after her husband's body is brought home?

11. Trace the mention of chrysanthemums through the story, attempting to explain their symbolic meaning.

THOMAS RADDALL

b. 1903

The wedding gift ❖ ❖ ❖

Thomas Raddall's story of how a socially ill-assorted couple come to wedlock is in striking contrast to D. H. Lawrence's account of how another such union ended. Notice how different is Raddall's attitude towards his characters. Lawrence's Elizabeth Bates is highly complex, viewed close-up through eyes that are affected by passionate personal involvement. Raddall's Kezia Barnes is convincingly flesh and blood, but she is part of an historical setting that the writer recreates imaginatively after careful study. His view is calmer, more distant; his characters come into simpler and brighter focus. He makes it impossible for us to imagine that his pair could end as Lawrence's couple did. The winner of several awards for his contributions to Canadian literature, Thomas Raddall has a solid reputation as both an historian of Nova Scotia and a writer of fiction. Among his historical novels are *Pride's Fancy* (1946), *A Muster of Arms* (1954), and *The Governor's Lady* (1959). His historical works include *Halifax, Warden of the North* (1948) and *The Path of Destiny* (1957). His mastery of the short story is represented in *The Wedding Gift and Other Stories* and *At the Tide's Turn* (1957). His early experiences as a wireless officer on board merchant vessels and at various east coast stations gave him an intimate knowledge of maritime winter storms, one of which plays an important role in "The Wedding Gift".

NOVA SCOTIA, in 1794. Winter. Snow on the ground. Two feet of it in the woods, less by the shore, except in drifts against Port Marriott's barns and fences; but enough to set sleigh bells ringing through the town, enough to require a multitude of paths and burrows from doors to streets, to carpet the wharves and the decks of the shipping, and to trim the ships' yards with tippets of ermine. Enough to require fires roaring in the town's chimneys, and blue wood smoke hanging low over the roof tops in the still December air. Enough to squeal under foot in the trodden places and to muffle the step everywhere else. Enough for the hunters, whose snowshoes now could overtake the floundering moose and caribou. Even enough for the always-complaining loggers, whose ox sleds now could haul their cut from every part of the woods. But not enough, not nearly enough snow for Miss Kezia Barnes, who was going to Bristol Creek to marry Mr. Hathaway.

Kezia did not want to marry Mr. Hathaway. Indeed she had told Mr. and Mrs. Barclay in a tearful voice that she didn't want to marry anybody. But Mr. Barclay had taken snuff and said "Ha! Humph!" in the severe tone he used when he was displeased; and Mrs. Barclay had sniffed and said it was a very good match for her, and revolved the cold blue eyes in her fat moon face, and said Kezia must not be a little fool.

There were two ways of going to Bristol Creek. One was by sea, in one of the fishing sloops. But the preacher objected to that. He was a pallid young man lately sent out from England by Lady Huntingdon's Connexion, and seasick five weeks on the way. He held Mr. Barclay in some awe, for Mr. Barclay had the best pew in the meetinghouse and was the chief pillar of godliness in Port Marriott. But young Mr. Mears was firm on this point. He would go by road, he said, or not at all. Mr. Barclay had retorted "Ha! Humph!" The road was twenty miles of horse path through the woods, now deep in snow. Also the path began at Harper's Farm on the far side of the harbour, and Harper had but one horse.

"I shall walk," declared the preacher calmly, "and the young woman can ride."

Kezia had prayed for snow, storms of snow, to bury the trail and keep anyone from crossing the cape to Bristol Creek. But now they were setting out from Harper's Farm, with Harper's big brown horse, and all Kezia's prayers had gone for naught. Like any anxious lover, busy Mr. Hathaway had sent Black Sam overland on foot to find out what delayed his wedding, and now Sam's day-old tracks marked for Kezia the road to marriage.

She was a meek little thing, as became an orphan brought up as house-help in the Barclay home; but now she looked at the preacher and saw how young and helpless he looked so far from his native Yorkshire, and how ill-clad for this bitter trans-Atlantic weather, and she spoke up.

"You'd better take my shawl, sir. I don't need it. I've got Miss Julia's old riding cloak. And we'll go ride-and-tie."

"Ride and what?" murmured Mr. Mears.

"I'll ride a mile or so, then I'll get down and tie the horse to a tree and walk on. When you come up to the horse, you mount and ride a mile or so, passing me on the way, and you tie him and walk on. Like that. Ride-and-tie, ride-and-tie. The horse gets a rest between."

Young Mr. Mears nodded and took the proffered shawl absently. It was a black thing that matched his sober broadcloth coat and smallclothes, his black woollen stockings, and his round black hat. At Mr. Barclay's suggestion he had borrowed a pair of moose-hide moccasins for the journey. As he walked a prayer-book in his coat-skirts bumped the back of his legs.

At the top of the ridge above Harper's pasture, where the narrow path led off through gloomy hemlock woods, Kezia paused for a last look back across the harbour. In the morning sunlight the white roofs of the little lonely town resembled a tidal wave flung up by the sea and frozen as it broke against the dark pine forest to the west. Kezia sighed, and young Mr. Mears was surprised to see tears in her eyes.

She rode off ahead. The saddle was a man's, of course, awkward to ride modestly, woman-fashion. As soon as she was out of the preacher's sight she rucked her skirts and slid a leg over to the other stirrup. That was better. There was a pleasant sensation of freedom about it, too. For a moment she forgot that she was going to Bristol Creek, in finery second-hand from the Barclay girls, in a new linen shift and drawers that she had sewn herself in the light of the kitchen candles, in white cotton stockings and a bonnet and shoes from Mr. Barclay's store, to marry Mr. Hathaway.

The Barclays had done well for her from the time when, a skinny weeping creature of fourteen, she was taken into the Barclay household and, as Mrs. Barclay so often said, "treated more like one of my own than a bond-girl from the poorhouse." She had first choice of the clothing cast off by Miss Julia and Miss Clara. She was permitted to sit in the same room, and learn what she could, when the schoolmaster came to give private lessons to the Barclay girls. She waited on table, of course, and helped in the kitchen, and made beds, and dusted and scrubbed. But then she had been taught to spin and to sew and to knit. And she was permitted, indeed encouraged, to sit with the Barclays in the meetinghouse, at the convenient end of the pew, where she could worship the Barclays' God and assist with the Barclay wraps at the beginning and end of the service. And now, to complete her rewards, she had been granted the hand of a rejected Barclay suitor.

Mr. Hathaway was Barclay's agent at Bristol Creek, where he sold rum and gunpowder and corn meal and such things to the fishermen and hunters, and bought split cod — fresh, pickled or dry — and ran a small sawmill, and cut and shipped firewood by schooner to Port Marriott, and managed a farm, all for a salary of fifty pounds, Halifax currency, per year. Hathaway was a most capable fellow, Mr. Barclay often acknowledged. But when after fifteen capable years he came seeking a wife, and cast a sheep's eye first at Miss Julia, and then at Miss Clara, Mrs. Barclay observed with a sniff that Hathaway was looking a bit high.

So he was. The older daughter of Port Marriott's most prosperous merchant was even then receiving polite attentions from Mr. Gamage, the new collector of customs, and a connection of the Halifax Gamages, as Mrs. Barclay was fond of pointing out. And Miss Clara was going to Halifax in the spring to learn the gentle art of playing the pianoforte, and incidentally to display her charms to the naval and military young gentlemen who thronged the Halifax drawing-rooms. The dear girls laughed behind their hands whenever long solemn Mr. Hathaway came to town aboard one of the Barclay vessels and called at the big house under the elms. Mrs. Barclay bridled at Hathaway's presumption, but shrewd Mr. Barclay narrowed his little black eyes and took snuff and said "Ha! Humph!"

It was plain to Mr. Barclay that an emergency had arisen. Hathaway was a good man — in his place; and Hathaway must be kept content there, to go on making profit for Mr. Barclay at a cost of only £50 a year. 'Twas a pity Hathaway couldn't satisfy himself with one of the fishermen's girls at the Creek, but there 'twas. If Hathaway had set his mind on a town miss, then a town miss he must have; but she must be the right kind, the sort who would content herself and Hathaway at Bristol Creek and not go nagging the man to remove and try his capabilities elsewhere. At once Mr. Barclay thought of Kezia — dear little Kezzie. A colourless little creature but quiet and well-mannered and pious, and only twenty-two.

Mr. Hathaway was nearly forty and far from handsome, and he had a rather cold, seeking way about him — useful in business of course — that rubbed women the wrong way. Privately Mr. Barclay thought Hathaway lucky to get Kezia. But it was a nice match for the girl, better than anything she could have expected. He impressed that upon her and introduced the suitor from Bristol Creek. Mr. Hathaway spent two or three evenings courting Kezia in the kitchen — Kezia in a quite good gown of Miss Clara's, gazing out at the November moon on the snow, murmuring now and again in the tones of someone in a rather dismal trance, while the kitchen help listened behind one door and the Barclay girls giggled behind another.

The decision, reached mainly by the Barclays, was that Mr. Hathaway should come to Port Marriott aboard the packet schooner on December twenty-third, to be married in the Barclay parlour and then take his bride home for Christmas. But an unforeseen circumstance had changed all this. The circumstance was a ship, "from Mogador in Barbary" as Mr. Barclay wrote afterwards in the salvage claim, driven off her course by gales and wrecked at the very entrance to Bristol Creek. She was a valuable wreck, laden with such queer things as goatskins in pickle, almonds, wormseed, pomegranate skins, and gum arabic, and capable Mr. Hathaway had lost no time in salvage for the benefit of his employer.

As a result he could not come to Port Marriott for a wedding or anything else. A storm might blow up at any time and demolish this fat prize. He dispatched a note by Black Sam, urging Mr. Barclay to send Kezia and the preacher by return. It was not the orthodox note of an impatient sweetheart, but it said that he had moved into his new house by the Creek and found it "extream empty lacking a woman", and it suggested delicately that while his days were full, the nights were dull.

Kezia was no judge of distance. She rode for what she considered a reasonable time and then slid off and tied the brown horse to a maple tree beside the path. She had brought a couple of lamp wicks to tie about her shoes, to keep them from coming off in the snow, and she set out afoot in the big splayed tracks of Black Sam. The soft snow came almost to her knees in places and she lifted her skirts high. The path was no wider than the span of a man's arms, cut out with axes years before. She stumbled over a concealed stump from time to time, and the huckleberry bushes dragged at her cloak, but the effort warmed her. It had been cold, sitting on the horse with the wind blowing up her legs.

After a time the preacher overtook her, riding awkwardly and holding the reins in a nervous grip. The stirrups were too short for his long black-stockinged legs. He called out cheerfully as he passed, "Are you all right, Miss?" She nodded, standing aside with her back to a tree. When he disappeared ahead, with a last flutter of black shawl tassels in the wind, she picked up her skirts and went on. The path climbed and dropped monotonously over a succession of wooded ridges. Here and there in a hollow she heard water running, and the creak of frosty poles underfoot, and knew she was crossing a small stream, and once the trail ran across a wide swamp on half-rotten corduroy, wind-swept and bare of snow.

She found the horse tethered clumsily not far ahead, and the tracks of the preacher going on. She had to lead the horse to a stump so she could mount, and when she passed Mr. Mears again she called out, "Please, sir, next time leave the horse by a stump or a rock so I can get on." In his quaint old-country accent he murmured, "I'm very sorry," and gazed down at the snow. She forgot she was riding astride until she had passed him, and then she flushed, and gave the indignant horse a cut of the switch. Next time she remembered and swung her right leg back where it should be, and tucked the skirts modestly about her ankles; but young Mr. Mears looked down at the snow anyway, and after that she did not trouble to shift when she overtook him.

The ridges became steeper, and the streams roared under the ice and snow in the swales. They emerged upon the high tableland between Port Marriott and Bristol Creek, a gusty wilderness of young hardwood scrub struggling up amongst the gray snags of an old forest fire, and now that they were out of the gloomy softwoods they could see a stretch of sky. It was blue-grey and forbidding, and the wind whistling up from the invisible sea felt raw on the cheek. At their next meeting Kezia said, "It's going to snow."

She had no knowledge of the trail but she guessed that they were not much more than half way across the cape. On this high barren the track was no longer straight and clear, it meandered amongst the meagre hardwood clumps where the path-makers had not bothered to cut, and only Black Sam's footprints really marked it for her unaccustomed eyes. The preacher nodded vaguely at her remark. The woods, like everything else about his chosen mission field, were new and very interesting, and he could not understand the alarm in her voice. He looked confidently at Black Sam's tracks.

Kezia tied the horse farther on and began her spell of walking. Her shoes were solid things, the kind of shoes Mr. Barclay invoiced as "a Common Strong sort, for women, Five Shillings"; but the snow worked into them and melted and saturated the leather. Her feet were numb every time she slid down from the horse and it took several minutes of stumbling through the snow to bring back an aching warmth. Beneath her arm she clutched the small bundle which contained all she had in the world – two flannel nightgowns, a shift of linen, three pairs of stout wool stockings – and of course Mr. Barclay's wedding gift for Mr. Hathaway.

Now as she plunged along she felt the first sting of snow on her face and, looking up, saw the stuff borne on the wind in small hard pellets that fell amongst the bare hardwoods and set up a whisper everywhere. When Mr. Mears rode up to her the snow was thick in their faces, like flung salt.

"It's a nor-easter!" she cried up to him. She knew the meaning of snow from the sea. She had been born in a fishing village down the coast.

"Yes," mumbled the preacher, and drew a fold of the shawl about his face. He disappeared. She struggled on, gasping, and after what seemed a tremendous journey came upon him standing alone and bewildered, looking off somewhere to the right.

"The horse!" he shouted. "I got off him, and before I could fasten the reins some snow fell off a branch – startled him, you know – and he ran off, over that way." He gestured with a mittened hand. "I must fetch him back," he added confusedly.

"No!" Kezia cried. "Don't you try. You'd only get lost. So would I. Oh, dear! This is awful. We'll have to go on, the best we can."

He was doubtful. The horse tracks looked very plain. But Kezia was looking at Black Sam's tracks, and tugging his arm. He gave in, and they struggled along for half an hour or so. Then the last trace of the old footprints vanished.

"What shall we do now?" the preacher asked, astonished.

"I don't know," whispered Kezia, and leaned against a dead pine stub in an attitude of weariness and indifference that dismayed him.

"We must keep moving, my dear, mustn't we? I mean, we can't stay here."

"Can't stay here," she echoed.

"Down there – a hollow, I think. I see some hemlock trees, or are they pines? – I'm never quite sure. Shelter, anyway."

"Shelter," muttered Kezia.

He took her by the hand and like a pair of lost children they dragged their steps into the deep snow of the hollow. The trees were tall spruces, a thick bunch in a ravine, where they had escaped the old fire. A stream thundered amongst them somewhere. There was no wind in this place, only the fine snow whirling thickly down between the trees like a sediment from the storm overhead.

"Look!" cried Mr. Mears. A hut loomed out of the whiteness before them, a small structure of moss-chinked logs with a roof of poles and birch-bark. It had an abandoned look. Long streamers of moss hung out between the logs. On the roof shreds of birch-bark wavered gently in the drifting snow. The door stood half open and a thin drift of snow lay along the split-pole floor. Instinctively Kezia went to the stone hearth. There were old ashes sodden with rain down the chimney and now frozen to a cake.

"Have you got flint and steel?" she asked. She saw in his eyes something dazed and forlorn. He shook his head, and she was filled with a sudden anger, not so much at him as at Mr. Barclay and that – that Hathaway, and all the rest of mankind. They ruled the world and made such a sorry mess of it. In a small fury she began to rummage about the hut.

There was a crude bed of poles and brushwood by the fireplace – brushwood so old that only a few brown needles clung to the twigs. A rough bench whittled from a pine log, with round birch sticks for legs. A broken earthenware pot in a corner. In another some ash-wood frames such as trappers used for stretching skins. Nothing else. The single window was covered with a stretched moose-bladder, cracked and dry rotten, but it still let in some daylight while keeping out the snow.

She scooped up the snow from the floor with her mittened hands, throwing it outside, and closed the door carefully, dropping the bar into place, as if she could shut out and bar the cold in such a fashion. The air inside was frigid. Their breath hung visible in the dim light from the window. Young Mr. Mears dropped on his wet knees and began to pray in a loud voice. His face was pinched with cold and his teeth rattled as he prayed. He was a pitiable object.

"Prayers won't keep you warm," said Kezia crossly.

He looked up, amazed at the change in her. She had seemed such a meek little thing. Kezia was surprised at herself, and surprisingly she went on, "You'd far better take off those wet moccasins and stockings and shake the snow out of your clothes." She set the example, vigorously shaking out her skirts and Miss Julia's cloak, and she turned her small back on him and took off her own shoes and stockings, and pulled on dry stockings from her bundle. She threw him a pair.

"Put those on."

He looked at them and at his large feet, hopelessly.

"I'm afraid they wouldn't go on."

She tossed him one of her flannel nightgowns. "Then take off your stockings and wrap your feet and legs in that."

He obeyed, in an embarrassed silence. She rolled her eyes upward, for his modesty's sake, and saw a bundle on one of the low rafters — the late owner's bedding, stowed away from mice. She stood on the bench and pulled down three bearskins, marred with bullet holes. A rank and musty smell arose in the cold. She considered the find gravely.

"You take them," Mr. Mears said gallantly. "I shall be quite all right."

"You'll be dead by morning, and so shall I," she answered vigorously, "if you don't do what I say. We've got to roll up in these."

"Together?" he cried in horror.

"Of course! To keep each other warm. It's the only way."

She spread the skins on the floor, hair uppermost, one overlapping another, and dragged the flustered young man down beside her, clutched him in her arms, and rolled with him, over, and over again, so that they became a single shapeless heap in the corner farthest from the draft between door and chimney.

"Put your arms around me," commanded the new Kezia, and he obeyed.

"Now," she said, "you can pray. God helps those that help themselves."

He prayed aloud for a long time, and privately called upon heaven to witness the purity of his thoughts in this strange and shocking situation. He said "Amen" at last; and "Amen", echoed Kezia, piously.

They lay silent a long time, breathing on each other's necks and hearing their own hearts – poor Mr. Mears' fluttering in an agitated way, Kezia's as steady as a clock. A delicious warmth crept over them. They relaxed in each other's arms. Outside, the storm hissed in the spruce tops and set up an occasional cold moan in the cracked clay chimney. The down-swirling snow brushed softly against the bladder pane.

"I'm warm now," murmured Kezia. "Are you?"

"Yes. How long must we stay here like this?"

"Till the storm's over, of course. Tomorrow, probably. Nor'easters usually blow themselves out in a day and a night, 'specially when they come up sharp, like this one. Are you hungry?"

"No."

"Abigail – that's the black cook at Barclay's – gave me bread and cheese in a handkerchief. I've got it in my bundle. Mr. Barclay thought we ought to reach Bristol Creek by supper time, but Nabby said I must have a bite to eat on the road. She's a good kind thing, old Nabby. Sure you're not hungry?"

"Quite. I feel somewhat fatigued but not hungry."

"Then we'll eat the bread and cheese for breakfast. Have you got a watch?"

"No, I'm sorry. They cost such a lot of money. In Lady Huntingdon's Connexion we – "

"Oh well, it doesn't matter. It must be about four o'clock – the light's getting dim. Of course, the dark comes very quick in a snowstorm."

"Dark," echoed young Mr. Mears drowsily. Kezia's hair, washed last night for the wedding journey, smelled pleasant so close to his face. It reminded him of something. He went to sleep dreaming of his mother, with his face snug in the curve of Kezia's neck and shoulder, and smiling, and muttering words that Kezia could not catch. After a time she kissed his cheek. It seemed a very natural thing to do.

Soon she was dozing herself, and dreaming, too; but her dreams were full of forbidding faces – Mr. Barclay's, Mrs. Barclay's, Mr. Hathaway's; especially Mr. Hathaway's. Out of a confused darkness Mr. Hathaway's hard acquisitive gaze searched her shrinking flesh like a cold wind. Then she was shuddering by the kitchen fire at Barclay's, accepting Mr. Hathaway's courtship and wishing she was dead. In the midst of that sickening wooing she wakened sharply.

It was quite dark in the hut. Mr. Mears was breathing quietly against her throat. But there was a sound of heavy steps outside, muffled in the snow and somehow felt rather than heard. She shook the young man and he wakened with a start, clutching her convulsively.

"Sh-h-h!" she warned. "Something's moving outside." She felt him stiffen.

"Bears?" he whispered.

Silly! thought Kezia. People from the old country could think of nothing but bears in the woods. Besides, bears holed up in winter. A caribou, perhaps. More likely a moose. Caribou moved inland before this, to the wide mossy bogs up the river, away from the coastal storms. Again the sound.

"There!" hissed the preacher. Their hearts beat rapidly together.

"The door – you fastened it, didn't you?"

"Yes," she said. Suddenly she knew.

"Unroll, quick!" she cried . . . "No, not this way – your way."

They unrolled, ludicrously, and the girl scrambled up and ran across the floor in her stockinged feet, and fumbled with the rotten door-bar. Mr. Mears attempted to follow but he tripped over the nightgown still wound about his feet, and fell with a crash. He was up again in a moment, catching up the clumsy wooden bench for a weapon, his bare feet slapping on the icy floor. He tried to shoulder her aside, crying "Stand back! Leave it to me!" and waving the bench uncertainly in the darkness.

She laughed excitedly. "Silly!" she said. "It's the horse." She flung the door open. In the queer ghostly murk of a night filled with snow they beheld a large dark shape. The shape whinnied softly and thrust a long face into the doorway. Mr. Mears dropped the bench, astonished.

"He got over his fright and followed us here somehow," Kezia said, and laughed again. She put her arms about the snowy head and laid her face against it.

"Good horse! Oh, good, good horse!"

"What are you going to do?" the preacher murmured over her shoulder. After the warmth of their nest in the furs they were shivering in this icy atmosphere.

"Bring him in, of course. We can't leave him out in the storm." She caught the bridle and urged the horse inside with expert clucking sounds. The animal hesitated, but fear of the storm and a desire for shelter and company decided him. In he came, tramping ponderously on the split-pole floor. The preacher closed and barred the door.

"And now?" he asked.

"Back to the furs. Quick! It's awful cold."

Rolled in the furs once more, their arms went about each other instinctively, and the young man's face found the comfortable nook against Kezia's soft throat. But sleep was difficult after that. The horse whinnied gently from time to time, and stamped about the floor. The decayed poles crackled dangerously under his hoofs whenever he moved, and Kezia trembled, thinking he might break through and frighten himself, and flounder about till he tumbled the crazy hut about their heads. She called out to him "Steady, boy! Steady!"

It was a long night. The pole floor made its irregularities felt through the thickness of fur; and because there seemed nowhere to put their arms but about each other the flesh became cramped, and spread its protest along the bones. They were stiff and sore when the first light of morning stained the window. They unrolled and stood up thankfully, and tramped up and down the floor, threshing their arms in an effort to fight off the gripping cold. Kezia undid her bundle in a corner and brought forth Nabby's bread and cheese, and they ate it sitting together on the edge of the brushwood bed with the skins about their shoulders. Outside the snow had ceased.

"We must set off at once," the preacher said. "Mr. Hathaway will be anxious."

Kezia was silent. She did not move, and he looked at her curiously. She appeared very fresh, considering the hardships of the previous day and the night. He passed a hand over his cheeks and thought how unclean he must appear in her eyes, with this stubble on his pale face.

"Mr. Hathaway – " he began again.

"I'm not going to Mr. Hathaway," Kezia said quietly.

"But – the wedding!"

"There'll be no wedding. I don't want to marry Mr. Hathaway. 'Twas Mr. Hathaway's idea, and Mr. and Mrs. Barclay's. They wanted me to marry him."

"What will the Barclays say, my dear?"

She shrugged. "I've been their bond-girl ever since I was

fourteen, but I'm not a slave like poor black Nabby, to be handed over, body and soul, whenever it suits."

"Your soul belongs to God," said Mr. Means devoutly.

"And my body belongs to me."

He was a little shocked at this outspokenness but he said gently, "Of course. To give oneself in marriage without true affection would be an offense in the sight of heaven. But what will Mr. Hathaway say?"

"Well, to begin with, he'll ask where I spent the night, and I'll have to tell the truth. I'll have to say I bundled with you in a hut in the woods."

"Bundled?"

"A custom the people brought with them from Connecticut when they came to settle in Nova Scotia. Poor folk still do it. Sweethearts, I mean. It saves fire and candles when you're courting on a winter evening. It's harmless – they keep their clothes on, you see, like you and me – but Mr. Barclay and the other Methody people are terrible set against it. Mr. Barclay got old Mr. Mings – he's the Methody preacher that died last year – to make a sermon against it. Mr. Mings said bundling was an invention of the devil."

"Then if you go back to Mr. Barclay – "

"He'll ask me the same question and I'll have to give him the same answer. I couldn't tell a lie, could I?" She turned a pair of round blue eyes and met his embarrassed gaze.

"No! No, you mustn't lie. Whatever shall we do?" he murmured in a dazed voice. Again she was silent, looking modestly down her small nose.

"It's so very strange," he floundered. "This country – there are so many things I don't know, so many things to learn. You – I – we shall have to tell the truth, of course. Doubtless I can find a place in the Lord's service somewhere else, but what about you, poor girl?"

"I heard say the people at Scrod Harbour want a preacher."

"But – the tale would follow me, wouldn't it, my dear? This – er – bundling with a young woman?"

" 'Twouldn't matter if the young woman was your wife."

"Eh?" His mouth fell open. He was like an astonished child, for all his preacher's clothes and the new beard on his jaws.

"I'm a good girl," Kezia said, inspecting her foot. "I can read and write, and know all the tunes in the psalter. And – and you need someone to look after you."

He considered the truth of that. Then he murmured uncertainly, "We'd be very poor, my dear. The Connexion gives some support, but of course – "

"I've always been poor," Kezia said. She sat very still but her cold fingers writhed in her lap.

He did something then that made her want to cry. He took hold of her hands and bowed his head and kissed them.

"It's strange – I don't even know your name, my dear."

"It's Kezia – Kezia Barnes."

He said quietly, "You're a brave girl, Kezia Barnes, and I shall try to be a good husband to you. Shall we go?"

"Hadn't you better kiss me, first?" Kezia said faintly.

He put his lips awkwardly to hers; and then, as if the taste of her clean mouth itself provided strength and purpose, he kissed her again, and firmly. She threw her arms about his neck.

"Oh, Mr. Mears!"

How little he knew about everything! He hadn't even known enough to wear two or three pairs of stockings inside those roomy moccasins, nor to carry a pair of dry ones. Yesterday's wet stockings were lying like sticks on the frosty floor. She showed him how to knead the hard-frozen moccasins into softness, and while he worked at the stiff leather she tore up one of her wedding bed-shirts and wound the flannel strips about his legs and feet. It looked very queer when she had finished, and they both laughed.

They were chilled to the bone when they set off, Kezia on the horse and the preacher walking ahead, holding the reins. When they regained the slope where they had lost the path, Kezia said, "The sun rises somewhere between east and southeast, this time of year. Keep it on your left shoulder a while. That will take us back towards Port Marriott."

When they came to the green timber she told him to shift the sun to his left eye.

"Have you changed your mind?" he asked cheerfully. The exercise had warmed him.

"No, but the sun moves across the sky."

"Ah! What a wise little head it is!"

They came over a ridge of mixed hemlock and hardwood and looked upon a long swale full of bare hackmatacks.

"Look!" the girl cried. The white slot of the axe path showed clearly in the trees at the foot of the swale, and again where it entered the dark mass of the pines beyond.

"Praise the Lord!" said Mr. Mears.

When at last they stood in the trail, Kezia slid down from the horse.

"No!" Mr. Mears protested.

"Ride-and-tie," she said firmly. "That's the way we came, and that's the way we'll go. Besides, I want to get warm."

He climbed up clumsily and smiled down at her.

"What shall we do when we get to Port Marriott, my dear?"

"Get the New Light preacher to marry us, and catch the packet for Scrod Harbour."

He nodded and gave a pull at his broad hat brim. She thought of everything. A splendid helpmeet for the world's wilderness. He saw it all very humbly now as a dispensation of Providence.

Kezia watched him out of sight. Then, swiftly, she undid her bundle and took out the thing that had lain there (and on her conscience) through the night – the tinderbox – Mr. Barclay's wedding gift to Mr. Hathaway. She flung it into the woods and walked on, skirts lifted, in the track of the horse, humming a psalm tune to the silent trees and the snow.

QUESTIONS

1. The writer of historical fiction must provide information about dress, customs, and attitudes of mind that are probably unfamiliar to his reader. And this information should seem a natural part of the story, not a veneer pasted on. How does Raddall solve this problem in "The Wedding Gift"?

2. (a) In this story shrewd, insensitive people try to prey upon simple, childlike people. Name each character mentioned in the opening section of the story and state which of these two groups he belongs to.
(b) What evidence in the opening section led you to make each of these judgments?
(c) Does Kezia's "experience" with Mr. Mears move her from one group to the other? To a place somewhere between the two? Explain your reasoning.

3. (a) On page 178, Kezia and Mr. Mears are described as wandering hand in hand "like two lost children", but both preceding and following events contrast the two. State this contrast and refer to incidents that make it plain.
(b) Which of these incidents illustrate Raddall's sense of comedy?

4. Do you feel the surprise at the very end of the story to be consistent with previous developments, or is it an implausible trick by the author? Justify your opinion.

5. What evidence in the story would justify the prediction that Kezia and her husband, unlike Elizabeth and Walter Bates in "Odour of Chrysanthemums", would have a satisfactory marriage?

6. Compare "The Wedding Gift" and "The Perfume Sea", considering theme, characters, and setting.

NATHANIEL HAWTHORNE

1804-1864

Dr. Heidegger's experiment

The descendant of one of the first families to settle in New England, Nathaniel Hawthorne inherited the Puritan tradition that man is by nature evil and can do nothing out of his own strength to redeem himself. As an educated man of letters, Hawthorne was not a prisoner of this narrow, pessimistic view of life, but it seems to have entered and suffused his imagination. His short stories and his best-known novels, *The Scarlet Letter* (1850), *The House of the Seven Gables* (1851), and *The Marble Faun* (1860), all investigate man's involvement in sin. Although written early in his career, "Dr. Heidegger's Experiment" is typical Hawthorne in its wry comment on humanity. In contrast to "The Perfume Sea", which emphasizes innocence and self-sacrifice, Hawthorne's fantasy treats the two opposite themes of guilt and vanity. In its use of symbols to develop a theme the story might also be compared with "The Hint of an Explanation".

THAT VERY SINGULAR MAN, old Dr. Heidegger, once invited four venerable friends to meet him in his study. There were three white-bearded gentlemen, Mr. Medbourne, Colonel Killigrew, and Mr. Gascoigne, and a withered gentlewoman, whose name was the Widow Wycherly. They were all melancholy old creatures, who had been unfortunate in life, and whose greatest misfortune it was that they were not long ago in their graves. Mr. Medbourne, in the vigor of his age, had been a prosperous merchant, but had lost his all by a frantic speculation, and was not little better than a mendicant. Colonel Killigrew had wasted his best years, and his health and substance, in the pursuit of sinful pleasures which had given birth to a brood of pains, such as the gout, and divers other torments of soul and body. Mr. Gascoigne was a ruined politician, a man of evil fame, or at least had been so, till time had buried him from the knowledge of the present generation, and made him obscure instead of infamous. As for the Widow Wycherly, tradition tells us that she was a great beauty in her day; but, for a long while past, she had lived in deep seclusion, on account of certain scandalous stories which had prejudiced the gentry of the town against her. It is a circumstance worth mentioning, that each of these three old gentlemen, Mr. Medbourne, Colonel Killigrew, and Mr. Gascoigne, were early lovers of the Widow Wycherly, and had once been on the point of cutting each other's throats for her sake. And, before proceeding farther, I will merely hint that Dr. Heidegger and all his four guests were sometimes thought to be a little beside themselves; as is not unfrequently the case with old people, when worried either by present troubles or woeful recollections.

"My dear old friends," said Dr. Heidegger, motioning them to be seated, "I am desirous of your assistance in one of those little experiments with which I amuse myself here in my study."

If all stories were true, Dr. Heidegger's study must have been a very curious place. It was a dim, old-fashioned chamber, festooned with cobwebs, and besprinkled with antique dust. Around the walls stood several oaken bookcases, the lower shelves of which were filled with rows of gigantic folios and black-letter quartos, and the upper with little parchment-covered duodecimos. Over the central bookcase was a bronze bust of Hippocrates, with which, according to some authorities, Dr. Heidegger was accustomed to hold consultations in all difficult cases of his practice. In the obscurest corner of the room stood a tall and narrow oaken closet, with its door ajar, within which doubtfully appeared a skeleton. Between two of the bookcases hung a looking-glass, presenting its high and dusty plate within a tarnished gilt frame.

Among many wonderful stories related of this mirror, it was fabled that the spirits of all the doctor's deceased patients dwelt within its verge, and would stare him in the face whenever he looked thitherward. The opposite side of the chamber was ornamented with the full-length portrait of a young lady, arrayed in the faded magnificence of silk, satin, and brocade, and with a visage as faded as her dress. Above half a century ago, Dr. Heidegger had been on the point of marriage with this young lady; but, being affected with some slight disorder, she had swallowed one of her lover's prescriptions, and died on the bridal evening. The greatest curiosity of the study remains to be mentioned; it was a ponderous folio volume, bound in black leather, with massive silver clasps. There were no letters on the back, and nobody could tell the title of the book. But it was well known to be a book of magic; and once, when a chambermaid had lifted it, merely to brush away the dust, the skeleton had rattled in its closet, the picture of the young lady had stepped one foot upon the floor, and several ghastly faces had peeped forth from the mirror; while the brazen head of Hippocrates frowned, and said, – "Forbear."

Such was Dr. Heidegger's study. On the summer afternoon of our tale, a small round table, as black as ebony, stood in the centre of the room, sustaining a cut-glass vase of beautiful form and elaborate workmanship. The sunshine came through the window, between the heavy festoons of two faded damask curtains, and fell directly across this vase; so that a mild splendor was reflected from it on the ashen visages of the five old people who sat around. Four champagne glasses were also on the table.

"My dear old friends," repeated Dr. Heidegger, "may I reckon on your aid in performing an exceedingly curious experiment?"

Now Dr. Heidegger was a very strange old gentleman, whose eccentricity had become the nucleus for a thousand fantastic stories. Some of these fables, to my shame be it spoken, might possibly be traced back to mine own veracious self; and if any passages of the present tale should startle the reader's faith, I must be content to bear the stigma of a fictionmonger.

When the doctor's four guests heard him talk of his proposed experiment, they anticipated nothing more wonderful than the murder of a mouse in an air pump, or the examination of a cobweb by the microscope, or some similar nonsense, with which he was constantly in the habit of pestering his intimates. But without waiting for a reply, Dr. Heidegger hobbled across the chamber, and returned with the same ponderous folio, bound in black leather, which common report affirmed to be a book of magic. Undoing the silver clasps, he opened the volume, and took from among its black-letter pages a rose, or what was once a rose, though now the green leaves and crimson petals had assumed one brownish hue, and the ancient flower seemed ready to crumble to dust in the doctor's hands.

"This rose," said Dr. Heidegger, with a sigh, "this same withered and crumbling flower, blossomed five-and-fifty years ago. It was given me by Sylvia Ward, whose portrait hangs yonder; and I meant to wear it in my bosom at our wedding. Five-and-fifty years it has been treasured between the leaves of this old volume. Now, would you deem it possible that this rose of half a century could ever bloom again?"

"Nonsense!" said the Widow Wycherly, with a peevish toss of her head. "You might as well ask whether an old woman's wrinkled face could ever bloom again."

"See!" answered Dr. Heidegger.

He uncovered the vase, and threw the faded rose into the water which it contained. At first, it lay lightly on the surface of the fluid, appearing to imbibe none of its moisture. Soon, however, a singular change began to be visible. The crushed and dried petals stirred, and assumed a deepening tinge of crimson, as if the flower were reviving from a deathlike slumber; the slender stalk and twigs of foliage became green; and there was the rose of half a century, looking as fresh as when Sylvia Ward had first given it to her lover. It was scarcely full flown; for some of its delicate red leaves curled modestly around its moist bosom, within which two or three dewdrops were sparkling.

"That is certainly a very pretty deception," said the doctor's friends; carelessly, however, for they had witnessed greater miracles at a conjurer's show; "pray how was it effected?"

"Did you never hear of the 'Fountain of Youth'?" asked Dr. Heidegger, "which Ponce de Leon, the Spanish adventurer, went in search of two or three centuries ago?"

"But did Ponce de Leon ever find it?" said the Widow Wycherly.

"No," answered Dr. Heidegger, "for he never sought it in the right place. The famous Fountain of Youth, if I am rightly informed, is situated in the southern part of the Floridian peninsula, not far from Lake Macaco. Its source is overshadowed by several gigantic magnolias, which, though numberless centuries old, have been kept as fresh as violets by the virtues of this wonderful water. An acquaintance of mine, knowing my curiosity in such matters, has sent me what you see in the vase."

"Ahem!" said Colonel Killigrew, who believed not a word of the doctor's story; "and what may be the effect of this fluid on the human frame?"

"You shall judge for yourself, my dear Colonel," replied Dr. Heidegger; "and all of you, my respected friends, are welcome to so much of this admirable fluid as may restore to you the bloom of youth. For my own part, having had much trouble in growing old, I am in no hurry to grow young again. With your permission, therefore, I will merely watch the progress of the experiment."

While he spoke, Dr. Heidegger had been filling the four champagne glasses with the water of the Fountain of Youth. It was apparently impregnated with an effervescent gas, for little bubbles were continually ascending from the depths of the glasses, and bursting in silvery spray at the surface. As the liquor diffused a pleasant perfume, the old people doubted not that it possessed cordial and comfortable properties; and, though utter skeptics as to its rejuvenescent power, they were inclined to swallow it at once. But Dr. Heidegger besought them to stay a moment.

"Before you drink, my respectable old friends," said he, "it would be well that, with the experience of a lifetime to direct you, you should draw up a few general rules for your guidance, in passing a second time through the perils of youth. Think what a sin and a shame it would be, if with your peculiar advantages, you should not become patterns of virtue and wisdom to all the young people of the age!"

The doctor's four venerable friends made him no answer, except by a feeble and tremulous laugh; so very ridiculous was the idea, that, knowing how closely repentance treads behind the steps of error, they should ever go astray again.

"Drink, then," said the doctor, bowing: "I rejoice that I have so well selected the subjects of my experiment."

With palsied hands, they raised the glasses to their lips. The liquor, if it really possessed such virtues as Dr. Heidegger imputed to it, could not have been bestowed on four human beings who needed it more wofully. They looked as if they had never known what youth or pleasure was, but had been the offspring of Nature's dotage, and always the gray, decrepit, sapless, miserable creatures, who now sat stooping round the doctor's table, without life enough in their souls or bodies to be animated even by the prospect of growing young again. They drank off the water, and replaced their glasses on the table.

Assuredly there was an almost immediate improvement in the aspect of the party, not unlike what might have been produced by a glass of generous wine, together with a sudden glow of cheerful sunshine brightening over all their visages at once. There was a healthful suffusion on their cheeks, instead of the ashen hue that had made them look so corpse-like. They gazed at one another, and fancied that some magic power had really begun to smooth away the deep and sad inscriptions which Father Time had been so long engraving on their brows. The Widow Wycherly adjusted her cap, for she felt almost like a woman again.

"Give us more of this wondrous water!" cried they, eagerly. "We are younger — but we are still too old! Quick — give us more!"

"Patience, patience!" quoth Dr. Heidegger, who sat watching the experiment with philosophic coolness. "You have been a long time growing old. Surely, you might be content to grow young in half an hour! But the water is at your service."

Again he filled their glasses with the liquor of youth, enough of which still remained in the vase to turn half the old people in the city to the age of their own grandchildren. While the bubbles were yet sparkling on the brim, the doctor's four guests snatched their glasses from the table, and swallowed the contents at a single gulp. Was it delusion? Even while the draught was passing down their throats, it seemed to have wrought a change on their whole systems. Their eyes grew clear and bright; a dark shade deepened among their silvery locks, they sat around the table, three gentlemen of middle age, and a woman hardly beyond her buxom prime.

"My dear widow, you are charming!" cried Colonel Killigrew, whose eyes had been fixed upon her face, while the shadows of age were flitting from it like darkness from the crimson daybreak.

The fair widow knew, of old, that Colonel Killigrew's compliments were not always measured by sober truth; so she started up and ran to the mirror, still dreading that the ugly visage of an old woman would meet her gaze. Meanwhile, the three gentlemen behaved in such a manner as proved that the water of the Fountain of Youth possessed some intoxicating qualities; unless, indeed, their exhilaration of spirits were merely a lightsome dizziness caused by the suddent removal of the weight of years. Mr. Gascoigne's mind seemed to run on political topics, but whether relating to the past, present, or future, could not easily be determined, since the same ideas and phrases have been in vogue these fifty years. Now he rattled forth full-throated sentences about patriotism, national glory, and the people's right; now he muttered some perilous stuff or other, in a sly and doubtful whisper, so cautiously that even his own conscience could scarcely catch the secret; and now again he spoke in measured accents, and a deeply deferential tone, as if a royal ear were listening to his well-turned periods. Colonel Killigrew all this time had been trolling forth a jolly bottlesong, and ringing his glass in symphony with the chorus, while his eyes wandered towards the buxom figure of the Widow Wycherly. On the other side of the table, Mr. Medbourne was involved in a calculation of dollars and cents, with which was strangely intermingled a project for supplying the East Indies with ice, by harnessing a team of whales to the polar icebergs.

As for the Widow Wycherly, she stood before the mirror curtsying and simpering to her own image, and greeting it as the friend whom she loved better than all the world beside. She thrust her face close to the glass, to see whether some long-remembered wrinkle or crow's-foot had indeed vanished. She examined whether the snow had so entirely melted from her hair, that the venerable cap could be safely thrown aside. At last, turning briskly away, she came with a sort of dancing step to the table.

"My dear old doctor," cried she, "pray favor me with another glass!"

"Certainly, my dear madam, certainly!" replied the complaisant doctor; "see! I have already filled the glasses."

There, in fact, stood the four glasses, brimful of this wonderful water, the delicate spray of which, as it effervesced from the surface, resembled the tremulous glitter of diamonds. It was now so nearly sunset that the chamber had grown duskier than ever; but a mild and moonlike splendor gleamed from within the vase, and rested alike on the four guests, and on the doctor's venerable figure. He sat in a high-backed, elaborately carved, oaken armchair, with a gray dignity of aspect that might have well befitted that very Father Time whose power had never been disputed save by this fortunate company. Even while quaffing the third draught of the Fountain of Youth, they were almost awed by the expression of his mysterious visage.

But, the next moment, the exhilarating gush of young life shot through their veins. They were now in the happy prime of youth. Age, with its miserable train of cares, and sorrows, and diseases, was remembered only as the trouble of a dream from which they had joyously awoke. The fresh gloss of the soul, so early lost, and without which the world's successive scenes had been but a gallery of faded pictures, again threw its enchantment over all their prospects. They felt like new-created beings in a new-created universe.

"We are young! We are young!" they cried exultingly.

Youth, like the extremity of age, had effaced the strongly-marked characteristics of middle life, and mutually assimilated them all. They were a group of merry youngsters, almost maddened with the exuberant frolicsomeness of their years. The most singular effect of their gayety was an impulse to mock the infirmity and decrepitude of which they had so lately been the victims. They laughed loudly at their old-fashioned attire, the wide-skirted coats and flapped waistcoats of the young men, and the ancient cap and gown of the blooming girl. One limped across the floor like a gouty grandfather; one set a pair of spectacles astride of his nose, and pretended to pore over the black-letter pages of the book of magic; a third seated himself in an armchair, and strove to imitate the venerable dignity of Dr. Heidegger. Then all shouted mirthfully, and leaped about the room. The Widow Wycherly – if so fresh a damsel could be called a widow – tripped up to the doctor's chair, with a mischievous merriment in her rosy face.

"Doctor, you dear old soul," cried she, "get up and dance

with me!" And then the four young people laughed louder than ever, to think what a queer figure the poor old doctor would cut.

"Pray excuse me," answered the doctor quietly. "I am old and rheumatic, and my dancing days were over long ago. But either of these gay young gentlemen will be glad of so pretty a partner."

"Dance with me, Clara!" cried Colonel Killigrew.

"No, no, I will be her partner!" shouted Mr. Gascoigne.

"She promised me her hand, fifty years ago!" exclaimed Mr. Medbourne.

They all gathered round her. One caught both her hands in his passionate grasp – another threw his arm about her waist – the third buried his hand among the glossy curls that clustered beneath the widow's cap. Blushing, panting, struggling, chiding, laughing, her warm breath fanning each of their faces by turns, she strove to disengage herself, yet still remained in their triple embrace. Never was there a livelier picture of youthful rivalship, with bewitching beauty for the prize. Yet, by a strange deception, owing to the duskiness of the chamber, and the antique dresses which they still wore, the tall mirror is said to have reflected the figures of the three old, gray, withered grandsires, ridiculously contending for the skinny ugliness of a shriveled grandam.

But they were young: their burning passions proved them so. Inflamed to madness by the coquetry of the girl-widow, who neither granted nor quite withheld her favors, the three rivals began to interchange threatening glances. Still keeping hold of the fair prize, they grappled fiercely at one another's throats. As they struggled to and fro, the table was overturned, and the vase dashed into a thousand fragments. The precious Water of Youth flowed in a bright stream across the floor moistening the wings of a butterfly, which grown old in the decline of summer, had alighted there to die. The insect fluttered lightly through the chamber, and settled on the snowy head of Dr. Heidegger.

"Come, come, gentlemen! – come, Madam Wycherly," exclaimed the doctor, "I really must protest against this riot."

They stood still, and shivered; for it seemed as if gray Time were calling them back from their sunny youth, far down into the chill and darksome vale of years. They looked at old Dr. Heidegger, who sat in his carved armchair, holding the rose of half a century, which he had rescued from among the fragments of the shattered vase. At the motion of his hand, the four rioters resumed their seats; the more readily, because their violent exertions had wearied them, youthful though they were.

"My poor Sylvia's rose!" ejaculated Dr. Heidegger, holding it in the light of the sunset clouds; "it appears to be fading again."

And so it was. Even while the party were looking at it, the flower continued to shrivel up, till it became as dry and fragile as when the doctor had first thrown it into the vase. He shook off the few drops of moisture which clung to its petals.

"I love it as well thus as in its dewy freshness," observed he, pressing the withered rose to his withered lips. While he spoke, the butterfly fluttered down from the doctor's snowy head, and fell upon the floor.

His guests shivered again. A strange chilliness, whether of the body or spirit they could not tell, was creeping gradually over them all. They gazed at one another, and fancied that each fleeting moment snatched away a charm, and left a deepening furrow where none had been before. Was it an illusion? Had the changes of a lifetime been crowded into so brief a space, and were they now four aged people, sitting with their old friend, Dr. Heidegger?

"Are we grown old again, so soon?" cried they, dolefully.

In truth they had. The Water of Youth possessed merely a virtue more transient than that of wine. The delirium which it created had effervesced away. Yes! they were old again. With a shuddering impulse, that showed her a woman still, the widow clasped her skinny hands before her face, and wished that the coffin lid were over it, since it could be no longer beautiful.

"Yes, friends, ye are old again," said Dr. Heidegger, "and lo! the Water of Youth is all lavished on the ground. Well – I bemoan it not; for if the fountain gushed at my very doorstep, I would not stoop to bathe my lips in it – no, though its delirium were for years instead of moments. Such is the lesson ye have taught me!"

But the doctor's four friends had taught no such lesson to themselves. They resolved forthwith to make a pilgrimage to Florida, and quaff at morning, noon, and night, from the Fountain of Youth.

QUESTIONS

1. When it was first printed in the *Knickerbocker Magazine*, Hawthorne called the story "The Fountain of Youth" but renamed it "Dr. Heidegger's Experiment" for reprinting in his book *Twice Told Tales*. Suggest reasons why he considered the second title an improvement.

2. There are numerous indications that Hawthorne is not writing in a tone of complete seriousness. How would you describe his humour in the story? Give an illustration from the story to support your description.

3. Hawthorne's nineteenth-century manner of addressing the reader directly, like a stage director halting the action while he comments to the audience, is not common in twentieth-century fiction. How does this narrative point of view affect his method of revealing character? Consider especially the first long paragraph.

4. Why is the detailed description of Dr. Heidegger's study essential to the story?

5. Hawthorne appears to have two contrasting feelings for his characters – pity and distaste. Is he able to harmonize these two attitudes, or do they destroy the story's unity of tone? Refer to the story to explain your view.

6. (a) What is the symbolic importance of the rose and the butterfly?
   (b) Pick out another symbol in the story and explain its significance.

7. Contrast this story with "The Perfume Sea", considering
   (a) the characters of Doree and Widow Wycherly,
   (b) the methods by which one story achieves the main effect of realism, the other the main effect of fantasy,
   (c) the comment on human nature implied by each story.

MARGARET LAURENCE
b. 1926

The perfume sea

A graduate of the University of Manitoba, Margaret Laurence is the wife of a civil engineer whose work has taken him to British Somaliland and Ghana. It was out of this African experience that Mrs. Laurence's first important work came – some brilliant short stories, a collection of Somali folk-tales and poetry, and her first novel *This Side of Jordan* (1960). Mrs. Laurence writes: "I have been fortunate in being able to observe two entirely different Africas. When we lived in Somaliland in East Africa, the tribal patterns of life were still very firmly established. In Ghana we found a totally different situation. We went to West Africa in 1952; independence was just coming up, and it was a period of great change and adjustment for both Africans and Europeans." "The Perfume Sea", first published in 1961, is a story of "change and adjustment" in Mrs. Laurence's lighter vein. Here is a crucial moment in human history seen from inside a beauty parlour and realized in terms of the "permanent wave". But while feminine vanity is presented as the only changeless element in a world of change, Mrs. Laurence, for all her lightness of touch, is not "making fun" of her Africans or her Europeans. In reading the story, probe for the deeper layers of human anxiety and hope beneath the comic surfaces. Margaret Laurence's shorter African stories have been collected in the volume *The Tomorrow - Tamer* (1963). Her most recent novels, *The Stone Angel* (1964) and *A Jest of God* (1966), have a Canadian setting.

"NO QUESTION OF IT," Mr. Archipelago said, delicately snipping a wisp of hair. "I am flotsam."

"Not jetsam?" Mrs. Webley-Pryce asked, blinking sharply watchful eyes as the scissored shreds fell down into her face. "I always get the two confused."

Outside, the small town was growing sluggish under the sedative sun of late morning. The one-footed beggar who squatted beside Mr. Archipelago's door had gone to sleep on the splintery wooden steps. Past the turquoise-and-red façade of Cowasjee's Silk Bazaar, in the rancid and shadowy room, the shrivelled Parsee sat, only half awake, folding a length of sari cloth and letting the silk slip through his fingers as he dreamed of a town in India, no less ill-smelling and dirty than this African one, but filled with the faces and speech of home. At the shop of K. Tachie (General Merchant), Tachie himself sat beside his cash register, surrounded by boxes and barrels. Kinglike, he perched on a high stool and roared abuse at his court of counter-clerks, while at the same time he managed to gulp a lurid carbonated grape beverage called Doko-Doko. At the Africa Star Chemists, a young shopgirl dozed, propping her brown arms against a carton of Seven Seas codliver oil. Down the street, in the Paradise Chop-Bar, a young man recalled those arms as he sloshed a rag over the tables in preparation for the customers who would soon be lifting the striped bedspread that hung across the doorway and shouting for beer and *kenkey*. In the Government Agent's office, and in the offices of Bridgeford & Knight, Exporters-Importers, Englishmen sighed and wilted and saw from their watches that they could not yet legitimately leave for lunch. Pariah dogs on the road snarled over a cat corpse; then, panting, tongues dribbling, defeated by sun, they crawled back to a shaded corner, where their scabrous hides were fondled by an old man in a hashish dream. Footsteps on the cracked and scorching pavement lagged. Even the brisk shoes of white men slackened and slowed. The market women walked tiredly, their headtrays heavy, their bare feet pressing the warm dust into ripples and dunes. Babies slung on their mothers' backs allowed their heads to loll forward and whimpered at the sweat that made sticky their faces. A donkey brayed disconsolately. Voices droned low. Laughter like melted honey poured slowly. Down by the shore, under a few scattered palm trees, the wives of fishermen drowsed over their net-mending. Only the children, the fire and gleam of them greater even than the harsh glint of sun, continued to leap and shout as before.

Mr. Archipelago riffled a comb through the winter straw of the lady's hair, and nuzzled his rotundity against her arm for the lightly spiteful pleasure of feeling her recoil. He moved back a decent pace. Under his white smock, the red and gold brocade waistcoat quivered with his belly's silent laughter.

"Flotsam, dear lady," he said. "I looked it up in the Concise Oxford."

On the other side of the room, Doree glanced up from the lustrous green with which she was enamelling the fingernails of her thin white hands, knuckle-swollen from years of cleansing other women's hair. Her mild myopic eyes were impressed, even awed. Her mouth, painted to emulate hardness, opened in a soft spontaneous astonishment.

"Can you beat it?" she said. "He looks up words all the time, and laughs like the dickens. I used to read the telephone book sometimes, in the nights, and wonder about those names and if they all belonged to real people, living somewhere, you know, and doing something. But I never laughed. What's it say for flotsam, Archipelago?"

Mr. Archipelago beamed. His shiny eyes were green as malachite. He stood on tiptoe, a plump pouter-pigeon of a man, puffing out his chest until the brocade waistcoat swelled. His hair, black as ripe olives, he only touched from time to time with pomade, but it gave the impression of having been crimped and perfumed.

"Wreckage found floating," he said proudly. "It said – 'wreckage found floating'."

"The very thing!" Doree cried, clapping her hands, but Mrs. Webley-Pryce looked aloof because she did not understand.

The air in the shop was syrupy with heat and perfume, and the odd puff of breeze that came in through the one window seemed to be the exhalation of a celestial fire-eater. Mrs.

Webley-Pryce, feeling the perspiration soaking through her linen dress, wriggled uncomfortably in her chair and tried to close her eyes to the unseemly and possibly septic litter around her. The shop was not really dirty, although to the fastidious English minds of lady customers it appeared so. Doree swept it faithfully every evening at closing time, but as her sight was so poor and she would not wear glasses, she often missed fragments of hair which gradually mingled with dust and formed themselves into small balls of grey and hazel-nut brown and bottled blonde. The curl-papers, too, had an uncanny way of escaping and drifting around the room like leaves fallen from some rare tree. Doree chain-smoked, so the ashtrays were nearly always full. Mr. Archipelago found her cigarette-butts charming, each with its orange kiss mark from the wide mouth he had never touched. But the ladies did not share his perception; they pushed the ashtrays away impatiently, hintingly, until with a sigh he emptied them into a wastepaper-basket and watched the ashes flutter like grey flakes of dandruff.

Sweat was gathering on Mr. Archipelago's smooth forehead, and his fingers were becoming slippery around the comb and scissors.

"The morning beer," he announced. "It is now time. For you, as well, Mrs. Webley-Pryce?"

"I think not, thanks," she replied coldly. "Nothing before sundown is my rule. Can't you hurry a little, Mr. Archipelago? At this rate it'll be midnight before my perm is finished."

"Pardon, pardon," said Mr. Archipelago, tilting the beer bottle. "One moment, and we fly to work. Like birds on the wing."

Out came the solutions, the flasks of pink and mauve liquid, the odour of ammonia competing with the coarse creamy perfumes. Out came clamps and pins and curl-papers, the jumbled contents of a dozen shelves and cupboards. In the midst of the debris, stirring it all like a magic potion, stood Mr. Archipelago, a fat and frantic wizard, refreshing himself occasionally with Dutch ale. He darted over to the mainstay of his alchemist's laboratory, an elaborate arrangement of electrically-heated metal rods, on which he placed the heavy clamps. He waited, arms folded, until the whole dangerous mechanism achieved the dull mysterious fire which was to turn Mrs. Webley-Pryce's base metal, as it were, to gold.

"You should sell that lot," Mrs. Webley-Pryce remarked. "Any museum in Europe would give you a good price."

At once he was on the defensive, his pride hurt.

"Let me tell you, dear lady, there isn't one beauty salon in the whole of Europe could give you a perm like this one does."

"I don't doubt that for one instant," she said with a short laugh.

Doree stood up, an emaciated yellow and white bird, a tall gaunt crane, her hair clinging like wet feathers around her squeezed-narrow shoulders. With her long hesitant stride she walked across the room, and held out her green lacquered hands.

"Sea pearl," she said. "Kind of different, anyhow. Africa Star Chemists just got it in. Like it?"

Shuddering slightly, Mrs. Webley-Pryce conceded that it was very handsome.

"Pearl reminds me," Mr. Archipelago said, returning to cheerfulness, "the Concise Oxford stated another thing for flotsam."

Mrs. Webley-Pryce looked at him with open curiosity and begged decorously to be told. Mr. Archipelago applied a dab of spit to a finger and casually tested the heat of the clamps.

"Precisely, it said 'oyster-spawn'! Think of that. Oyster-spawn. And that is me, too, eh?"

Doree laughed until she began to cough, and he frowned at her, for they were both worried by this cough and she could not stop smoking for more than an hour at a time.

"I don't see — " Mrs. Webley-Pryce probed.

"A little joke," Mr. Archipelago explained. "Not a very good one, perhaps, but we must do the best with what we have. My father, as I may have told you, was an Armenian sailor."

"Oh yes," Mrs. Webley-Pryce said, disappointed, holding her breath as he placed the first hot clamp on her tightly wound-up hair. "I believe you did mention it. Odd — Archipelago never seems like an Armenian name to me, somehow."

"It isn't."

"Oh?"

Mr. Archipelago smiled. He enjoyed talking about himself. He allowed himself a degree of pride in the fact that no one could ever be sure where the truth ended and the tinted unreality began. With the Englishmen to whom he administered haircuts, Mr. Archipelago talked sparingly. They seemed glum and taciturn to him, or else overly robust, with a kind of dogged heartiness that made him at once wary. But with the lady customers it was a different matter. He had a genuine sympathy for them. He did not chide, even to himself, their hunger. If one went empty for long enough, one became hungry. His tales were the manna with which it was his pleasure to nourish his lady customers. Also, he was shrewd. He knew his conversation was an attraction, no less than the fact that he was the only hairdresser within a hundred miles; it was his defence against that noxious invention, the home-permanent.

"It would have been difficult for my mother to give me my father's name," he said, "as she never knew it. She was — I may have mentioned — an Italian girl. She worked in a wineshop in Genoa. It smelled of Barbera and stale fish and — things you would prefer I did not speak about. I grew up there. That Genoa! Never go there. A port town, a sailors' town. The most saddening city in the world, I think. The ships are always mourning. You hear those wailing voices even in your sleep. The only place I ever liked in all Genoa was the Staglieno cemetery, up on the hills. I used to go there and sit beside the tombs of the rich, a small fat boy with the white marble angels — so compassionate they looked, and so costly — I believed then that each was the likeness of a lady buried beneath. Then I would look over at the fields of rented graves nearby. The poor rent graves for one, two, five years — I can't remember exactly. The body must be taken out if the rent cannot be paid. In death, as in life, the rent must always be paid."

"How horrible," Mrs. Webley-Pryce said. "Look here — are you sure this clamp isn't too hot? I think it's burning my neck. Oh thanks, that's better. It's your mother's name, then?"

Doree glared. Mrs. Webley-Pryce was the wife of the Government Agent, but she had married late and had lived in Africa only one year — she had not yet learned that however eager one might be, the questions must always be judicious, careful. But Mr. Archipelago was bland. He did not mind the curiosity of his lady customers.

"No, dear lady, it is not her name. Why should a person not pick his own name? It sounds Italian. I liked it. It suits me. Do you know what it means?"

"Well, of course," Mrs. Webley-Pryce said uncertainly. "An archipelago is — well, it's — "

"A sea with many islands, according to the Concise Oxford. That has been my life. A sea with many islands."

"This is one of them, I suppose?"

"The most enduring so far," he replied. "Twelve years I have been here."

"Really? That's a long time. You'll go back, though, someday?"

"I have no wish to go back," Mr. Archipelago answered offhandedly. "I would like to die here and be buried in my own garden. Perhaps if I were buried under the wild orchids they would grow better. I have tried every other kind of fertilizer."

"You can't be serious," Mrs. Webley-Pryce protested. "About not going back, I mean."

"Why not? I like it here."

"But it's so far from everything. So far from home."

"For you, perhaps," Mr. Archipelago said. "But then, you are not a true expatriate. You may stay twenty years, but you are a visitor. Your husband, though — does he anticipate with pleasure the time when he will retire and go back to England?"

She looked at him in surprise.

"No — he dreads it, as a matter of fact. That's understandable, though. His work is here, his whole life. He's been here a long time, too, you know. But it's rather different. He was sent out here. He had to come."

"Did he?"

"Of course," she said. "If a person goes in for colonial administration, he must go to a colony, mustn't he?"

"Indeed he must," Mr. Archipelago said agreeably. "If he goes in for colonial administration, it is the logical step."

"But for a hairdresser," she said, "it's not the sort of place most people would exactly choose — "

"Aha — now we come to it. You are one of those who believe that I did not choose to come here, then? That I was, perhaps, forced to leave my own country?"

"I didn't mean that — " Mrs. Webley-Pryce floundered. "And I suppose that it's a blessing for the European women that there's someone in a tiny station like this who can do hair — "

"Even if it is only Archipelago with his equipment that belongs in a museum. Well, well. Tell me, madam — what is the current theory about me? It changes, you know. This interests me greatly. No, please — I am not offended. You must not think so. Only curious, just as you are curious about me. Once, I remember, I was said to have been a counterfeiter. Another time, I had deserted my wife and family. Through the years, it has been this and that. Perhaps one of them is true. Or perhaps not. To maintain dignity, one must have at least one secret — don't you agree?"

Mrs. Webley-Pryce gave him a sideways glance.

"I have heard," she admitted, "about there having been some trouble. I'm sure it couldn't have been true, though — "

But Mr. Archipelago neither confirmed nor denied. He tested a curl, and finding it satisfactory, he began to remove the mass of iron from the hair. Mrs. Webley-Pryce, embarrassed by his silence, turned to Doree, who was applying bleach to her own long yellow hair.

"Speaking of names, I've always meant to ask you about yours, Doree. It's rather unusual, isn't it?"

"Yeh," Doree said, through her mane. "I used to be Doreen."

"Oh?" Once more the lilt in the voice of the huntress.

Doree spoke of herself rarely. She did not possess Mr. Archipelago's skill or his need, and when she talked about her own life she usually blurted unwillingly the straight facts because she could not think of anything else to say. Her few fabrications were obvious; she wrenched them out aggressively, knowing that no one would believe her. Now she was caught off guard.

"I had my own shop once," she said in her gentle rasping voice. "It had a sign up — DOREEN/BEAUTY INCORPORATED. Classy. Done in those gilt letters. You buy them separately and stick them up. The state of my dough wasn't so classy, though. So when the goddam 'N' fell off, I figured it was cheaper to change my name to fit the sign."

Gratified, Mrs. Webley-Pryce tittered.

"And just where was your shop?"

Now it was Mr. Archipelago's turn to glare. It was permissible to question him minutely, but not Doree. Customers were supposed to understand this rule. He saw Doree's eyes turn vague, and he longed to touch her hand, to comfort and reassure her. But it was better not to do such a thing. He did not want her to misunderstand his devotion, or to be in any way alarmed by a realization of its existence. Instead, he slithered a still-hot clamp down on Mrs. Webley-Pryce's neck, causing a faint smell of singed skin and a gasp of pain.

"It was in Montreal, if you must know," Doree said harshly.

Last time someone asked, the answer was Chicago, and

once, daringly, Mexico City. Mr. Archipelago himself did not know. She had simply walked into his shop one day, and where she came from, or why, did not matter to him. When they were alone, he and Doree never questioned each other. Their evening conversation was of the day's small happenings.

"Montreal — " Mrs. Webley-Pryce said thoughtfully. Perhaps David and I will go to some place like that. There's nothing much left for administrative men in England."

"You're leaving?" Mr. Archipelago asked, startled. "You're leaving Africa?"

"Yes, of course — that's what I meant when I said David dreaded — didn't you know?"

"But — why?" he asked in dismay, for recently she had been patronizing the shop regularly. "Why?"

"Dear me," she said, with an effort at brightness, "you are behind the times, aren't you? Didn't you know this colony will be self-governing soon? They don't want us here any more."

"I knew it was coming," Mr. Archipelago said, "but I had not realized it was so soon. Strange. I read the newspapers. I talk with Mr. Tachie, my landlord, who is a very political man. But — ah well, I tend my garden, and try to get wild orchids to grow here beside the sea, where the soil is really much too sandy for them, and I do the ladies' hair and drink beer and talk to Doree. I think nothing will ever change in this place — so insignificant, surely God will forget about it and let it be. But not so. How many will be going?"

"Oh, I don't know — most of the Europeans in government service — perhaps all. I expect some of those in trade will remain."

Her tone implied that Mr. Archipelago would be left with a collection of lepers, probably hairless.

"There are not enough of them," he murmured, "to keep me in business."

He groped on a shelf for another beer and opened it with perspiring hands. He thought of the sign outside his establishment. Not a gilt-lettered sign, to be sure, but nicely done in black and aquamarine, with elegant spidery letters:

ARCHIPELAGO
English-Style Barber
European Ladies' Hairdresser

"A sea with many islands," he said, addressing only himself. "Sometimes it happens that a person discovers he has built his house upon an island that is sinking."

A large green house by the shore sheltered Mr. Archipelago. Once he had lived there alone, but for the past five years he had not been alone. Doree's presence in his house had been, he knew, a popular topic of discussion at the morning coffee parties in the European cantonment. He did not blame the ladies for talking, but it did give him a certain satisfaction to know that their actual information on the subject was extremely slight. Neither he nor Doree had ever spoken of their domestic arrangements to customers. And their cook-steward, Attah, under the impression that he was protecting his employers' reputations, had never told a living soul that the two shared only living and dining-rooms and that neither had ever entered the private apartments of the other.

Mr. Archipelago's dwelling was not close either to the white cantonment or to the African houses. It was off by itself, on a jut of land overlooking a small bay. The sprawling overgrown garden was surrounded by a high green wall which enabled Mr. Archipelago in the late afternoons to work outside clad only in his underwear and a round white linen hat. He had no wish to tame the garden, which was a profusion of elephant grass, drooping casuarina trees, frowsy banana palms, slender paw-paw, and all manner of flowering shrubs—hibiscus, purple bougainvillaea, and the white Rose of Sharon, whose blossoms turned to deep blush as they died. Into this cherished disorder, Mr. Archipelago carefully introduced wild orchids, which never survived for long, and clumps of hardy canna lilies that bloomed pink and ragged. He grew pineapples, too, and daily prodded angrily with his stick at the speared clusters which consistently refused to bear fruit the size of that sold for a mere shilling in the African market. The favourite of his domain, however, was the sensitive plant, an earth vine which, if its leaves were touched even lightly, would softly and stubbornly close. Mr. Archipelago liked to watch the sensitive plant's closing. Nothing in this world could stop its self-containment; it was not to be bribed or cajoled; it had integrity. But he seldom touched it, for the silent and seemingly conscious inturning of each leaf made him feel clumsy and lacking in manners.

Just as the garden was Mr. Archipelago's special province, so the long verandah was Doree's. Here flew, uncaged, four grey African parrots, their wings tipped with scarlet. Sometimes they departed for a while, and sulked in the branches of the frangipani tree. Doree never attempted to catch them, nor would she even lure them with seeds or snails. Mr. Archipelago believed she almost wished one of them would find itself able to leave the sanctuary and return to the forest. But they had lived inside the verandah for too long. They could not have fended for themselves, and they must have known it. They always came back to be fed.

Mr. Archipelago could well have done without some of the visitors to Doree's menagerie. He did not mind the little geckos that clung transparent to the walls, like lizards of glass, nor the paunchy toads whose tongues hunted the iridescent green flies. But the trays containing all the morsels which Doree imagined to be choice fare for spiders — these sometimes drew scorpions and once a puff-adder. Doree would not kill even the lethal guests. She shooed them carefully out at broom-point, assuring the sweating Mr. Archipelago that they had no wish to harm anyone — they wanted only to be shown how to escape. Perhaps her faith protected her, or her lack of fear, for within her sanctuary no live thing seemed to her to be threatening. In any event, she had never been touched by the venom of wild creatures.

She had a chameleon, too, of which she was extremely fond, an eerie bright green reptile with huge eyes and a long tail curled up like a tape-measure. Mr. Archipelago once ventured to suggest that she might find a prettier pet. Doree's large pale eyes squinted at him reproachfully.

"What do you want me to do, anyway? Conk him on the head because he's not a goddam butterfly?"

Mr. Archipelago, appalled at his blunder, answered humbly.

"Am I God, that I should judge a creature? It is not the chameleon that is ugly, but I, for thinking him so. And now, looking at him more carefully, and seeing his skin grow darker against that dark branch where he is, I can see that he must be appreciated according to his own qualities, and not compared with butterflies, who are no doubt gaudy but who do not possess this interesting ability. You are right — he is beautiful."

"I don't get it," Doree said. "I never said he was beautiful."

"Well, then, I did. I do."

"You're what they call 'round the bend', Archipelago. Never mind. Maybe so am I."

"We suit each other," he replied.

The evenings were spent quietly. They did not go out anywhere, nor did they entertain. They had always been considered socially non-existent by the European community, while in the Africans' view they were standard Europeans and therefore apart. Mr. Archipelago and Doree did not mind. They preferred their own company. Mr. Archipelago possessed a gramophone which vied in antiquity with the wave-machine. Often after dinner he played through his entire repertoire of fourteen records, mainly Italian opera. He particularly liked to listen to Pagliacci, in order to criticize it.

"Hear that!" he would cry to the inattentive Doree. "How sorry he is for himself! A storm of the heart — what a buffoon. Do you know his real tragedy? Not that he had to laugh when his heart was breaking — that is a commonplace. No — the unfortunate fact is that he really is a clown. Even in his desolation. A clown."

Doree, sitting on the mock-Persian carpet whose richness was not lessened for her by its label "Made in Brussels", would placidly continue to talk to her two favourite parrots. She called them Brasso and Silvo, and Mr. Archipelago understood that this christening was meant as a compliment to him, these being the closest to Italian names she could manage.

After work, Mr. Archipelago's scarlet waistcoat was discarded in favour of an impressive smoking-jacket. It was a pale bluish-green Indian brocade, and the small cockerels on it were worked in threads of gold. Although it was a rather warm garment, Mr. Archipelago suffered his sweat for the sake of magnificence.

"You look just like one of those what-d'you-call-'ems – you know, sultans," Doree had once said admiringly.

He remembered the remark each evening when he donned the jacket. Momentarily endowed with the hauteur of Haroun al Raschid, he would saunter nonchalantly through the Baghdad of his own living-room.

Frequently they brought out their perfumes, of which they had a great variety, bottles and flagons of all colours and intricate shapes – crowns and hearts and flowers, diamonded, bubbled, baubled, angular, and smooth. The game was to see how many could be identified by smell alone, the vessel masked, before the senses began to flag. Mr. Archipelago did not love the perfumes for themselves alone, nor even for their ability to cover the coarse reek of life. Each one, sniffed like snuff, conjured up for him a throng of waltzing ladies, whirling and spinning eternally on floors of light, their grey gowns swaying, ladies of gentle dust.

Mr. Archipelago and Doree got along well with their one servant. Attah regularly told them the gossip of the town, although they cared about it not at all. He tended to be cantankerous; he would not be argued with; he served for meals the dishes of his own choice. They accepted him philosophically, but on one point they were adamant. They would not allow Attah's wife and family to live within the walls of the compound. The family lived, instead, in the town. Mr. Archipelago and Doree never ceased to feel sorry about this separation, but they could not help it. They could not have endured to have the voices of children threatening their achieved and fragile quiet.

Outside the green wall, however, and far from the sugared humidity of the small shop, events occurred. Governments made reports and politicians made speeches. Votes were cast. Supporters cheered and opponents jeered. Flags changed, and newspapermen typed furiously, recording history to meet a deadline. Along the shore, loin-clothed fishermen, their feet firm in the wet sand, grinned and shrugged, knowing they would continue to burn their muscles like quick torches, soon consumed, in the sea-grappling that claimed them now as always, but sensing, too, that the land in which they set their returning feet was new as well as old, and that they, unchanged, were new with it.

In the town, the white men began to depart one by one, as their posts were filled by Africans. And in Mr. Archipelago's shop, the whirr of the hair-dryer was heard less and less.

Late one night Doree came downstairs in her housecoat, an unheard-of thing for her. Mr. Archipelago was sitting like a gloomy toad in his high-backed wicker armchair. He glanced up in surprise.

"It's my imagination again," she said. "It's been acting up."

Doree suffered periodic attacks of imagination, like indigestion or migraine. She spoke of it always as though it were an affliction of a specific organ, as indeed it was, for her phrenology charts placed the imagination slightly above the forehead, on the right side. Mr. Archipelago brought another wicker chair for her and gave her a little creme-de-cacao in her favourite liqueur glass, a blinding snow-shadow blue, frosted with edelweiss.

"It's two months," Doree said, sipping, "since the Webley-Pryces left. I don't know how many are gone now. Almost all,

I guess. I heard today that Bridgeford & Knight are putting in an African manager. The last perm we gave was nearly a month ago. This week only three haircuts and one shampoo-and-set. Archipelago – what are we going to do?"

He looked at her dumbly. He could give her no comfort.

"Could we go someplace else?" she went on. "Sierra Leone? Liberia?"

"I have thought of that," he said. "Yes, perhaps we shall have to consider it."

They both knew they did not have sufficient money to take them anywhere else.

"Please – " He hesitated. "You must not be upset, or I cannot speak at all – "

"Go on," she said roughly. "What is it?"

"Did you know," Mr. Archipelago questioned sadly, "that if an expatriate is without funds, he can go to the consulate of his country, and they will send him back?"

She lowered her head. Her yellow hair, loose, fell like unravelled wool around her, scarfing the bony pallor of her face.

"I've heard that – yes."

Mr. Archipelago pushed away his creme-de-cacao, the sweetness of which had begun to nauseate him. His incongruously small feet in their embroidered slippers pattered across the concrete floor. He returned with Dutch ale.

"I have never asked," he said. "And you have never asked, and now I must break the rule. Could you go back? Could you, Doree, if there was nothing else to do?"

Doree lit a cigarette from the end of the last one.

"No," she replied in a steady, strained voice. "Not even if there was nothing else to do."

"Are you sure?"

"My God – " she said. "Yes, I'm sure all right."

Mr. Archipelago did not ask why. He brought his hands together in a staccato clap.

"Good. We know where we stand. Enough of this, then."

"No," she said. "What about you?"

"It is very awkward," he said, "but unfortunately I cannot go back, either."

She did not enquire further. For her, too, his word was sufficient.

"But Archipelago, the Africans won't let us stay if we're broke. We're not their responsibility — "

"Wait — " Mr. Archipelago said. "I have just remembered something."

Beside his chair, a carved wooden elephant bore a small table on its back. Mr. Archipelago groped underneath and finally opened a compartment in the beast's belly. He took out an object wrapped in tissue paper.

"I have always liked this elephant," he said. "See — a concealed hiding place. Very cloak-and-dagger. A treasure — no, a toy — such as Columbus might have brought back from his travels. He was once in West Africa, you know, as a young seaman, at one of the old slave-castles not far from here. And he, also, came from Genoa. Well, well. There the similarity ends. This necklace is one I bought many years ago. I have always saved it. I thought I was being very provident — putting away one gold necklace to insure me against disaster. It is locally made — crude, as you can see, but heavy. Ashanti gold, and quite valuable."

Doree looked at it without interest.

"Very nice," she said. "But we can't live off that forever."

"No, but it will give you enough money to live in the city until you find work. More Europeans will be staying there, no doubt, and we know there are several beauty salons. At least it is a chance. For me, the worst would be for you not to have any chance — "

Mr. Archipelago perceived that he had revealed too much. He squirmed and sweated, fearful that she would misunderstand. But when he looked at her, he saw in her eyes not alarm but surprise.

"The necklace and all — " Doree said slowly. "You'd do that — for me?"

Mr. Archipelago forgot about himself in the urgency of convincing her.

"For you, Doree," he said. "Of course, for you. If only it were more — "

"But — it's everything — "

"Yes, everything," he said bitterly. "All I have to offer. A fragment of gold."

"I want you to know," she said, her voice rough with tears, "I want you to know I'm glad you offered. Now put the necklace back in the elephant and let's leave it there. We may need it worse, later."

"You won't take it?" he cried. "Why not?"

"Because you haven't told me yet what's gonna happen to you," Doree said. "And anyway, I don't want to go to another place."

He could not speak. She hurried on.

"If I wasn't here," she said, with a trembling and apologetic laugh, "who'd remind you to put on your hat in the boiling sun? Who'd guess the perfumes with you?"

"I would miss you, of course," he said in a low voice. "I would miss you a great deal."

She turned on him, almost angrily.

"Don't you think I'd miss you?" she cried. "Don't you know how it would be — for me?"

They stared at each other, wide-eyed, incredulous. Mr. Archipelago lived through one instant of unreasonable and terrifying hope. Then, abruptly, be became once more aware of himself, oddly swathed in Indian brocade and holding in his fat perspiring hands an ale-glass and a gold necklace.

Doree's eyes, too, had become distant and withdrawn. She was twisting a sweat-lank strand of her hair around one wrist.

"We're getting ourselves into a stew over nothing," she said at last. "Nobody's gonna be leaving. Everything will be just the same as always. Listen, Archipelago, I got a hunch we're due for a lucky break. I'm sure of it. Once I met a spiritualist — a nice old dame — I really went for that ouija-board stuff in those days — well, she told me I had natural ability. I had the right kind of an aura. Yeh, sure it's phony, I know that. But my hunches are hardly ever wrong. Shall we shake on it?"

Gravely, they shook hands and drank to the lucky break. Mr. Archipelago began to tell stories about the tourists with whom, as a boy, he used to practise his shaky English, and how nervous they always were of getting goat's milk in their tea.

They talked until the pressure lamp spluttered low and the floor beneath it was littered with the beige and broken wings of moths. Doree went upstairs then, singing a snatch of an African highlife tune in her warm raw voice. But later, Mr. Archipelago, queasy with beer and insomnia, heard once again the sound that used to be so frequent when she first came to this house, her deep and terrible crying in her sleep.

They had had no customers at all for a fortnight, but still they opened the shop each morning and waited until exactly four o'clock to close it. One morning Tachie strolled in, prosperous in a new royal blue cloth infuriatingly patterned with golden coins. He was a large man; the warm room with its sweet cloying air seemed too small to hold his brown ox-shoulders, his outflung arms, his great drum of a voice.

"Mistah Arch'pelago, why you humbug me? Two month, and nevah one penny I getting. You t'ink I rich too much? You t'ink I no need for dis money?"

Mr. Archipelago, standing beside his idle transmutation machine and sagging gradually like a scarlet balloon with the air sinking out of it, made one unhopeful effort at distracting Tachie.

"Can I offer you a beer, Mr. Tachie? A light refreshing ale at this time of day — "

Tachie grimaced.

"You t'ink I drink beer wey come from my shop an' nevah been pay at all? No, I t'ank you. I no drink dis beer — he too cost, for me. Mistah Arch'pelago, you trouble me too much. What we do, eh?"

Mr. Archipelago's skin looked sallower than usual. His eyes were dull and even his crisp neat hair had become limp. Doree held out large and pitying hands towards him, but she could not speak.

"In life as in death, the rent must be paid," he said. "We have been dreaming, dreaming, while the world moved on, and now we waken to find it so changed we do not know what to do. We wanted only to stay and not to harm anyone, but of course you are right, Mr. Tachie, to remind us it is not enough. One must always have a product to sell that someone wants to buy. We do not have much of anything any more, but we will try to pay our debts before we move on. Perhaps a museum will buy my wave-machine after all."

Doree put her hands over her face, and Tachie, horrified, looked from one to the other, still unable to grasp the actuality of their despair.

"You no got money — at all? De time wey I come for you shop, I anger too much for you. Now angry can no stay for me. My friend, I sorry. Befoah God, I too sorry. But what I can do?"

"It is not your concern," Mr. Archipelago said with dignity. "We do not expect you to let us stay. We are not appealing for charity."

But Tachie could not stop justifying himself.

"I look-a de shop, I see Eur'pean womans all dey gone, I see you no got lucky. But I no savvy propra. I t'ink you got money you put for bank. Now I see wit' my eye you tell me true, you no got nothing. But what I can do? I no be rich man. I got shop, I got dis place. But I got plenty plenty family, all dey come for me, all dey say 'Tachie, why you no give we more?' My own pickin dey trouble me too much. My daughtah Mercy, she big girl, all time she saying 'meka you buy for me one small new cloth, meka you buy powdah for face, meka you buy shoe same city girl dey wear it — ' "

Mr. Archipelago peered sharply at Tachie.

"Your daughter — facepowder — shoes — she, too, is changed — "

"I tell you true. Mistah Arch'pelago, why you're looking so?"

The balloon that was Mr. Archipelago suddently became re-inflated. He began to spin on one foot, whistled a Viennese waltz, bounced across the room, grasped Doree's hand, drew her into his comprehension and his laughter. Together they waltzed, absurd, relieved, triumphant.

"Mr. Tachie, you are a bringer of miracles!" Mr. Archipelago cried. "There it was, all the time, and we did not see it. We, even we, Doree, will make history – you will see."

Tachie frowned, bewildered.

"I see it happen so, for white men, wen dey stay too long for dis place. Dey crez'. Mistah Arch'pelago meka you drink some small beer. Den you head he come fine."

"No, no, not beer," Mr. Archipelago replied, puffing out his waistcoat. "Here – a flask kept for medicinal purposes or special celebrations. A brandy, Mr. Tachie! A brandy for the history-makers!"

He and Doree laughed until they were weak. And Tachie, still not understanding, but pleased that they were in some lunatic fashion pleased, finally laughed with them and consented to drink the unpaid-for brandy.

That evening they painted the new sign. They worked until midnight with tins and brushes spread out on the dining-room table, while Brasso and Silvo squawked and stared. The sign was black and gilt, done in optimistically plump lettering:

ARCHIPELAGO & DOREE
Barbershop
All-Beauty Salon
African Ladies A Specialty

The men of the town continued, not unnaturally, to have their hair cut by the African barbers who plied their trade under the niim tree in the market. The African women, however, showed great interest in the new sign. They gathered in little groups and examined it. The girls who had attended school read the words aloud to their mothers and aunts. They murmured together. Their laughter came in soft gusts, like the sound of the wind through the casuarina branches. But not one of them would enter the shop.

Several times Mr. Archipelago saw faces peeping in at the window, scrutinizing every detail of the room. But as soon as he looked, the curious ones lowered their eyes and quickly walked away.

The hair-straightening equipment (obtained second-hand, and on credit, through Tachie) remained unused. Each day Doree dusted and set back on the counter the unopened make-up base which she had hurriedly ordered from the city when she discovered that the Africa Star Chemists, slightly behind the times, sold only shades of ivory and peach.

Another week, and still no customers. Then one morning, as Mr. Archipelago was opening his second bottle of Dutch ale, Mercy Tachie walked in.

"Please, Mr. Archipelago — " she began hesitantly. "I am thinking to come here for some time, but I am not sure what I should do. We have never had such a place in our town before, you see. So all of us are looking, but no one wishes to be the first. Then my father, he said to me today that I should be the first, because if you are having no customers, he will never be getting his money from you."

Mercy was about sixteen. She was clad in traditional cloth, but her face was thickly daubed with pale powder that obscured her healthy skin. She stood perfectly still in the centre of the room, her hands clasped in front of her, her face expressionless. Mr. Archipelago looked in admiration at the placidity of her features, a repose which he knew concealed an extreme nervousness and perhaps even panic, for in her life there had not been many unfamiliar things. He motioned her to a chair, and she sat down woodenly.

"Good," he said. "Doree and I welcome you. Now — can you help us to know a little, the way you want to look?"

Mercy's splendid eyes were blank no longer; they turned to him appealingly.

"I would like to look like a city girl, please," Mercy Tachie said. "That is what I would like the most."

"A city girl — " Mr. Archipelago ran a finger lightly over the chalky powder on her face. "That is why you wear this mask, eh? Ladies never know when they are beautiful — strange. They must be chic — God is not a good enough craftsman. Fortunate, I suppose, for us. Ah well. Yes, we will make you look like a city girl, if that is what you would like the most."

Confused by his sigh and smile, Mercy felt compelled to explain herself.

"I was going for seven years to the mission school here, you see, and all my life I am never knowing any place outside this town. But someday, maybe, I will be living in some big place, and if so, I would not want to feel like a bushgirl. So I wish to know how it is proper to have my hair, and what to do for the face. You do not think I am foolish?"

Mr. Archipelago shook his head.

"I think the whole world is foolish," he said. "But you are no more foolish than anyone else, and a great deal less so than many."

Doree, who felt his reply to be unsatisfactory, placed her splay-hands on the girl's dark wiry hair.

"Not to worry," she said. "We'll straighten your hair just enough to set it and style it. We'll take that goop off your face. You got lovely skin — not a wrinkle — you shouldn't cover it up like that. We'll give you a complete make-up job. Doll, you'll be a queen."

And Mercy Tachie, her eyes trusting, smiled.

"Do you think so? Do you really think it will be so?"

The air was redolent once more with the potions and unguents, the lotions and shampoos and lacquers, the nostril-pinching pungency of ammonia and the fragrance of bottled colognes. The snik-snik-snik of Mr. Archipelago's scissors was the theme of a small-scale symphony; overtones and undertones were provided by the throb of the dryer and the strident blues-chanting of Doree as she paced the room like a priestess. Mercy began to relax.

"My friends, they also would like to come here, I think, if they like the way I will look," she confided. "Mr. Archipelago, you will be staying here? You will not be leaving now?"

"Perhaps we will be staying," he said. "We must wait and see if your friends like the way you look."

Mercy pursed her lips pensively.

"Will you not go back, someday," she ventured, "to your own country? For the sake of your family?"

Doree glared, but Mr. Archipelago was bland. He had never minded the curiosity of his lady customers.

"The charming questions," he said. "They begin again. Good. No – I have no family."

"Oh, I thought it must be so!" Mercy cried.

"I beg your pardon?"

Once more she became self-conscious. She folded her hands and looked at the floor.

"I have heard," she said apologetically, "that you were leaving your own country many years ago because you had some bad trouble – maybe because you thought you might go to prison. But I am never believing that story, truly. Always I think you had some different kind of trouble. My aunt Abenaa, you know, she lost all her family – husband and three children – when their house burned down, and after that she left her village and came to live here, in my father's house, and never again will she go to that village."

"You think it was that way, for me?" he said.

"I think it – yes."

Mr. Archipelago straightened his waistcoat over his belly. In his eyes there appeared momentarily a certain sadness, a certain regret. But when he replied, his voice expressed nothing except a faint acceptable tenderness.

"You are kind. Perhaps the kindest of all my ladies."

At last the ritual was accomplished, and Mercy Tachie

looked at herself in the cracked and yellowing wall-mirror. Slowly, she turned this way and that, absorbing only gradually the details – the soft-curled hair whorled skilfully down onto her forehead, the face with its crimson lipstick and its brown make-up that matched her own skin. Then she smiled.

"Oh – " she breathed. "It is just like the pictures I have seen in *Drum* magazine – the girls, African girls, who know how everything is done in the new way. Oh, now I will know, too!"

"Do you think your friends will overcome their shyness now?" Mr. Archipelago asked.

"I will make sure of it," Mercy promised. "You will see."

They sat quietly in the shop after Mercy had left. They felt spent and drained, but filled and renewed as well. Doree stretched her long legs and closed her eyes. Mr. Archipelago bulged in his carved rocking-chair, and cradled to and fro peacefully, his shoes off and his waistcoat unbuttoned.

The crash of noise and voices from outside startled them. They ran to the open door. Spilling down the street was an impromptu procession. Every girl in town appeared to be there, hips and shoulders swaying, unshod feet stepping lightly, hands clapping, cloths of blue and magenta and yellow fluttering around them like the flags of nations while they danced. A few of the older women were there, too, buxom and lively, their excited laughter blaring like a melody of raucous horns. At the front of the parade walked Mercy Tachie in new red high-heeled shoes, her head held high to display her proud new hair, her new face alight with pleasure and infinite hope. Beside Mercy, as her guard and her champions, there pranced and jittered half a dozen young men, in khaki trousers and brilliantly flower-printed shirts. One held her hand – he was her own young man. Another had a guitar, and another a gourd rattle. They sang at full strength, putting new words to the popular highlife "Everybody Likes Saturday Night".

"Everybody like Mercy Tachie,
Everybody like Mercy Tachie,
Everybody everybody
Everybody everybody
Everybody say she fine pas' all — "

Mr. Archipelago turned to Doree. Gravely, they shook hands.

"By an act of Mercy," Mr. Archipelago said, "we are saved."

They walked along the shore in the moist and cooling late afternoon. The palm boughs rustled soothingly. The sound reminded Mr. Archipelago of taffeta, the gowns of the whispering ladies, twirling forever in a delicate minuet of dust, the ladies watched over by pale and costly marble angels, the dove-grey and undemanding ladies of his insomnia, eternally solacing, eternally ladies.

He watched Doree. She had discovered a blue crab, clownishly walking sideways, a great round crab with red and comic protruding eyes, and she stooped to examine it more carefully, to enjoy its grotesque loveliness. But it did not know that it need not be afraid, so it ran away.

"Archipelago," Doree said, "now that it's over, and we're here to stay, I guess I oughta tell you."

"No," he said. "There is nothing you need tell me."

"Yes," she insisted. "You know when you asked me if I could go back, and I said I couldn't? Well, I guess I didn't give you the straight goods, in a way — "

"I know," Mr. Archipelago said quietly. "There was no troubled past. I have always known that."

"Have you?" she said, mild-eyed, not really surprised. "How did you know?"

He glanced at her face, at the heavy make-up that covered the ageing features, ravaged and virginal.

"Because," he replied slowly, "for me it was the same. I, too, had no past. The white ladies and now the brown ladies — they have never guessed. I did not intend that they should.

It is not their concern. But we know, Doree, why we are here and why we stay."

"Yes," she said," I guess we do know. I guess we both know that. So we don't need to talk about it any more, do we?"

"No," he promised. "No more."

"And whatever happens," she went on, "even if we go broke, you won't get any more fancy ideas about me finding a better job somewhere else?"

"The new sign – " he reminded her. "Have you forgotten what it says?"

"That's right," she said. " 'Archipelago & Doree'. Yeh, that's right."

Mr. Archipelago sniffed the brine-laden wind.

"Smell the sea, Doree? A perfume for our collection."

She smiled. "What shall we call it?"

"Oh, nothing too ornate," he said lightly. "Perhaps *eau d'exile* would do."

The sea spray was bitter and salt, but to them it was warm, too. They watched on the sand their exaggerated shadows, one squat and bulbous, the other bone-slight and clumsily elongated, pigeon and crane. The shadows walked with hands entwined like children who walk through the dark.

QUESTIONS

1. What use does the author make of "Archipelago" and "flotsam" in preparing us for the underlying theme of the story?

2. Mr. Archipelago is from Genoa – the home of Christopher Columbus. But his memory of the city is of its graveyard. Doree is evasive about her origins. Is there any significance in the author's emphasis on the origins of both the main characters?

3. What do you learn about Mr. Archipelago from his garden, particularly from the wild orchids and the "sensitive plant"?

4. What do you learn about Doree from her "menagerie", and her refusal to kill "even the lethal guests"?

5. Why does Mercy Tachie tell Mr. Archipelago that she could never believe the gossip that he left his own country because of "some bad trouble"? And why does Mr. Archipelago hear this with "a certain sadness, a certain regret"?

6. How does the author relate the "perfume sea" (with the acceptance of exile – *eau d'exile*) to the earlier perfume ritual which for Archipelago conjured up "a throng of waltzing ladies"?

7. Why, at the end, is each able to admit the truth about the past – without regret?

PART FOUR
MAN AND HIS SYMBOLS

LOREN EISELEY

b. 1907

The bird and the machine ❖ ❖

In both this essay and the story that follows it, a pair of hawks symbolize the mystery, terror, and beauty of life. The title suggests the relationship of the essay to a theme that Loren Eiseley has developed in several books. In *The Immense Journey* (1957), *The Firmament of Time* (1960), *Francis Bacon and the Modern Dilemma* (1961), and *The Mind as Nature* (1962) he has repeatedly stressed the danger that modern man, in exploiting the substance of nature, may become blinded to its soul, and to his own soul as well. As former head of the Department of Anthropology at the University of Pennsylvania and as present University Professor in the History of Science, Eiseley has a secure grasp of the methods of science; however, in order to express his wonder at life's immense journey through time, he uses here the poet's resources of image and connotation.

I SUPPOSE their little bones have years ago been lost among the stones and winds of those high glacial pastures. I suppose their feathers blew eventually into the piles of tumbleweed beneath the straggling cattle fences and rotted there in the mountain snows, along with dead steers and all the other things that drift to an end in the corners of the wire. I do not quite know why I should be thinking of birds over the *New York Times* at breakfast, particularly the birds of my youth half a continent away. It is a funny thing what the brain will do with memories and how it will treasure them and finally bring them into odd juxtapositions with other things, as though it wanted to make a design, or get some meaning out of them, whether you want it or not, or even see it.

It used to seem marvelous to me, but I read now that there are machines that can do these things in a small way, machines that can crawl about like animals, and that it may not be long now until they do more things – maybe even make themselves – I saw that piece in the *Times* just now. And then they will, maybe – well, who knows – but you read about it more and more with no one making any protest, and already they can add better than we and reach up and hear things through the dark and finger the guns over the night sky.

This is the new world that I read about at breakfast. This is the world that confronts me in my biological books and journals, until there are times when I sit quietly in my chair and try to hear the little purr of the cogs in my head and the tubes flaring and dying as the messages go through them and the circuits snap shut or open. This is the great age, make no mistake about it; the robot has been born somewhat appropriately along with the atom bomb, and the brain they say now is just another type of more complicated feedback system. The engineers have its basic principles worked out; it's mechanical, you know; nothing to get superstitious about; and man can always improve on nature once he gets the idea. Well, he's got it all right and that's why, I guess, that I sit here in my chair, with the article crunched in my hand, remembering those two birds and that blue mountain sunlight. There is another magazine article on my desk that reads "Machines Are Getting Smarter Every Day". I don't deny it, but I'll still stick with the birds. It's life I believe in, not machines.

Maybe you don't believe there is any difference. A skeleton is all joints and pulleys, I'll admit. And when man was in his simpler stages of machine building in the eighteenth century, he quickly saw the resemblances. "What," wrote Hobbes, "is the heart but a spring, and the nerves but so many strings, and the joints but so many wheels, giving motion to the whole body?" Tinkering about in their shops it was inevitable in the end that men would see the world as a huge machine "subdivided into an infinite number of lesser machines".

The idea took on with a vengeance. Little automatons toured the country – dolls controlled by clock-work. Clocks described as little worlds were taken on tours by their designers. They were made up of moving figures, shifting scenes and other remarkable devices. The life of the cell was unknown. Man, whether he was conceived as possessing a soul or not, moved and jerked about like these tiny puppets. A human being thought of himself in terms of his own tools and implements. He had been fashioned like the puppets he produced and was only a more clever model made by a greater designer.

Then in the nineteenth century, the cell was discovered, and the single machine in its turn was found to be the product of millions of infinitesimal machines – the cells. Now, finally, the cell itself dissolves away into an abstract chemical machine – and that into some intangible, inexpressible flow of energy. The secret seems to lurk all about, the wheels get smaller and smaller, and they turn more rapidly, but when you try to seize it the life is gone – and so, by popular definition, some would say that life was never there in the first place. The wheels and the cogs are the secret and we can make them better in time – machines that will run faster and more accurately than real mice to real cheese.

I have no doubt it can be done, though a mouse harvesting seeds on an autumn thistle is to me a fine sight and more complicated, I think, in his multiform activity, than a machine "mouse" running a maze. Also, I like to think of the possible shape of the future brooding in mice, just as it brooded once in a rather ordinary mousy insectivore who became a man. It leaves a nice fine indeterminate sense of wonder that even an electronic brain hasn't got, because you know perfectly well that if the electronic brain changes, it will be because of something man has done to it. But what man will do to himself he doesn't really know. A certain scale of time and a ghostly intangible thing called change are ticking in him. Powers and potentialities like the oak in the seed, or a red and awful ruin. Either way, it's impressive; and the mouse has it, too. Or those birds, I'll never forget those birds — yet before I measured their significance, I learned the lesson of time first of all. I was young then and left alone in a great desert — part of an expedition that had scattered its men over several hundred miles in order to carry on research more effectively. I learned there that time is a series of planes existing superficially in the same universe. The tempo is a human illusion, a subjective clock ticking in our own kind of protoplasm.

As the long months passed, I began to live on the slower planes and to observe more readily what passed for life there. I sauntered, I passed more and more slowly up and down the canyons in the dry baking heat of midsummer. I slumbered for long hours in the shade of huge brown boulders that had gathered in tilted companies out on the flats. I had forgotten the world of men and the world had forgotten me. Now and then I found a skull in the canyons, and these justified my remaining there. I took a serene cold interest in these discoveries. I had come, like many a naturalist before me, to view life with a wary and subdued attention. I had grown to take pleasure in the divested bone.

I sat once on a high ridge that fell away before me into a waste of sand dunes. I sat through hours of a long afternoon. Finally, as I glanced beside my boot an indistinct configuration caught my eye. It was a coiled rattlesnake, a big one. How long he had sat with me I do not know. I had not frightened him. We were both locked in the sleep-walking tempo of the earlier world, baking in the same high air and sunshine. Perhaps he had been there when I came. He slept on as I left, his coils, so ill discerned by me, dissolving once more among the stones and gravel from which I had barely made him out.

Another time I got on a higher ridge, among some tough little wind-warped pines half covered over with sand in a basin-like depression that caught everything carried by the air up to those heights. There were a few thin bones of birds, some cracked shells of indeterminable age, and the knotty fingers of pine roots bulged out of shape from their long and agonizing grasp upon the crevices of the rock. I lay under the pines in the sparse shade and went to sleep once more.

It grew cold finally, for autumn was in the air by then, and the few things that lived thereabouts were sinking down into an even chillier scale of time. In the moments between sleeping and waking I saw the roots about me and slowly, slowly, a foot in what seemed many centuries, I moved my sleep-stiffened hands over the scaling bark and lifted my numbed face after the vanishing sun. I was a great awkward thing of knots and aching limbs, trapped up there in some long, patient endurance that involved the necessity of putting living fingers into rock and by slow, aching expansion bursting those rocks asunder. I suppose, so thin and slow was the time of my pulse by then, that I might have stayed on to drift still deeper into the lower cadences of the frost, or the crystalline life that glistens pebbles, or shines in a snowflake, or dreams in the meteoric iron between the worlds.

It was a dim descent, but time was present in it. Somewhere far down in that scale the notion struck me that one might come the other way. Not many months thereafter I joined some colleagues heading higher into a remote windy tableland where huge bones were reputed to protrude like boulders from the turf. I had drowsed with reptiles and moved with the century-long pulse of trees; now, lethargically, I was climbing back up some invisible ladder of quickening hours. There had been talk of birds in connection with my duties. Birds are intense, fast-living creatures — reptiles, I suppose one might say, that have escaped out of the heavy sleep of time, transformed fairy creatures dancing over sunlit meadows. It is a youthful fancy, no doubt, but because of something that happened up there among the escarpments of that range, it remains with me a lifelong impression. I can never bear to see a bird imprisoned.

We came into that valley through the trailing mists of a spring night. It was a place that looked as though it might never have known the foot of man, but our scouts had been ahead of us and we knew all about the abandoned cabin of stone that lay far up on one hillside. It had been built in the land rush of the last century and then lost to the cattlemen again as the marginal soils failed to take to the plow.

There were spots like this all over that country. Lost graves marked by unlettered stones and old corroding rim-fire cartridge cases lying where somebody had made a stand among the boulders that rimmed the valley. They are all that remain of the range wars; the men are under the stones now. I could see our cavalcade winding in and out through the mist below us: torches, the reflection of the truck lights on our collecting tins, and the far-off bumping of a loose dinosaur thigh bone in the bottom of a trailer. I stood on a rock a moment looking down and thinking what it cost in money and equipment to capture the past.

We had, in addition, instructions to lay hands on the present. The word had come through to get them alive — birds, reptiles, anything. A zoo somewhere abroad needed restocking. It was one of those reciprocal matters in which science involves itself. Maybe our museum needed a stray ostrich egg and this was the pay-off. Anyhow, my job was to help capture some birds and that was why I was there before the trucks.

The cabin had not been occupied for years. We intended to clean it out and live in it, but there were holes in the roof and the birds had come in and were roosting in the rafters. You could depend on it in a place like this where everything blew away, and even a bird needed some place out of the weather and away from coyotes. A cabin going back to nature in a wild place draws them till they come in, listening at the eaves, I imagine, pecking softly among the shingles till they find a hole and then suddenly the place is theirs and man is forgotten.

Sometimes of late years I find myself thinking the most beautiful sight in the world might be the birds taking over New York after the last man has run away to the hills. I will never live to see it, of course, but I know just how it will sound because I've lived up high and I know the sort of watch birds keep on us. I've listened to sparrows tapping tentatively on the outside of air conditioners when they thought no one was listening, and I know how other birds test the vibrations that come up to them through the television aerials.

"Is he gone?" they ask, and the vibrations come up from below, "Not yet, not yet."

Well, to come back, I got the door open softly and I had the spotlight all ready to turn on and blind whatever birds there were so they couldn't see to get out through the roof. I had a short piece of ladder to put against the far wall where there was a shelf on which I expected to make the biggest haul. I had all the information I needed just like any skilled assassin. I pushed the door open, the hinges squeaking only a little. A bird or two stirred – I could hear them – but nothing flew and there was a faint starlight through the holes in the roof.

I padded across the floor, got the ladder up and the light ready, and slithered up the ladder till my head and arms were over the shelf. Everything was dark as pitch except for the starlight at the little place back of the shelf near the eaves. With the light to blind them, they'd never make it. I had them. I reached my arm carefully over in order to be ready to seize whatever was there and I put the flash on the edge of the shelf where it would stand by itself when I turned it on. That way I'd be able to use both hands.

Everything worked perfectly except for one detail – I didn't know what kind of birds were there. I never thought about it at all, and it wouldn't have mattered if I had. My orders were to get something interesting. I snapped on the flash and sure enough there was a great beating and feathers flying, but instead of my having them, they, or rather he, had me. He had my hand, that is, and for a small hawk not much bigger than my fist he was doing all right. I heard him give one short metallic cry when the light went on and my hand descended on the bird beside him; after that he was busy with his claws and his beak was sunk in my thumb. In the struggle I knocked the lamp over on the shelf, and his mate got her sight back and whisked neatly through the hole in the roof and off among the stars outside. It all happened in fifteen seconds and you might think I would have fallen down the ladder, but no, I had a professional assassin's reputation to keep up, and the bird, of course, made the mistake of thinking the hand was the enemy and not the eyes behind it. He chewed my thumb up pretty effectively and lacerated my hand with his claws, but in the end I got him, having two hands to work with.

He was a sparrow hawk and a fine young male in the prime of life. I was sorry not to catch the pair of them, but as I dripped blood and folded his wings carefully, holding him by the back so that he couldn't strike again, I had to admit the two of them might have been more than I could have handled under the circumstances. The little fellow had saved his mate by diverting me, and that was that. He was born to it, and made no outcry now, resting in my hand hopelessly, but peering toward me in the shadows behind the lamp with a fierce, almost indifferent glance. He neither gave nor expected mercy and something out of the high air passed from him to me, stirring a faint embarrassment.

I quit looking into that eye and managed to get my huge carcass with its fist full of prey back down the ladder. I put the bird in a box too small to allow him to injure himself by struggle and walked out to welcome the arriving trucks. It had been a long day, and camp still to make in the darkness. In the morning that bird would be just another episode. He would go back with the bones in the truck to a small cage in a city where he would spend the rest of his life. And a good thing, too. I sucked my aching thumb and spat out some blood. An assassin has to get used to these things. I had a professional reputation to keep up.

In the morning, with the change that comes on suddenly in that high country, the mist that had hovered below us in the valley was gone. The sky was a deep blue, and one could see for miles over the high outcroppings of stone. I was up early and brought the box in which the little hawk was imprisoned out onto the grass where I was building a cage. A wind as cool as a mountain spring ran over the grass and stirred my hair. It was a fine day to be alive. I looked up and all around and at the hole in the cabin roof out of which the other little hawk had fled. There was no sign of her anywhere that I could see.

"Probably in the next county by now," I thought cynically, but before beginning work I decided I'd have a look at my last night's capture.

Secretively, I looked again all around the camp and up and down and opened the box. I got him right out in my hand with his wings folded properly and I was careful not to startle him. He lay limp in my grasp and I could feel his heart pound under the feathers but he only looked beyond me and up.

I saw him look that last look away beyond me into a sky so full of light that I could not follow his gaze. The little breeze flowed over me again, and nearby a mountain aspen shook all its tiny leaves. I suppose I must have had an idea then of what I was going to do, but I never let it come up into consciousness. I just reached over and laid the hawk on the grass.

He lay there a long minute without hope, unmoving, his eyes still fixed on that blue vault above him. It must have been that he was already so far away in heart that he never felt the release from my hand. He never even stood. He just lay with his breast against the grass.

In the next second after that long minute he was gone. Like a flicker of light, he had vanished with my eyes full on him, but without actually seeing even a premonitory wing beat. He was gone straight into that towering emptiness of light and crystal that my eyes could scarcely bear to penetrate. For another long moment there was silence. I could not see him. The light was too intense. Then from far up somewhere a cry came ringing down.

I was young then and had seen little of the world, but when I heard that cry my heart turned over. It was not the cry of the hawk I had captured; for, by shifting my position against the sun, I was now seeing further up. Straight out of the sun's eye, where she must have been soaring restlessly above us for untold hours, hurtled his mate. And from far up, ringing from peak to peak of the summits over us, came a cry of such unutterable and ecstatic joy that it sounds down across the years and tingles among the cups on my quiet breakfast table.

I saw them both now. He was rising fast to meet her. They met in a great soaring gyre that turned to a whirling circle and a dance of wings. Once more, just once, their two voices, joined in a harsh wild medley of question and response, struck and echoed against the pinnacles of the valley. Then they were gone forever somewhere into those upper regions beyond the eyes of men.

I am older now, and sleep less, and have seen most of what there is to see and am not very much impressed any more, I suppose, by anything. "What Next in the Attributes of Machines?" my morning headline runs. "It Might Be the Power to Reproduce Themselves."

I lay the paper down and across my mind a phrase floats insinuatingly: "It does not seem that there is anything in the construction, constituents, or behavior of the human being which it is essentially impossible for science to duplicate and synthesize. On the other hand . . ."

All over the city the cogs in the hard, bright mechanisms have begun to turn. Figures move through computers, names are spelled out, a thoughtful machine selects the fingerprints of a wanted criminal from an array of thousands. In the laboratory an electronic mouse runs swiftly through a maze toward the cheese it can neither taste nor enjoy. On the second run it does better than a living mouse.

"On the other hand . . ." Ah, my mind takes up, on the other hand the machine does not bleed, ache, hang for hours in the empty sky in a torment of hope to learn the fate of another machine, nor does it cry out with joy nor dance in the air with the fierce passion of a bird. Far off, over a distance greater than space, that remote cry from the heart of heaven makes a faint buzzing among my breakfast dishes and passes on and away.

QUESTIONS

1. The essay develops with poetic intensity a contrast that the noncommittal title only implies. What is this contrast?

2. What different effects are achieved by the image of decay in the first paragraph
   (a) as you begin reading the essay,
   (b) in retrospect, after you have finished the essay?

3. In paragraphs 2 and 3 Eiseley mentions the achievements of a mechanistic age, with an ironic pretence of being impressed by them. How does he indicate to us his actual suspicion of these achievements? Pick out the sentence in which he states his real position.

4. Why does he include the brief historical outline of how the mechanistic view of life developed?

5. Before narrating the crucial episode of the hawks, the author writes an impressionistic description of two previous experiences on a barren plateau. What knowledge came to him there? What is the relationship between these two experiences and the later one?

6. (a) Eiseley describes with artistic care the setting for his decision. Why is the setting important?
   (b) Describing the moment, he says, "I saw him look that last look away beyond me into a sky so full of light that I could not follow

his gaze." And, as the bird rejoins its mate, "I could not see him. The light was too intense." We can accept these statements about the light as literal truths, but in their context of emotionally persuasive prose, what additional meaning do they convey?

7. What does the concluding section contribute to the essay?

LIAM O'FLAHERTY

b. 1897

The hawk ✦ ✦ ✦

Liam O'Flaherty has written more than a dozen novels, one of which, *The Informer* (1925), was made into a movie that is now regarded as a classic. In 1935 O'Flaherty went to Hollywood to work on the screenplay of *The Informer* and has resided mainly in the United States since then. Like his countryman Frank O'Connor he has done some of his best writing in his short stories. These are collected in *The Short Stories of Liam O'Flaherty* (1956). As is true of some of his other fiction, the setting for "The Hawk" is O'Flaherty's birthplace, the awesomely desolate Aran islands that lie off the west coast of Ireland. His description of the hawk's passion for its mate and its furious encounter with man suits the mood of this wild, high place and resembles Eiseley's account in the preceding essay, although the outcome is very different.

HE BREASTED the summit of the cliff and then rose in wide circles to the clouds. When their undertendrils passed about his outstretched wings, he surged straight inland. Gliding and dipping his wings at intervals, he roamed across the roof of the firmament, with his golden hawk's eyes turned down, in search of prey, toward the bright earth that lay far away below, beyond the shimmering emptiness of the vast blue sky.

Once the sunlight flashed on his grey back, as he crossed an open space between two clouds. Then again he became a vague, swift shadow, rushing through the formless vapour. Suddenly his fierce heart throbbed, as he saw a lark, whose dewy back was jewelled by the radiance of the morning light, come rising toward him from a green meadow. He shot forward at full speed, until he was directly over his mounting prey. Then he began to circle slowly, with his wings stiff and his round eyes dilated, as if in fright. Slight tremors passed along his skin, beneath the compact armour of his plumage – like a hunting dog that stands poised and quivering before his game.

The lark rose awkwardly at first, uttering disjointed notes as he leaped and circled to gain height. Then he broke into full-throated song and soared straight upward, drawn to heaven by the power of his glorious voice, and fluttering his wings like a butterfly.

The hawk waited until the songbird had almost reached the limit of his climb. Then he took aim and stooped. With his wings half-closed, he raked like a meteor from the clouds. The lark's warbling changed to a shriek of terror as he heard the fierce rush of the charging hawk. Then he swerved aside, just in time to avoid the full force of the blow. Half-stunned, he folded his wings and plunged headlong toward the earth, leaving behind a flutter of feathers that had been torn from his tail by the claws of his enemy.

When he missed his mark, the hawk at once opened wide his wings and canted them to stay his rush. He circled once more above his falling prey, took aim, and stooped again. This time the lark did nothing to avoid the kill. He died the instant he was struck; his inert wings unfolded. With his head dangling from his limp throat, through which his lovely song had just been poured, he came tumbling down, convoyed by the closely circling hawk. He struck earth on a patch of soft brown sand, beside a shining stream.

The hawk stood for a few moments over his kill, with his lewd purple tongue lolling from his open beak and his black-barred breast heaving from the effort of pursuit. Then he secured the carcass in his claws, took wing, and flew off to the cliff where his mate was hatching on a broad ledge, beneath a massive tawny-gold rock that rose, over-arching, to the summit.

It was a lordly place, at the apex of a narrow cove, and so high above the sea that the roar of the breaking waves reached there only as a gentle murmur. There was no other sound within the semicircle of towering limestone walls that rose sheer from the dark water. Two months before, a vast crowd of other birds had lived on the lower edges of the cliffs, making the cove merry with their cries as they flew out to sea and back again with fish. Then one morning the two young hawks came there from the east to mate.

For hours the rockbirds watched them in terror, as the interlopers courted in the air above the cove, stooping past each other from the clouds down to the sea's edge, and then circling up again, wing to wing, winding their garland of love. At noon they saw the female draw the male into a cave, and heard his mating screech. Then they knew the birds of death had come to nest in their cove. So they took flight. That afternoon the mated hawks gambolled in the solitude that was now their domain, and at sundown the triumphant male brought his mate to nest on this lofty ledge, from which a pair of ravens had fled.

Now, as he dropped the dead lark beside her on the ledge, she lay there in a swoon of motherhood. Her beak rested on one of the sticks that formed her rude bed, and she looked down at the distant sea through half-closed eyes. Uttering cries of tenderness, he trailed his wings and marched around the nest on his bandy legs, pushing against her sides, caressing her back with his throat, and gently pecking at her crest. He had circled her four times, before she awoke from her stupor. Then she raised her head suddenly, opened her beak, and screamed. He screamed in answer and leaped upon the carcass of the lark. Quickly he severed its head, plucked its feathers, and offered her the naked, warm meat. She opened her mouth wide, swallowed the huge morsel in one movement, and again rested her beak on the stick. Her limp body spread out once more around the pregnant eggs, as she relapsed into her swoon.

His brute soul was exalted by the consciousness that he

had achieved the fullness of the purpose for which nature had endowed him. Like a hound stretched out in a sleep before a blazing fire, dreaming of the day's long chase, he relived the epic of his mating passion, while he strutted back and forth among the disgorged pellets and the bloody remains of eaten prey with which the rock was strewn.

Once he went to the brink of the ledge, flapped his wings against his breast, and screamed in triumph, as he looked out over the majestic domain that he had conquered with his mate. Then again he continued to march, rolling from side to side in ecstasy, as he recalled his moments of tender possession and the beautiful eggs that were warm among the sticks.

His exaltation was suddenly broken by a sound that reached him from the summit of the cliff. He stood motionless, close to the brink, and listened with his head turned to one side. Hearing the sound again from the summit, the same tremor passed through the skin within his plumage, as when he had soared, poised, above the mounting lark. His heart also throbbed as it had done then, but not with the fierce desire to exercise his power. He knew that he had heard the sound of human voices, and he felt afraid.

He dropped from the ledge and flew, close to the face of the cliff, for a long distance toward the west. Then he circled outward, swiftly, and rose to survey the intruders. He saw them from on high. There were three humans near the brink of the cliff, a short way east of the nest. They had secured the end of a stout rope to a block of limestone. The tallest of them had tied the other end to his body, and then attached a small brown sack to his waist belt.

When the hawk saw the tall man being lowered down along the face of the cliff to a protruding ledge that was on a level with the nest, his fear increased. He knew that the men had come to steal his mate's eggs; yet he felt helpless in the presence of the one enemy that he feared by instinct. He spiralled still higher and continued to watch in agony.

The tall man reached the ledge and walked carefully to its western limit. There he signalled to his comrades, who hauled up the slack of his rope. Then he braced himself, kicked the brink of the ledge, and swung out toward the west, along the blunt face of the cliff, using the taut rope as a lever. He landed on the eastern end of the ledge where the hawk's mate was sitting on her nest, on the far side of a bluff. His comrades again slackened the rope, in answer to his signal, and he began to move westward, inch by inch, crouched against the rock.

The hawk's fear vanished as he saw his enemy relentlessly move closer to the bluff. He folded his wings and dove headlong down to warn his mate. He flattened out when he came level with the ledge and screamed as he flew past her. She took no notice of the warning. He flew back and forth several times, screaming in agony, before she raised her head and answered him. Exalted by her voice, he circled far out to sea and began to climb.

Once more he rose until the undertendrils of the clouds passed about his outstretched wings and the fierce cold of the upper firmament touched his heart. Then he fixed his golden eyes on his enemy and hovered to take aim. At this moment of supreme truth, as he stood poised, it was neither pride in his power nor the intoxication of the lust to kill that stiffened his wings and the muscles of his breast. He was drawn to battle by the wild, sad tenderness aroused in him by his mate's screech.

He folded his wings and stooped. Down he came, relentlessly, straight at the awe-inspiring man that he no longer feared. The two men on the cliff top shouted a warning when they saw him come. The tall man on the ledge raised his eyes. Then he braced himself against the cliff to receive the charge. For a moment, it was the eyes of the man that showed fear, as they looked into the golden eyes of the descending hawk. Then he threw up his arms, to protect his face, just as the hawk struck. The body of the doomed bird glanced off the thick cloth that covered the man's right arm and struck the cliff with a dull thud. It rebounded and went tumbling down.

When the man came creeping round the bluff, the mother hawk stood up in the nest and began to scream. She leaped at him and tried to claw his face. He quickly caught her, pinioned her wings, and put her in his little sack. Then he took the eggs.

Far away below, the body of the dead hawk floated, its broken wings outstretched on the foam-embroidered surface of the dark water, and drifted seaward with ebbing tide.

QUESTIONS

1. (a) At the literal level this is a story about the climax of a bird's life – its mating and its death. But it also expresses the author's perception of life. What comment about life does he seem to be making? If the hawk may be regarded as a symbol, what does it symbolize?
   (b) Compare O'Flaherty's statement about life with that of Loren Eiseley in "The Bird and the Machine".

2. When a writer chooses the mind of an animal for his narrative point of view, he runs the danger of letting the animal's thoughts and emotions seem too much like those of a human being. This danger is especially great in writing of birds, whose intelligence is very slight, although their emotions are intense. In what passages of the story do you think he is particularly successful in overcoming this problem? In what passages, if any, does he let the hawk seem too "human"?

3. What is the function in the story of the preliminary incident of the hawk's kill?

4. How does the point of view shift in the first two paragraphs of the second part of the story? Why is the flashback inserted at this point in the narrative?

5. The relations of the mated hawks are described with a strange mixture of beauty and ugliness. Why does O'Flaherty blend these two opposites? Where else in the story do you notice a similar juxtaposition of the beautiful and the repulsive?

6. (a) What effect on the reader does the author want to achieve in the final section of the story?
(b) Examine the image in the last sentence. What qualities in the image itself and in the rhythm of the language conveying it make this an emotionally moving conclusion?

GRAHAM GREENE

b. 1904

The hint of an explanation ✦ ✦

This story is a good example in little of the preoccupation with the theme of evil which has characterized the serious novels of Graham Greene from *Brighton Rock* (1938) to *The Comedians* (1965). And there is a touch, too, in this story of that fine art of situation and suspense, which marks Graham Greene's famous "thrillers" or, as he calls them, "entertainments" – stories like *Stamboul Train* (1932) and *Confidential Agent* (1939). In "The Hint of an Explanation", which appeared in a collection of Graham Greene's called *Twenty-One Stories* (1960), our author once again, as in novels like *The Power and the Glory* (1940) and *The Heart of the Matter* (1948), defines his great theme in specifically Roman Catholic terms. Here, as elsewhere, he does not hesitate to rest his central effect and purpose on a theological conviction which he knows may not be shared by all his readers. And all his readers – indeed many of his most devoted readers – do not share his convictions, his Catholic faith. At the core of this story is to be found the Catholic belief in the doctrine of Transubstantiation, the belief that the bread and wine consecrated in the Mass are changed to the true Body and Blood of Christ. A proper critical exercise for you in reading this story is to decide whether or not the success of the story depends on your own agreement or disagreement with Greene's theology. If you do not agree, is a "willing suspension of disbelief" (Coleridge's phrase) possible and sufficient? Is it enough to understand what Greene believes? If so, what values – artistic, dramatic, psychological, moral – might the story have for both Catholic and non-Catholic readers?

A LONG TRAIN JOURNEY on a late December evening, in this new version of peace, is a dreary experience. I suppose that my fellow traveller and I could consider ourselves lucky to have a compartment to ourselves, even though the heating apparatus was not working, even though the lights went out entirely in the frequent Pennine tunnels and were too dim anyway for us to read our books without straining the eyes, and though there was no restaurant car to give at least a change of scene. It was when we were trying simultaneously to chew the same kind of dry bun bought at the same station buffet that my companion and I came together. Before that we had sat at opposite ends of the carriage, both muffled to the chin in overcoats, both bent low over type we could barely make out, but as I threw the remains of my cake under the seat our eyes met, and he laid his book down.

By the time we were half-way to Bedwell Junction we had found an enormous range of subjects for discussion; starting with buns and the weather, we had gone on to politics, the Government, foreign affairs, the atom bomb, and by an inevitable progression, God. We had not, however, become either shrill or acid. My companion, who now sat opposite me, leaning a little forward, so that our knees nearly touched, gave such an impression of serenity that it would have been impossible to quarrel with him, however much our views differed, and differ they did profoundly.

I had soon realized I was speaking to a Catholic — to someone who believed — how do they put it? — in an omnipotent and omniscient Deity, while I am what is loosely called an Agnostic. I have a certain intuition (which I do not trust, founded as it may well be on childish experiences and needs) that a God exists, and I am surprised occasionally into belief by the extraordinary coincidences that beset our path like the traps set for leopards in the jungle, but intellectually I am revolted at the whole notion of such a God who can so abandon his creatures to the enormities of Free Will. I found myself expressing this view to my companion who listened quietly and with respect. He made no attempt to interrupt — he showed none of the impatience or the intellectual arrogance I have grown to expect from Catholics; when the lights of a wayside station flashed across his face that had escaped hitherto the rays of the one globe working in the compartment, I caught a glimpse suddenly of—what? I stopped speaking, so strong was the impression. I was carried back ten years, to the other side of the great useless conflict, to a small town, Gisors in Normandy. I was again, for a moment, walking on the ancient battlements and looking down across the grey roofs, until my eyes for some reason lit on one stony "back" out of the many, where the face of a middle-aged man was pressed against a window pane (I suppose that face has ceased to exist now, just as I believe the whole town with its medieval memories has been reduced to rubble). I remembered saying to myself with astonishment, "That man is happy—completely happy." I looked across the compartment at my fellow traveller, but his face was already again in shadow. I said weakly, "When you think what God—if there is a God—allows. It's not merely the physical agonies, but think of the corruption, even of children...."

He said, "Our view is so limited," and I was disappointed at the conventionality of his reply. He must have been aware of my disappointment (it was as though our thoughts were huddled as closely as ourselves for warmth), for he went on, "Of course there is no answer here. We catch hints"... and then the train roared into another tunnel and the lights again went out. It was the longest tunnel yet; we went rocking down it and the cold seemed to become more intense with the darkness, like an icy fog (perhaps when one sense—of sight—is robbed, the others grow more acute). When we emerged into the mere grey of night and the globe lit up once more, I could see that my companion was leaning back on his seat.

I repeated his last words as a question, "Hints?"

"Oh, they mean very little in cold print—or cold speech," he said, shivering in his overcoat. "And they mean nothing at all to another human being than the man who catches them. They are not scientific evidence—or evidence at all for that matter. Events that don't, somehow, turn out as they were intended — by the human actors, I mean, or by the thing behind the human actors."

"The thing?"

"The word Satan is so anthropomorphic." I had to lean forward now: I wanted to hear what he had to say. I am — I really am, God knows — open to conviction. He said, "One's words are so crude, but I sometimes feel pity for that thing. It is so continually finding the right weapon to use against its Enemy and the weapon breaks in its own breast. It sometimes seems to me so — powerless. You said something just now about the corruption of children. It reminded me of something in my own childhood. You are the first person — except for one — that I have thought of telling it to, perhaps because you are anonymous. It's not a very long story, and in a way it's relevant."

I said, "I'd like to hear it."

"You mustn't expect too much meaning. But to me there seems to be a hint. That's all. A hint."

He went slowly on, turning his face to the pane, though he could have seen nothing real in the whirling world outside except an occasional signal lamp, a light in a window, a small country station torn backwards by our rush, picking his words with precision. He said, "When I was a child they taught me to serve at Mass. The church was a small one, for there were very few Catholics where I lived. It was a market town in East Anglia, surrounded by flat chalky fields and ditches — so many ditches. I don't suppose there were fifty Catholics all told, and for some reason there was a tradition of hostility to us. Perhaps it went back to the burning of a Protestant martyr in the sixteenth century — there was a stone marking the place near where the meat stalls stood on Wednesdays. I was only half aware of the enmity, though I knew that my school nickname of Popey Martin had something to do with my religion, and I had heard that my father was nearly excluded from the Constitutional Club when he first came to the town.

"Every Sunday I had to dress up in my surplice and serve

Mass. I hated it — I have always hated dressing up in any way (which is funny when you come to think of it), and I never ceased to be afraid of losing my place in the service and doing something which would put me to ridicule. Our services were at a different hour from the Anglican, and as our small, far-from-select band trudged out of the hideous chapel the whole of the townsfolk seemed to be on the way past to the proper church — I always thought of it as the proper church. We had to pass the parade of their eyes, indifferent, supercilious, mocking; you can't imagine how seriously religion can be taken in a small town, if only for social reasons.

"There was one man in particular; he was one of the two bakers in the town, the one my family did not patronize. I don't think any of the Catholics patronized him because he was called a free-thinker — an odd title, for, poor man, no one's thoughts were less free than his. He was hemmed in by his hatred — his hatred of us. He was very ugly to look at, with one wall eye and a head the shape of a turnip, with the hair gone on the crown, and he was unmarried. He had no interests, apparently, but his baking and his hatred, though now that I am older I begin to see other sides to his nature — it did contain, perhaps, a certain furtive love. One would come across him suddenly, sometimes, on a country walk, especially if one was alone and it was Sunday. It was as though he rose from the ditches and the chalk smear on his clothes reminded one of the flour on his working overalls. He would have a stick in his hand and stab at the hedges, and if his mood were very black he would call out after you strange abrupt words that were like a foreign tongue — I know the meaning of those words, of course, now. Once the police went to his house because of what a boy said he had seen, but nothing came of it except that the hate shackled him closer. His name was Blacker, and he terrified me.

"I think he had a particular hatred of my father — I don't know why. My father was manager of the Midland Bank, and it's possible that at some time Blacker may have had unsatisfactory dealings with the bank — my father was a very cautious man who suffered all his life from anxiety about money — his own and other people's. If I try to picture Blacker now I see him walking along a narrowing path between high windowless walls, and at the end of the path stands a small boy of ten — me. I don't know whether it's a symbolic picture or the memory of one of our encounters — our encounters somehow got more and more frequent. You talked just now about the corruption of children. That poor man was preparing to revenge himself on everything he hated — my father, the Catholics, the God whom people persisted in crediting, and that by corrupting me. He had evolved a horrible and ingenious plan.

"I remember the first time I had a friendly word from him. I was passing his shop as rapidly as I could when I heard his voice call out with a kind of sly subservience as though he were an under servant. 'Master David,' he called, 'Master David,' and I hurried on. But the next time I passed that way he was at his door (he must have seen me coming) with one of those curly cakes in his hand that we called Chelsea buns. I didn't want to take it, but he made me, and then I couldn't be other than polite when he asked me to come into his parlour behind the shop and see something very special.

"It was a small electric railway — a rare sight in those days, and he insisted on showing me how it worked. He made me turn the switches and stop and start it, and he told me that I could come in any morning and have a game with it. He used the word 'game' as though it were something secret, and it's true that I never told my family of this invitation and of how, perhaps twice a week those holidays, the desire to control that little railway became overpowering, and looking up and down the street to see if I were observed, I would dive into the shop."

Our larger, dirtier, adult train drove into a tunnel and the light went out. We sat in darkness and silence, with the noise of the train blocking our ears like wax. When we were through we didn't speak at once and I had to prick him into continuing. "An elaborate seduction," I said.

"Don't think his plans were as simple as that," my companion said, "or as crude. There was much more hate than love, poor man, in his make-up. Can you hate something you don't believe in? And yet he called himself a free-thinker. What an impossible paradox, to be free and to be so obsessed. Day by day all through those holidays his obsession must have grown, but he kept a grip; he bided his time. Perhaps that thing I spoke of gave him the strength and the wisdom. It was only a week from the end of the holidays that he spoke to me of what concerned him so deeply.

"I heard him behind me as I knelt on the floor, coupling two coaches. He said, 'You won't be able to do this, Master David, when school starts.' It wasn't a sentence that needed any comment from me any more than the one that followed, 'You ought to have it for your own, you ought,' but how skilfully and unemphatically he had sowed the longing, the idea of a possibility. . . . I was coming to his parlour every day now; you see I had to cram every opportunity in before the hated term started again, and I suppose I was becoming accustomed to Blacker, to that wall eye, that turnip head, that nauseating subservience. The Pope, you know, describes himself as 'The servant of the servants of God,' and Blacker – I sometimes think that Blacker was 'the servant of the servants of . . . ' well, let it be.

"The very next day, standing in the doorway watching me play, he began to talk to me about religion. He said, with what untruth even I recognized, how much he admired the Catholics; he wished he could believe like that, but how could a baker believe? He accented 'a baker' as one might say a biologist, and the tiny train spun round the gauge O track. He said, 'I can bake the things you eat just as well as any Catholic can,' and disappeared into his shop. I hadn't the faintest idea what he meant. Presently he emerged again, holding in his hand a little wafer. 'Here,' he said, 'eat that and tell me. . . .' When I put it in my mouth I could tell that it was made in the same way as our wafers for communion – he had got the shape a little wrong, that was all, and I felt guilty and irrationally scared. 'Tell me,' he said, 'what's the difference?'

" 'Difference?' I asked.

" 'Isn't that just the same as you eat in church?'

"I said smugly, 'It hasn't been consecrated.'

"He said, 'Do you think if I put the two of them under a microscope, you could tell the difference?' But even at ten I had the answer to that question. 'No,' I said, 'the – accidents don't change,' stumbling a little on the word 'accidents' which had suddenly conveyed to me the idea of death and wounds.

"Blacker said with sudden intensity, 'How I'd like to get one of your ones in my mouth – just to see. . . .'

"It may seem odd to you, but this was the first time that the idea of transubstantiation really lodged in my mind. I had learnt it all by rote; I had grown up with the idea. The Mass was as lifeless to me as the sentences in *De Bello Gallico*; communion a routine like drill in the school-yard, but here suddenly I was in the presence of a man who took it seriously, as seriously as the priest whom naturally one didn't count – it was his job. I felt more scared than ever.

"He said, 'It's all nonsense, but I'd just like to have it in my mouth.'

" 'You could if you were a Catholic,' I said naïvely. He gazed at me with his one good eye like a Cyclops. He said, 'You serve at Mass, don't you? It would be easy for you to get at one of those things. I tell you what I'd do – I'd swap this electric train for one of your wafers – consecrated, mind. It's got to be consecrated.'

" 'I could get you one out of the box,' I said. I think I still imagined that his interest was a baker's interest – to see how they were made.

" 'Oh, no,' he said. 'I want to see what your God tastes like.'

" 'I couldn't do that.'

" 'Not for a whole electric train, just for yourself? You wouldn't have any trouble at home. I'd pack it up and put a label inside that your Dad could see – "For my bank man ager's little boy from a grateful client." He'd be pleased as Punch with that.'

"Now that we are grown men it seems a trivial temptation, doesn't it? But try to think back to your own childhood. There was a whole circuit of rails on the floor at our feet, straight rails and curved rails, and a little station with porters and passengers, a tunnel, a foot-bridge, a level crossing, two signals, buffers, of course – and above all, a turntable. The tears of longing came into my eyes when I looked at the turntable. It was my favourite piece – it looked so ugly and practical and true. I said weakly, 'I wouldn't know how.'

"How carefully he had been studying the ground. He must have slipped several times into Mass at the back of the church. It would have been no good, you understand, in a little town like that, presenting himself for communion. Everybody there knew him for what he was. He said to me, 'When you've been given communion you could just put it under your tongue a moment. He serves you and the other boy first, and I saw you once go out behind the curtain straight afterwards. You'd forgotten one of those little bottles.'

" 'The cruet,' I said.

" 'Pepper and salt.' He grinned at me jovially, and I – well, I looked at the little railway which I could no longer come and play with when term started. I said, 'You'd just swallow it, wouldn't you?'

" 'Oh, yes,' he said. 'I'd just swallow it.'

"Somehow I didn't want to play with the train any more that day. I got up and made for the door, but he detained me, gripping my lapel. He said, 'This will be a secret between you and me. Tomorrow's Sunday. You come along here in the afternoon. Put it in an envelope and post it in. Monday morning the train will be delivered bright and early.'

" 'Not tomorrow,' I implored him.

" 'I'm not interested in any other Sunday,' he said. 'It's your only chance.' He shook me gently backwards and forwards. 'It will always have to be a secret between you and me,' he said. 'Why, if anyone knew they'd take away the train and there'd be me to reckon with. I'd bleed you something awful. You know how I'm always about on Sunday walks. You can't avoid a man like me. I crop up. You wouldn't ever be safe in your own house. I know ways to get into houses when people are asleep.' He pulled me into the shop after him and opened a drawer. In the drawer was an odd-looking key and a cut-throat razor. He said, 'That's a master key that opens all locks and that – that's what I bleed people with.' Then he patted my cheek with his plump floury fingers and said, 'Forget it. You and me are friends.'

"That Sunday Mass stays in my head, every detail of it, as though it had happened only a week ago. From the moment of the Confession to the moment of Consecration it had a terrible importance; only one other Mass has ever been so important to me – perhaps not even one, for this was a solitary Mass which would never happen again. It seemed as final as the last Sacrament, when the priest bent down and put the wafer in my mouth where I knelt before the altar with my fellow server.

"I suppose I had made up my mind to commit this awful act – for, you know, to us it must always seem an awful act – from the moment when I saw Blacker watching from the back of the church. He had put on his best Sunday clothes, and as though he could never quite escape the smear of his profession, he had a dab of dried talcum on his cheek, which he had presumably applied after using that cut-throat of his. He was watching me closely all the time, and I think it was fear – fear of that terrible undefined thing called bleeding – as much as covetousness that drove me to carry out my instructions.

"My fellow server got briskly up and taking the communion plate preceded Father Carey to the altar rail where the other Communicants knelt. I had the Host lodged under my tongue: it felt like a blister. I got up and made for the curtain to get the cruet that I had purposely left in the sacristy. When I was there I looked quickly round for a hiding place and saw an old copy of the *Universe* lying on a chair. I took the Host from my mouth and inserted it between two sheets – a little damp mess of pulp. Then I thought: perhaps Father Carey has put the paper out for a particular purpose and he will find the Host before I have time to remove it, and the enormity of my act began to come home to me when I tried to imagine what punishment I should incur. Murder is sufficiently trivial to have its appropriate punishment, but for this act the mind boggled at the thought of any retribution at all. I tried to remove the Host, but it had stuck clammily between the pages and in desperation I tore out a piece of the newspaper and screwing the whole thing up, stuck it in my trousers pocket. When I came back through the curtain carrying the cruet my eyes met Blacker's. He gave me a grin of encouragement and unhappiness – yes, I am sure, unhappiness. Was it perhaps that the poor man was all the time seeking something incorruptible?

"I can remember little more of that day. I think my mind was shocked and stunned and I was caught up too in the family bustle of Sunday. Sunday in a provincial town is the day for relations. All the family are at home and unfamiliar cousins and uncles are apt to arrive packed in the back seats of other people's cars. I remember that some crowd of that kind descended on us and pushed Blacker temporarily out of the foreground of my mind. There was somebody called Aunt Lucy with a loud hollow laugh that filled the house with mechanical merriment like the sound of recorded laughter from inside a hall of mirrors, and I had no opportunity to go out alone even if I had wished to. When six o'clock came and Aunt Lucy and the cousins departed and peace returned, it was too late to go to Blacker's and at eight it was my own bed-time.

"I think I had half forgotten what I had in my pocket. As I emptied my pocket the little screw of newspaper brought quickly back the Mass, the priest bending over me, Blacker's grin. I laid the packet on the chair by my bed and tried to go to sleep, but I was haunted by the shadows on the wall where the curtains blew, the squeak of furniture, the rustle in the chimney, haunted by the presence of God there on the chair. The Host had always been to me – well, the Host. I knew theoretically, as I have said, what I had to believe, but suddenly, as someone whistled in the road outside, whistled secretively, knowingly, to me, I knew that this which I had beside my bed was something of infinite value – something a man would pay for with his whole peace of mind, something that was so hated one could love it as one loves an outcast or a bullied child. These are adult words and it was a child of ten who lay scared in bed, listening to the whistle from the road, Blacker's whistle, but I think he felt fairly clearly what I am describing now. That is what I meant when I said this Thing, whatever it is, that seizes every possible weapon against God, is always, everywhere, disappointed at the moment of success. It must have felt as certain of me as Blacker did. It must have felt certain, too, of Blacker. But I wonder, if one knew what happened later to that poor man, whether one would not find again that the weapon had been turned against its own breast.

"At last I couldn't bear that whistle any more and got out of bed. I opened the curtains a little way, and there right under my window, the moonlight on his face, was Blacker. If I had stretched my hand down, his fingers reaching up could almost have touched mine. He looked up at me, flashing the one good eye, with hunger – I realise now that near-success must have developed his obsession almost to the point of madness. Desperation had driven him to the house. He whispered up at me, 'David, where is it?'

"I jerked my head back at the room. 'Give it me,' he said, 'quick. You shall have the train in the morning.'

"I shook my head. He said, 'I've got the bleeder here, and the key. You'd better toss it down.'

" 'Go away,' I said, but I could hardly speak with fear.

" 'I'll bleed you first and then I'll have it just the same.'

" 'Oh no, you won't,' I said. I went to the chair and picked it – Him – up. There was only one place where He was safe. I couldn't separate the Host from the paper, so I swallowed both. The newsprint stuck like a prune skin to the back of my throat, but I rinsed it down with water from the ewer. Then I went back to the window and looked down at Blacker. He began to wheedle me. 'What have you done with it, David? What's the fuss? It's only a bit of bread,' looking so longingly and pleadingly up at me that even as a child I wondered whether he could really think that, and yet desire it so much.

" 'I swallowed it,' I said.

" 'Swallowed it?'

" 'Yes,' I said. 'Go away.' Then something happened which seems to me now more terrible than his desire to corrupt or my thoughtless act: he began to weep — the tears ran lopsidedly out of the one good eye and his shoulders shook. I only saw his face for a moment before he bent his head and strode off, the bald turnip head shaking, into the dark. When I think of it now, it's almost as if I had seen that Thing weeping for its inevitable defeat. It had tried to use me as a weapon and now I had broken in its hands and it wept its hopeless tears through one of Blacker's eyes."

The black furnaces of Bedwell Junction gathered around the line. The points switched and we were tossed from one set of rails to another. A spray of sparks, a signal light changed to red, tall chimneys jetting into the grey night sky, the fumes of steam from stationary engines — half the cold journey was over and now remained the long wait for the slow cross-country train. I said, "It's an interesting story. I think I should have given Blacker what he wanted. I wonder what he would have done with it."

"I really believe," my companion said, "that he would first of all have put it under his microscope — before he did all the other things I expect he had planned."

"And the hint?" I said. "I don't quite see what you mean by that."

"Oh, well," he said vaguely, "you know for me it was an odd beginning, that affair, when you come to think of it," but I should never have known what he meant had not his coat, when he rose to take his bag from the rack, come open and disclosed the collar of a priest.

I said, "I suppose you think you owe a lot to Blacker."

"Yes," he said. "You see, I am a very happy man."

QUESTIONS

1. Why does Greene choose the train journey as the setting for this story?

2. What is gained by having the story told from the point of view of an agnostic?

3. Why does the speaker refer to evil as "the Thing" rather than as "Satan"?

4. What is Blacker's motive? And why does the author permit him "a certain furtive love"?

5. "Can you hate something you don't believe in?"

6. What "explanation" does the story "hint" at? How?

JOHN UPDIKE

b. 1932

Pigeon feathers ✦ ✦ ✦

One of the most highly praised younger American writers, John Updike has written several novels: *The Poorhouse Fair* (1959), *Rabbit, Run* (1960), *The Centaur* (1963), and *Of the Farm* (1965). He also writes poems and stories for *The New Yorker* Magazine, on which he was a staff writer for two years. The poems have been collected in *Telegraph Poles* (1963) and *A Child's Calendar* (1965), the stories in *Pigeon Feathers and Other Stories* (1962), and *Olinger Stories* (1964). Updike's fiction expresses the yearning of our restless age to find a rock of certainty on which to take a stand. The terrifying loss of belief in God experienced by David in this story is a universal phase in growing up – a time of blindness while the eyes of childhood struggle to accommodate themselves to the appalling glare of life's full spectrum; but the story has particular force in an age when even some clergymen pose the question, "Is God dead?" Updike consciously employs image and symbol to dramatize David's painful awakening to a new awareness of his place in the scheme of things.

WHEN THEY MOVED to Firetown, things were upset, displaced, rearranged. A red cane-back sofa that had been the chief piece in the living room at Olinger was here banished, too big for the narrow country parlor, to the barn, and shrouded under a tarpaulin. Never again would David lie on its length all afternoon eating raisins and reading mystery novels and science fiction and P. G. Wodehouse. The blue wing chair had stood for years in the ghostly, immaculate guest bedroom, gazing through the windows curtained with dotted swiss toward the telephone wires and horse-chestnut trees and opposite houses, was here established importantly in front of the smutty little fireplace that supplied, in those first cold April days, their only heat. As a child, David had been afraid of the guest bedroom — it was there that he, lying sick with the measles, had seen a black rod the size of a yardstick jog along at a slight slant beside the edge of the bed and vanish when he screamed — and it was disquieting to have one of the elements of its haunted atmosphere basking by the fire, in the center of the family, growing sooty with use. The books that at home had gathered dust in the case beside the piano were here hastily stacked, all out of order, in the shelves that the carpenters had built along one wall below the deep-silled windows. David, at fourteen, had been more moved than a mover; like the furniture, he had to find a new place, and on the Saturday of the second week he tried to work off some of his disorientation by arranging the books.

It was a collection obscurely depressing to him, mostly books his mother had acquired when she was young: college anthologies of Greek plays and Romantic poetry, Will Durant's *Story of Philosophy*, a soft-leather set of Shakespeare with string bookmarks sewed to the bindings, *Green Mansions* boxed and illustrated with woodcuts, *I, the Tiger*, by Manuel Komroff, novels by names like Galsworthy and Ellen Glasgow and Irvin S. Cobb and Sinclair Lewis and "Elizabeth". The odor of faded taste made him feel the ominous gap between himself and his parents, the insulting gulf of time that existed before he was born. Suddenly he was tempted to dip into this time. From the heaps of books piled around him on the worn old floorboards, he picked up Volume II of a four-volume set of *The Outline of History*, by H. G. Wells. Once David had read *The Time Machine* in an anthology; this gave him a small grip on the author. The book's red binding had faded to orange-pink on the spine. When he lifted the cover, there was a sweetish, attic-like smell, and his mother's maiden name written in unfamiliar handwriting on the flyleaf — an upright, bold, yet careful signature, bearing a faint relation to the quick scrunched backslant that flowed with marvelous consistency across her shopping lists and budget accounts and Christmas cards to college friends from this same, vaguely menacing long ago.

He leafed through, pausing at drawings, done in an old-fashioned stippled style, of bas-reliefs, masks, Romans without pupils in their eyes, articles of ancient costume, fragments of pottery found in unearthed homes. He knew it would be interesting in a magazine, sandwiched between ads and jokes, but in this undiluted form history was somehow sour. The print was determinedly legible, and smug, like a lesson book. As he bent over the pages, yellow at the edges, they seemed rectangles of dusty glass through which he looked down into unreal and irrelevant worlds. He could see things sluggishly move, and an unpleasant fullness came into his throat. His mother and grandmother fussed in the kitchen; the puppy, which they had just acquired, for "protection in the country", was cowering, with a sporadic panicked scrabble of claws, under the dining table that in their old home had been reserved for special days but that here was used for every meal.

Then, before he could halt his eyes, David slipped into Wells' account of Jesus. He had been an obscure political agitator, a kind of hobo, in a minor colony of the Roman Empire. By an accident impossible to reconstruct, he (the small *h* horrified David) survived his own crucifixion and presumably died a few weeks later. A religion was founded on the freakish incident. The credulous imagination of the times retrospectively assigned miracles and supernatural pretensions to Jesus; a myth grew, and then a church, whose theology at most points was in direct contradiction of the simple, rather communistic teachings of the Galilean.

It was as if a stone that for weeks and even years had been gathering weight in the web of David's nerves snapped them and plunged through the page and a hundred layers of paper underneath. These fantastic falsehoods – plainly untrue; churches stood everywhere, the entire nation was founded "under God" – did not at first frighten him; it was the fact that they had been permitted to exist in an actual human brain. This was the initial impact — that at a definite spot in time and space a brain black with the denial of Christ's divinity had been suffered to exist; that the universe had not spit out this ball of tar but allowed it to continue in its blasphemy, to grow old, win honors, wear a hat, write books that, if true, collapsed everything into a jumble of horror. The world outside the deep-silled windows — a rutted lawn, a whitewashed barn, a walnut tree frothy with fresh green — seemed a haven from which he was forever sealed off. Hot washrags seemed pressed against his cheeks.

He read the account again. He tried to supply out of his ignorance objections that would defeat the complacent march of these black words, and found none. Survivals and misunderstandings more far-fetched were reported daily in the papers. But none of them caused churches to be built in every town. He tried to work backwards through the churches, from their brave high fronts through their shabby, ill-attended interiors back into the events at Jerusalem, and felt himself surrounded by shifting gray shadows, centuries of history, where he knew nothing. The thread dissolved in his hands. Had Christ ever come to him, David Kern, and said, "Here. Feel the wound in My side"? No; but prayers had been answered. What prayers? He had prayed that Rudy Mohn, whom he had purposely tripped so he cracked his head on their radiator, not die, and he had not died. But for all the blood, it was just a cut; Rudy came back the same day, wearing a bandage and repeating the same teasing words. He could never have died. Again, David had prayed for two separate war-effort posters he had sent away for to arrive tomorrow, and though they did not, they did arrive, some days later, together, popping through the clacking letter slot like a rebuke from God's mouth: *I answer your prayers in My way, in My time.* After that, he had made his prayers less definite, less susceptible of being twisted into a scolding. But what a tiny, ridiculous coincidence this was, after all, to throw into battle against H. G. Wells' engines of knowledge!

Indeed, it proved the enemy's point: Hope bases vast premises on foolish accidents, and reads a word where in fact only a scribble exists.

His father came home. Though Saturday was a free day for him, he had been working. He taught school in Olinger and spent all his days performing, with a curious air of panic, needless errands. Also, a city boy by birth, he was frightened of the farm and seized any excuse to get away. The farm had been David's mother's birthplace; it had been her idea to buy it back. With an ingenuity and persistence unparalleled in her life, she had gained that end, and moved them all here – her son, her husband, her mother. Granmom, in her prime, had worked these fields alongside her husband, but now she dabbled around the kitchen futilely, her hands waggling with Parkinson's disease. She was always in the way. Strange, out in the country, amid eighty acres, they were crowded together. His father expressed his feelings of discomfort by conducting with Mother an endless argument about organic farming. All through dusk, all through supper, it rattled on.

"Elsie, I *know*, I know from my education, the earth is nothing but chemicals. It's the only damn thing I got out of four years of college, so don't tell me it's not true."

"George, if you'd just walk out on the farm you'd know it's not true. The land has a *soul*."

"Soil, has, no, soul," he said, enunciating stiffly, as if to a very stupid class. To David he said, "You can't argue with a femme. Your mother's a real femme. That's why I married her, and now I'm suffering for it."

"*This* soil has no soul," she said, "because it's been killed with superphosphate. It's been burned bare by Boyer's tenant farmers." Boyer was the rich man they had bought the farm from. "It used to have a soul, didn't it, Mother? When you and Pop farmed it?"

"Ach, yes; I guess." Granmom was trying to bring a forkful of food to her mouth with her less severely afflicted hand. In her anxiety she brought the other hand up from her lap. The crippled fingers, dull red in the orange light of the kerosene lamp in the center of the table, were welded by paralysis into one knobbed hook.

"Only human indi-vidu-als have souls," his father went on, in the same mincing, lifeless voice. "Because the Bible tell us so." Done eating, he crossed his legs and dug into his ear with a match miserably; to get at the thing inside his head he tucked in his chin, and his voice came out low-pitched at David. "When God made your mother, He made a real femme."

"George, don't you read the papers? Don't you know that between the chemical fertilizers and the bug sprays we'll all be dead in ten years? Heart attacks are killing every man in the country over forty-five."

He sighed wearily; the yellow skin of his eyelids wrinkled as he hurt himself with the match. "There's no connection," he stated, spacing his words with pained patience, "between the heart — and chemical fertilizers. It's alcohol that's doing it. Alcohol and milk. There is too much — cholesterol — in the tissues of the American heart. Don't tell me about chemistry, Elsie; I majored in the damn stuff for four years."

"Yes and I majored in Greek and I'm not a penny wiser. Mother, put your waggler *away*!" The old woman started, and the food dropped from her fork. For some reason, the sight of her bad hand at the table cruelly irritated her daughter. Granmom's eyes, worn bits of crazed crystal embedded in watery milk, widened behind her cockeyed spectacles. Circles of silver as fine as thread, they clung to the red notches they had carved over the years into her little white beak. In the orange flicker of the kerosene lamp her dazed misery seemed infernal. David's mother began, without noise, to cry. His father did not seem to have eyes at all; just jaundiced sockets of wrinkled skin. The steam of food clouded the scene. It was horrible but the horror was particular and familiar, and distracted David from the formless dread that worked, sticky and sore, within him, like a too large wound trying to heal.

He had to go to the bathroom, and took a flashlight down through the wet grass to the outhouse. For once, his fear of spiders there felt trivial. He set the flashlight, burning, beside him, and an insect alighted on its lens, a tiny insect, a mosquito or flea, made so fine that the weak light projected its X-ray onto the wall boards: the faint rim of its wings, the blurred strokes, magnified, of its long hinged legs, the dark cone at the heart of its anatomy. The tremor must be its heart beating. Without warning, David was visited by an exact vision of death: a long hole in the ground, no wider than your body, down which you are drawn while the white faces above recede. You try to reach them but your arms are pinned. Shovels pour dirt into your face. There you will be forever, in an upright position, blind and silent, and in time no one will remember you, and you will never be called. As strata of rock shift, your fingers elongate, and your teeth are distended sideways in a great underground grimace indistinguishable from a strip of chalk. And the earth tumbles on, and the sun expires, and unaltering darkness reigns where once there were stars.

Sweat broke out on his back. His mind seemed to rebound off a solidness. Such extinction was not another threat, a graver sort of danger, a kind of pain; it was qualitatively different. It was not even a conception that could be voluntarily pictured; it entered him from outside. His protesting nerves swarmed on its surface like lichen on a meteor. The skin of his chest was soaked with the effort of rejection. At the same time that the fear was dense and internal, it was dense and all around him; a tide of clay had swept up to the stars; space was crushed into a mass. When he stood up, automatically hunching his shoulders to keep his head away from the spider webs, it was with a numb sense of being cramped between two huge volumes of rigidity. That he had even this small freedom to move surprised him. In the narrow shelter of that rank shack, adjusting his pants, he felt — his first spark of comfort — too small to be crushed.

But in the open, as the beam of the flashlight skidded with

frightened quickness across the remote surfaces of the barn and the grape arbor and the giant pine that stood by the path to the woods, the terror descended. He raced up through the clinging grass pursued, not by one of the wild animals the woods might hold, or one of the goblins his superstitious grandmother had communicated to his childhood, but by spectres out of science fiction, where gigantic cinder moons fill half the turquoise sky. As David ran, a gray planet rolled inches behind his neck. If he looked back, he would be buried. And in the momentum of his terror, hideous possibilities – the dilation of the sun, the triumph of the insects, the crabs on the shore in *The Time Machine* – wheeled out of the vacuum of make-believe and added their weight to his impending oblivion.

He wrenched the door open; the lamps within the house flared. The wicks burning here and there seemed to mirror one another. His mother was washing the dishes in a little pan of heated pump-water; Granmom fluttered near her elbow apprehensively. In the living room – the downstairs of the little square house was two long rooms – his father sat in front of the black fireplace restlessly folding and unfolding a newspaper as he sustained his half of the argument. "Nitrogen, phosphorus, potash: these are the three replaceable constituents of the soil. One crop of corn carries away hundreds of pounds of" – he dropped the paper into his lap and ticked them off on three fingers – "nitrogen, phosphorus, potash."

"Boyer didn't grow corn."

"*Any* crop, Elsie. The human animal – "

"You're killing the *earth*worms, George!"

"The human animal, after thousands and *thou*sands of years, learned methods whereby the chemical balance of the soil may be maintained. Don't carry me back to the Dark Ages."

"When we moved to Olinger the ground in the garden was like slate. Just one summer of my cousin's chicken dung and the earthworms came back."

"I'm sure the Dark Ages were a fine place to the poor devils born in them, but I don't want to go there. They give me the creeps." Daddy stared into the cold pit of the fireplace and clung to the rolled newspaper in his lap as if it alone were keeping him from slipping backwards and down, down.

Mother came into the doorway brandishing a fistful of wet forks. "And thanks to your DDT there soon won't be a bee left in the country. When I was a girl here you could eat a peach without washing it."

"It's primitive, Elsie. It's Dark Age stuff."

"Oh what do *you* know about the Dark Ages?"

"I know I don't want to go back to them."

David took from the shelf, where he had placed it this afternoon, the great unabridged Webster's Dictionary that his grandfather had owned. He turned the big thin pages, floppy as cloth, to the entry he wanted, and read

> soul . . . 1. An entity conceived as the essence, substance, animating principle, or actuating cause of life, or of the individual life, esp. of life manifested in psychical activities; the vehicle of individual existence, separate in nature from the body and usually held to be separable in existence.

The definition went on, into Greek and Egyptian conceptions, but David stopped short on the treacherous edge of antiquity. He needed to read no further. The careful overlapping words shingled a temporary shelter for him. "Usually held to be separable in existence" – what could be fairer, more judicious, surer?

His father was saying, "The modern farmer can't go around sweeping up after his cows. The poor devil has thousands and *thou*sands of acres on his hands. Your modern farmer uses a scientifically-arrived-at mixture, like five-ten-five, or six-twelve-six, or *three*-twelve-six, and spreads it on with this wonderful modern machinery which of course we can't afford. Your modern farmer can't *afford* medieval methods."

Mother was quiet in the kitchen; her silence radiated waves of anger.

"Now now Elsie; don't play the femme with me. Let's discuss this calmly like two rational twentieth-century people. Your organic farming nuts aren't attacking five-ten-five; they're attacking the chemical fertilizer crooks. The monster firms."

A cup clinked in the kitchen. Mother's anger touched David's face; his cheeks burned guiltily. Just by being in the living room he was associated with his father. She appeared in the doorway with red hands and tears in her eyes, and said to the two of them, "I knew you didn't want to come here but I didn't know you'd torment me like this. You talked Pop into his grave and now you'll kill me. Go ahead, George, more power to you; at least I'll be buried in good ground." She tried to turn and met an obstacle and screamed, "Mother, stop hanging on my *back*! Why don't you go to *bed*?"

"Let's all go to bed," David's father said, rising from the blue wing chair and slapping his thigh with a newspaper. "This reminds me of death." It was a phrase of his that David had heard so often he never considered its sense.

Upstairs, he seemed to be lifted above his fears. The sheets on his bed were clean. Granmom had ironed them with a pair of flatirons saved from the Olinger attic; she plucked them hot off the stove alternately, with a wooden handle called a goose. It was a wonder, to see how she managed. In the next room, his parents grunted peaceably; they seemed to take their quarrels less seriously than he did. They made comfortable scratching noises as they carried a little lamp back and forth. Their door was open a crack, so he saw the light shift and swing. Surely there would be, in the last five minutes, in the last second, a crack of light, showing the door from the dark room to another, full of light. Thinking of it this vividly frightened him. His own dying, in a specific bed in a specific room, specific walls mottled with wallpaper, the dry whistle of his breathing, the murmuring doctors, the nervous relatives going in and out, but for him no way out but down into the funnel. *Never touch a doorknob again.* A whisper, and his parents' light was blown out. David prayed to be reassured. Though the experiment frightened him, he lifted his hands high into the darkness above his face and begged Christ to touch them. Not hard or long: the faintest, quickest grip would be final for a lifetime. His hands waited in the air, itself a substance, which seemed to move through his fingers; or was it the pressure of his pulse? He returned his hands to beneath the covers uncertain if they had been touched or not. For would not Christ's touch *be* infinitely gentle.

Through all the eddies of its aftermath, David clung to this thought about his revelation of extinction: that there, in the outhouse, he had struck a solidness qualitatively different, a rock of horror firm enough to support any height of construction. All he needed was a little help; a word, a gesture, a nod of certainty, and he would be sealed in, safe. The assurance from the dictionary had melted in the night. Today was Sunday, a hot fair day. Across a mile of clear air the church bells called, *Celebrate, celebrate.* Only Daddy went. He put on a coat over his rolled-up shirtsleeves and got into the little old black Plymouth parked by the barn and went off, with the same pained hurried grimness of all his actions. His churning wheels, as he shifted too hastily into second, raised plumes of red dust on the dirt road. Mother walked to the far field, to see what bushes needed cutting. David, though he usually preferred to stay in the house, went with her. The puppy followed at a distance, whining as it picked its way through the stubble but floundering off timidly if one of them went back to pick it up and carry it. When they reached the crest of the far field, his mother asked, "David, what's troubling you?"

"Nothing. Why?"

She looked at him sharply. The greening woods cross-hatched the space beyond her half-gray hair. Then she showed him her profile, and gestured toward the house, which they had left a half-mile behind them. "See how it sits in the land? They don't know how to build with the land any more. Pop always said the foundations were set with the compass. We must try to get a compass and see. It's supposed to face due south; but south feels a little more *that* way to me." From the side, as she said these things, she seemed handsome and young. The smooth sweep of her hair over her ear seemed white with a purity and calm that made her feel foreign to him. He had never regarded his parents as consolers of his troubles; from the beginning they had seemed to have more troubles than he. Their confusion had flattered him into an illusion of strength; so now on this high clear ridge he jealously guarded the menace all around them, blowing like a breeze on his fingertips, the possibility of all this wide scenery sinking into darkness. The strange fact that though she came to look at the brush she carried no clippers, for she had a fixed prejudice against working on Sundays, was the only consolation he allowed her to offer.

As they walked back, the puppy whimpering after them, the rising dust behind a distant line of trees announced that Daddy was speeding home from church. When they reached the house he was there. He had brought back the Sunday paper and the vehement remark, "Dobson's too intelligent for these farmers. They just sit there with their mouths open and don't hear a thing the poor devil's saying."

"What makes you think farmers are unintelligent? This country was made by farmers. George Washington was a farmer."

"They are, Elsie. They are unintelligent. George Washington's dead. In this day and age only the misfits stay on the farm. The lame, the halt, the blind. The morons with one arm. Human garbage. They remind me of death, sitting there with their mouths open."

"My *father* was a farmer."

"He was a frustrated man, Elsie. He never knew what hit him. The poor devil meant so well, and he never knew which end was up. Your mother'll bear me out. Isn't that right, Mom? Pop never knew what hit him?"

"Ach, I guess not," the old woman quavered, and the ambiguity for the moment silenced both sides.

David hid in the funny papers and sports section until one-thirty. At two, the catechetical class met at the Firetown church. He had transferred from the catechetical class of the Lutheran church in Olinger, a humiliating comedown. In Olinger they met on Wednesday nights, spiffy and spruce, in the atmosphere of a dance. Afterwards, blessed by the brick-faced minister from whose lips the word "Christ" fell like a burning stone, the more daring of them went with their Bibles to a luncheonette and smoked. Here in Firetown, the girls were dull white cows and the boys narrow-faced brown goats in old men's suits, herded on Sunday afternoons into a threadbare church basement that smelled of stale hay. Because his father had taken the car on one of his endless errands to Olinger, David walked, grateful for the open air and the silence. The catechetical class embarrassed him, but today he placed hope in it, as the source of the nod, the gesture, that was all he needed.

Reverend Dobson was a delicate young man with great dark eyes and small white shapely hands that flickered like protesting doves when he preached; he seemed a bit misplaced in the Lutheran ministry. This was his first call. It was a split parish; he served another rural church twelve miles away. His iridescent green Ford, new six months ago, was spattered to the windows with red mud and rattled from bouncing on the rude back roads, where he frequently got lost, to the malicious satisfaction of many. But David's mother liked him, and, more pertinent to his success, the Haiers, the sleek family of feed merchants and innkeepers and tractor salesmen who dominated the Firetown church, liked him. David liked him, and felt liked in turn; sometimes in class, after some special stupidity, Dobson directed toward him out of those wide black eyes a mild look of disbelief, a look that, though flattering, was also delicately disquieting.

Catechetical instruction consisted of reading aloud from a work booklet answers to problems prepared during the week, problems like, "I am the ______, the ______, and the ______, saith the Lord." Then there was a question period in which no one ever asked any questions. Today's theme was the last third of the Apostles' Creed. When the time came for questions, David blushed and asked, "About the Resurrection of the Body – are we conscious between the time when we die and the Day of Judgment?"

Dobson blinked, and his fine little mouth pursed, suggesting that David was making difficult things more difficult. The faces of the other students went blank, as if an indiscretion had been committed.

"No, I suppose not," Reverend Dobson said.

"Well, where is our soul, then, in this gap?"

The sense grew, in the class, of a naughtiness occurring. Dobson's shy eyes watered, as if he were straining to keep up the formality of attention, and one of the girls, the fattest, simpered toward her twin, who was a little less fat. Their chairs were arranged in a rough circle. The current running around the circle panicked David. Did everybody know something he didn't know?

"I suppose you could say our souls are asleep," Dobson said.

"And then they wake up, and there is the earth like it always is, and all the people who have ever lived? Where will Heaven be?"

Anita Haier giggled. Dobson gazed at David intently, but with an awkward, puzzled flicker of forgiveness, as if there existed a secret between them that David was violating. But David knew of no secret. All he wanted was to hear Dobson repeat the words he said every Sunday morning. This he would not do. As if these words were unworthy of the conversational voice.

"David, you might think of Heaven this way: as the way the goodness Abraham Lincoln did lives after him."

"But is Lincoln conscious of it living on?" He blushed no longer with embarrassment but in anger; he had walked here in good faith and was being made a fool.

"Is he conscious now? I would have to say no; but I don't think it matters." His voice had a coward's firmness; he was hostile now.

"You don't."

"Not in the eyes of God, no." The unction, the stunning impudence, of this reply sprang tears of outrage in David's eyes. He bowed them to his book, where short words like Duty, Love, Obey, Honor, were stacked in the form of a cross.

"Were there any other questions, David?" Dobson asked with renewed gentleness. The others were rustling, collecting their books.

"No." He made his voice firm, though he could not bring up his eyes.

"Did I answer your question fully enough?"

"Yes."

In the minister's silence the shame that should have been his crept over David: the burden and fever of being a fraud were placed upon *him*, who was innocent, and it seemed, he knew, a confession of this guilt that on the way out he was unable to face Dobson's stirred gaze, though he felt it probing the side of his head.

Anita Haier's father gave him a ride down the highway as far as the dirt road. David said he wanted to walk the rest, and figured that his offer was accepted because Mr. Haier did not want to dirty his bright blue Buick with dust. This was all right; everything was all right, as long as it was clear. His indignation at being betrayed, at seeing Christianity betrayed, had hardened him. The straight dirt road reflected his hardness. Pink stones thrust up through its packed surface. The April sun beat down from the center of the afternoon half of the sky; already it had some of summer's heat. Already the fringes of weeds at the edges of the road were bedraggled with dust. From the reviving grass and scruff of the fields he walked between, insects were sending up a monotonous, automatic chant. In the distance a tiny figure in his father's coat was walking along the edge of the woods. His mother. He wondered what joy she found in such walks; to him the brown stretches of slowly rising and falling land expressed only a huge exhaustion.

Flushed with fresh air and happiness, she returned from her walk earlier than he had expected, and surprised him at his grandfather's Bible. It was a stumpy black book, the boards worn thin where the old man's fingers had held them; the spine hung by one weak hinge of fabric. David had been looking for the passage where Jesus says to the one thief on the cross, "Today shalt thou be with me in paradise." He had never tried reading the Bible for himself before. What was so embarrassing about being caught at it, was that he detested the apparatus of piety. Fusty churches, creaking hymns, ugly Sunday-school teachers, and their stupid leaflets – he hated everything about them but the promise they held out, a promise that in the most perverse way, as if the homeliest crone in the kingdom were given the Prince's hand, made every good and real thing, ball games and jokes and pert-breasted girls, possible. He couldn't explain this to his mother. There was no time. Her solicitude was upon him.

"David, what are you doing?"

"Nothing."

"What are you doing at Grandpop's Bible?"

"Trying to read it. This is supposed to be a Christian country, isn't it?"

She sat down on the green sofa, which used to be in the sun parlor at Olinger, under the fancy mirror. A little smile still lingered on her face from the walk. "David, I wish you'd talk to me."

"What about?"

"About whatever it is that's troubling you. Your father and I have both noticed it."

"I asked Reverend Dobson about Heaven and he said it was like Abraham Lincoln's goodness living after him."

He waited for the shock to strike her. "Yes?" she said, expecting more.

"That's all."

"And why didn't you like it?"

"Well; don't you see? It amounts to saying there isn't any Heaven at all."

"I don't see that it amounts to that. What do you want Heaven to be?"

"Well, I don't know. I want it to be *some*thing. I thought he'd tell me what it was. I thought that was his job." He was becoming angry, sensing her surprise at him. She had assumed that Heaven had faded from his head years ago. She had imagined that he had already entered, in the secrecy of silence, the conspiracy that he now knew to be all around him.

"David," she asked gently, "don't you ever want to rest?"

"No. Not forever."

"David, you're so young. When you get older, you'll feel differently."

"Grandpa didn't. Look how tattered this book is."

"I never understood your grandfather."

"Well, I don't understand ministers who say it's like Lincoln's goodness going on and on. Suppose you're not Lincoln?"

"I think Reverend Dobson made a mistake. You must try to forgive him."

"It's not a *question* of his making a mistake! It's a question of dying and never moving or seeing or hearing anything ever again."

"But" – in exasperation – "darling, it's so *greedy* of you to want more. When God has given us this wonderful April day, and given us this farm, and you have your whole life ahead of you – "

"You think, then, that there is God?"

"Of course I do" – with deep relief, that smoothed her features into a reposeful oval. He had risen and was standing too near her for his comfort. He was afraid she would reach out and touch him.

"He made everything? You feel that?"

"Yes."

"Then who made Him?"

"Why, Man. Man." The happiness of this answer lit up her face radiantly, until she saw his gesture of disgust. She was so simple, so illogical; such a femme.

"Well that amounts to saying there is none."

Her hand reached for his wrist but he backed away. "David, it's a mystery. A miracle. It's a miracle more beautiful than any Reverend Dobson could have told you about. You don't say houses don't exist because Man made them."

"No. God has to be different."

"But, David, you have the *evidence*. Look out the window at the sun; at the fields."

"Mother, good grief. Don't you see" — he rasped away the roughness in his throat — "if when we die there's nothing, all your sun and fields and what not are all, ah, *horror*? It's just an ocean of horror."

"But David, it's not. It's so clearly not that." And she made an urgent opening gesture with her hands that expressed, with its suggestion of a willingness to receive his helplessness, all her grace, her gentleness, her love of beauty, gathered into a passive intensity that made him intensely hate her. He would not be wooed away from the truth. *I am the Way, the Truth ...*

"No," he told her. "Just let me alone."

He found his tennis ball behind the piano and went outside to throw it against the side of the house. There was a patch high up where the brown stucco that had been laid over the sandstone masonry was crumbling away; he kept trying with the tennis ball to chip more pieces off. Superimposed upon his deep ache was a smaller but more immediate worry; that he had hurt his mother. He heard his father's car rattling on the straightaway, and went into the house, to make peace before he arrived. To his relief, she was not giving off the stifling damp heat of her anger, but instead was cool, decisive, maternal. She handed him an old green book, her college text of Plato.

"I want you to read the Parable of the Cave," she said.

"All right," he said, though he knew it would do no good. Some story by a dead Greek just vague enough to please her. "Don't worry about it, Mother."

"I *am* worried. Honestly, David, I'm sure there will be something for us. As you get older, these things seems to matter a great deal less."

"That may be. It's a dismal thought, though."

His father bumped at the door. The locks and jambs stuck here. But before Granmom could totter to the latch and let him in, he had knocked it open. He had been in Olinger dithering with track meet tickets. Although Mother usually kept her talks with David a confidence, a treasure between them, she called instantly, "George, David is worried about death!"

He came to the doorway of the living room, his shirt pocket bristling with pencils, holding in one hand a pint box of melting ice cream and in the other the knife with which he was about to divide it into four sections, their Sunday treat. "Is the kid worried about death? Don't give it a thought, David. I'll be lucky if I live till tomorrow, and I'm not worried. If they'd taken a buckshot gun and shot me in the cradle I'd be better off. The *world*'d be better off. Hell, I think death is a wonderful thing. I look forward to it. Get the garbage out of the way. If I had the man here who invented death, I'd pin a medal on him."

"Hush, George. You'll frighten the child worse than he is."

This was not true; he never frightened David. There was no harm in his father, no harm at all. Indeed, in the man's steep self-disgust the boy felt a kind of ally. A distant ally. He saw his position with a certain strategic coldness. Nowhere in the world of other people would he find the hint, the nod, he needed to begin to build his fortress against death. They none of them believed. He was alone. In that deep hole.

In the months that followed, his position changed little.

School was some comfort. All those sexy, perfumed people, wisecracking, chewing gum, all of them doomed to die, and none of them noticing. In their company David felt that they would carry him along into the bright, cheap paradise reserved for them. In any crowd, the fear ebbed a little; he had reasoned that somewhere in the world there must exist a few people who believed what was necessary, and the larger the crowd, the greater the chance that he was near such a soul, within calling distance, if only he was not too ignorant, too ill-equipped, to spot him. The sight of clergymen cheered him; whatever they themselves thought, their collars were still a sign that somewhere, at some time, someone had recognized that we cannot, *cannot*, submit to death. The sermon topics posted outside churches, the flip, hurried pieties of disc jockeys, the cartoons in magazines showing angels or devils — on such scraps he kept alive the possibility of hope.

For the rest, he tried to drown his hopelessness in clatter and jostle. The pinball machine at the luncheonette was a merciful distraction; as he bent over its buzzing, flashing board of flippers and cushions, the weight and constriction in his chest lightened and loosened. He was grateful for all the time his father wasted in Olinger. Every delay postponed the moment when they must ride together down the dirt road into the heart of the dark farmland, where the only light was the kerosene lamp waiting on the dining-room table, a light that drowned their food in shadow and made it sinister.

He lost his appetite for reading. He was afraid of being ambushed again. In mystery novels people died like dolls being discarded; in science fiction enormities of space and time conspired to crush the humans; and even in P. G. Wodehouse he felt a hollowness, a turning away from reality that was implicitly bitter, and became explicit in the comic figures of futile clergymen. All gaiety seemed minced out on the skin of a void. All quiet hours seemed invitations to dread.

Even on weekends, he and his father contrived to escape the farm; and, when, some Saturdays, they did stay home, it was to do something destructive — tear down an old henhouse or set huge brush fires that threatened, while Mother shouted and flapped her arms, to spread to the woods. Whenever his father worked, it was with rapt violence; when he chopped kindling, fragments of the old henhouse boards flew like shrapnel and the ax-head was always within a quarter of an inch of flying off the handle. He was exhilarating to watch, sweating and swearing and sucking bits of saliva back into his lips.

School stopped. His father took the car in the opposite direction, to a highway construction job where he had been hired for the summer as a timekeeper, and David was stranded in the middle of acres of heat and greenery and blowing pollen and the strange, mechanical humming that lay invisibly in the weeds and alfalfa and dry orchard grass.

For his fifteenth birthday his parents gave him, with jokes about him being a hillbilly now, a Remington .22. It was somewhat like a pinball machine to take it out to the old kiln in the woods where they dumped their trash, and set up tin cans on the kiln's sandstone shoulder and shoot them off one by one. He'd take the puppy, who had grown long legs and a rich coat of reddish fur – he was part chow. Copper hated the gun but loved the boy enough to accompany him. When the flat acrid crack rang out, he would race in terrified circles that would tighten and tighten until they brought him, shivering, against David's legs. Depending upon his mood, David would shoot again or drop to his knees and comfort the dog. Giving this comfort to a degree returned comfort to him. The dog's ears, laid flat against his skull in fear, were folded so intricately, so – he groped for the concept – *surely*. Where the dull-studded collar made the fur stand up, each hair showed a root of soft white under the length, black-tipped, of the metal-color that had lent the dog its name. In his agitation Copper panted through nostrils that were elegant slits, like two healed cuts, or like the keyholes of a dainty lock of black, grained wood. His whole whorling, knotted, jointed body was a wealth of such embellishments. And in the smell of the dog's hair David seemed to descend through many finely differentiated layers of earth: mulch, soil, sand, clay, and the glittering mineral base.

But when he returned to the house, and saw the books arranged on the low shelves, fear returned. The four adamant volumes of Wells like four thin bricks, the green Plato that had puzzled him with its queer softness and tangled purity, the dead Galsworthy and "Elizabeth", Grandpa's mammoth dictionary, Grandpa's Bible, the Bible that he himself had received on becoming a member of the Firetown Lutheran Church — at the sight of these, the memory of his fear reawakened and came around him. He had grown stiff and stupid in its embrace. His parents tried to think of ways to entertain him.

"David, I have a job for you to do," his mother said one evening at the table.

"What?"

"If you're going to take that tone perhaps we'd better not talk."

"What tone? I didn't take any tone."

"Your grandmother thinks there are too many pigeons in the barn."

"Why?" David turned to look at his grandmother, but she sat there staring at the burning lamp with her usual expression of bewilderment.

Mother shouted, "Mom, he wants to know why!"

Granmom made a jerky, irritable motion with her bad hand, as if generating the force for utterance, and said, "They foul the furniture."

"That's right," Mother said. "She's afraid for that old Olinger furniture that we'll never use. David, she's been after me for a month about those poor pigeons. She wants you to shoot them."

"I don't want to kill anything especially," David said.

Daddy said, "The kid's like you are, Elsie. He's too good for this world. Kill or be killed, that's my motto."

His mother said loudly, "Mother, he doesn't want to do it."

"Not?" The old lady's eyes distended as if in horror, and her claw descended slowly to her lap.

"Oh, I'll do it, I'll do it tomorrow," David snapped, and a pleasant crisp taste entered his mouth with the decision.

"And I had thought, when Boyer's men made the hay, it would be better if the barn doesn't look like a rookery," his mother added needlessly.

A barn, in day, is a small night. The splinters of light between the dry shingles pierce the high roof like stars, and the rafters and cross-beams and built-in ladders seem, until your eyes adjust, as mysterious as the branches of a haunted forest. David entered silently, the gun in one hand. Copper whined desperately at the door, too frightened to come in with the gun yet unwilling to leave the boy. David stealthily turned, said "Go away," shut the door on the dog, and slipped the bolt across. It was a door within a door; the double door for wagons and tractors was as high and wide as the face of a house.

The smell of old straw scratched his sinuses. The red sofa, half-hidden under its white-splotched tarpaulin, seemed assimilated into this smell, sunk in it, buried. The mouths of empty bins gaped like caves. Rusty oddments of farming — coils of baling wire, some spare tines for a harrow, a handleless shovel — hung on nails driven here and there in the thick wood. He stood stock-still a minute; it took a while to separate the cooing of the pigeons from the rustling in his ears. When he had focused on the cooing, it flooded the vast interior with its throaty, bubbling outpour: there seemed no other sound. They were up behind the beams. What light there was leaked through the shingles and the dirty glass windows at the far end and the small round holes, about as big as basketballs, high on the opposite stone side walls, under the ridge of the roof.

A pigeon appeared in one of these holes, on the side toward the house. It flew in, with a battering of wings, from the outside, and waited there, silhouetted against its pinched bit of sky, preening and cooing in a throbbing, thrilled, tentative way. David tiptoed four steps to the side, rested his gun against the lowest rung of a ladder pegged between two upright beams, and lowered the gunsight into the bird's tiny, jauntily cocked head. The slap of the report seemed to come off the stone wall behind him, and the pigeon did not fall. Neither did it fly. Instead it stuck in the round hole, pirouetting rapidly and nodding its head as if in frantic agreement. David shot the bolt back and forth and had aimed again before the spent cartridge had stopped jingling on the boards by his feet. He eased the tip of the sight a little lower, into the bird's breast, and took care to squeeze the trigger with perfect evenness. The slow contraction of his hand abruptly sprang the bullet; for a half-second there was doubt, and then the pigeon fell like a handful of rags, skimming down the barn wall into the layer of straw that coated the floor of the mow on this side.

Now others shook loose from the rafters, and whirled in the dim air with a great blurred hurtle of feathers and noise. They would go for the hole; he fixed his sight on the little moon of blue, and when a pigeon came to it, shot him as he was walking the ten inches of stone that would have carried him into the open air. This pigeon lay down in that tunnel of stone, unable to fall either one way or the other, although he was alive enough to lift one wing and cloud the light. It would sink back, and he would suddenly lift it again, the feathers flaring. His body blocked that exit. David raced to the other side of the barn's main aisle, where a similar ladder was symmetrically placed, and rested his gun on the same rung. Three birds came together to this hole; he got one, and two got through. The rest resettled in the rafters.

There was a shallow triangular space behind the cross beams supporting the roof. It was here they roosted and hid. But either the space was too small, or they were curious, for now that his eyes were at home in the dusty gloom David could see little dabs of gray popping in and out. The cooing was shriller now; its apprehensive tremolo made the whole volume of air seem liquid. He noticed one little smudge of a head that was especially persistent in peeking out; he marked the place, and fixed his gun on it, and when the head appeared again, had his finger tightened in advance on the trigger. A parcel of fluff slipped off the beam and fell the barn's height onto a canvas covering some Olinger furniture, and where its head had peeked out there was a fresh prick of light in the shingles.

Standing in the center of the floor, fully master now, disdaining to steady the barrel with anything but his arm, he killed two more that way. He felt like a beautiful avenger. Out of the shadowy ragged infinity of the vast barn roof these impudent things dared to thrust their heads, presumed to dirty its starred silence with their filthy timorous life, and he cut them off, tucked them back neatly into the silence. He had the sensation of a creator; these little smudges and flickers that he was clever to see and even cleverer to hit in the dim recesses of the rafters – out of each of them he was making a full bird. A tiny peek, probe, dab of life, when he hit it, blossomed into a dead enemy, falling with good, final weight.

The imperfection of the second pigeon he had shot, who was still lifting his wing now and then up in the round hole, nagged him. He put a new clip into the stock. Hugging the gun against his body, he climbed the ladder. The barrel sight scratched his ear; he had a sharp, garish vision, like a color slide, of shooting himself and being found tumbled on the barn floor among his prey. He locked his arm around the top rung – a fragile, gnawed rod braced between uprights – and shot into the bird's body from a flat angle. The wing folded, but the impact did not, as he had hoped, push the bird out of the hole. He fired again, and again, and still the little body, lighter than air when alive, was too heavy to budge from its high grave. From up here he could see green trees and a brown corner of the house through the hole. Clammy with the cobwebs that gathered between the rungs, he pumped a full clip of eight bullets into the stubborn shadow, with no success. He climbed down, and was struck by the silence in the barn. The remaining pigeons must have escaped out the other hole. That was all right; he was tired of it.

He stepped with his rifle into the light. His mother was coming to meet him, and it tickled him to see her shy away from the carelessly held gun. "You took a chip out of the house," she said. "What were those last shots about?"

"One of them died up in that little round hole and I was trying to shoot it down."

"Copper's hiding behind the piano and won't come out. I had to leave him."

"Well don't blame me. *I* didn't want to shoot the poor devils."

"Don't smirk. You look like your father. How many did you get?"

"Six."

She went into the barn, and he followed. She listened to the silence. Her hair was scraggly, perhaps from tussling with the dog. "I don't suppose the others will be back," she said wearily. "Indeed, I don't know why I let Mother talk me into it. Their cooing was such a comforting noise." She began to gather up the dead pigeons. Though he didn't want to touch them, David went into the mow and picked up by its tepid, horny, coral-colored feet the first bird he had killed. Its wings unfolded disconcertingly, as if the creature had been held together by threads that now were slit. It did not weigh much. He retrieved the one on the other side of the barn; his mother got the three in the middle and led the way across the road to the little southern slope of land that went down toward the foundations of the vanished tobacco shed. The ground was too steep to plant and mow; wild strawberries grew in the tangled grass. She put her burden down and said, "We'll have to bury them. The dog will go wild."

He put his two down on her three; the slick feathers let the bodies slide liquidly on one another. He asked, "Shall I get you the shovel?"

"Get it for yourself; *you* bury them. They're your kill. And be sure to make the hole deep enough so he won't dig them up." While he went to the tool shed for the shovel, she went into the house. Unlike her, she did not look up, either at the orchard to the right of her or at the meadow on her left, but instead held her head rigidly, tilted a little, as if listening to the ground.

He dug the hole, in a spot where there were no strawberry plants, before he studied the pigeons. He had never seen a bird this close before. The feathers were more wonderful than dog's hair, for each filament was shaped within the shape of the feather, and the feathers in turn were trimmed to fit a pattern that flowed without error across the bird's body. He lost himself in the geometrical tides as the feathers now broadened and stiffened to make an edge for flight, now softened and constricted to cup warmth around the mute flesh. And across the surface of the infinitely adjusted yet somehow effortless mechanics of the feathers played idle designs of color, no two alike, designs executed, it seemed, in a controlled rapture, with a joy that hung level in the air above and behind him. Yet these birds bred in the millions and were exterminated as pests. Into the fragrant open earth he dropped one broadly banded in slate shades of blue, and on top of it another, mottled all over in rhythms of lilac and gray. The next was almost wholly white, but for a salmon glaze at its throat. As he fitted the last two, still pliant, on the top, and stood up, crusty coverings were lifted from him, and with a feminine, slipping sensation along his nerves that seemed to give the air hands, he was robed in this certainty: that the God who had lavished such craft upon these worthless birds would not destroy His whole Creation by refusing to let David live forever.

QUESTIONS

1. Why would you describe the basic conflict in this story as an inner one?

2. How does the opening paragraph foreshadow David's impending conflict? (Note particularly the symbols of the red cane-back sofa and the blue wing chair.)

3. One of Christ's central teachings is contained in this statement: "I am the resurrection and the life: he that believeth in me, though he were dead, yet shall he live." Why does David's reading the chapter in Wells' *Outline of History* begin to topple his faith in this promise?

4. Explain why the place and the time of the year make an appropriate setting for David's mental and spiritual crisis.

5. What part in the boy's crisis is played by his parents' frequent arguments about farming methods?

6. In the 20th century a widening rift has developed between science – the study of the physical world, and the humanities – the study of man through his art, literature, and history. Some readers have believed that David's mother and father symbolize this division. What evidence in the story might lead to this conclusion?

7. Updike makes wide use of images and symbols of death.
   (a) Trace through the story his use of the hole or funnel as one such image.
   (b) How does he make us aware that Granmom is a symbol of death? In what way is she connected with David's "rebirth" at the end of the story?
   (c) How does Updike contrast David's observation of the mosquito, whose image is projected by the light of his flashlight, with what he sees in the dead pigeons?
   (d) How valid is David's final insight?

8. "The Hawk", "The Bird and the Machine", and "Pigeon Feathers" are quite different pieces of writing. However, all three employ rich imagery and at least some symbolism. Compare them in these two respects.

WALLACE STEGNER

b. 1909

Specifications for a hero ❖ ❖ ❖

Stegner's vivid boyhood memories of south-western Saskatchewan remind us of how recently the Canadian West was a frontier. In 1914 the author accompanied his parents from Montana to a homestead near the town of Whitemud, close to the Cypress Hills and just a few miles north of the United States-Canada border. Here he spent his boyhood and adopted a code of behaviour that he could never afterwards quite shake off. A generation previously, the Cypress Hills area had been buffalo and Indian country. At the time of the Stegners' arrival, its period as a short-grass range for Texas cattle was just ending, and a few years ahead lay the dust-bowl era of the thirties. In "Specifications for a Hero" he explains the impact on his boyish mind of the tough code of the cowboy, who was so soon to vanish from the Saskatchewan scene. Wallace Stegner is a noted biographer, historian, and novelist. Three of his books that show his skill in these respective literary types are *Beyond the Hundredth Meridian* (1954), *Mormon Country* (1942), and *A Shooting Star* (1961). *Wolf Willow* (1962), in which the following selection appears as one of a series of related essays and stories, shows him employing all three skills. He has also written short stories, collected in *The Women on the Wall* (1950) and *The City of the Living* (1956), and is Director of the Creative Writing Center at Stanford University, California.

IN OUR TOWN, as in most towns, everybody had two names — the one his parents had given him and the one the community chose to call him by. Our nicknames were an expression of the folk culture, and they were more descriptive than honorific. If you were underweight, you were called Skinny or Slim or Sliver; if overweight, Fat or Chubby if left-handed, Lefty; if spectacled, Four Eyes. If your father was the minister, your name was Preacher Kid, and according to the condition and colour of your hair you were Whitey, Blacky, Red, Rusty, Baldy, Fuzzy, or Pinky. If you had a habit of walking girls in the brush after dusk, you were known as Town Bull or T.B. If you were small for your age, as I was, your name was Runt or Peewee. The revelation of your shape at the town swimming hole by the footbridge could tag you for life with the label Birdlegs. The man who for a while ran one of our two grocery stores was universally known as Jew Meyer.

Like the lingo we spoke, our nicknames were at odds with the traditional and educational formalisms; along with them went a set of standard frontier attitudes. What was appropriate for Jimmy Craig in his home or in church or in school would have been shameful to Preacher Kid Craig down at the bare-naked hole. When we were digging a cave in the cutbank back of my house, and someone for a joke climbed up on top and jumped up and down, and the roof caved in on P.K. and he had to be dug out and revived by artificial respiration, even P.K. thought the hullabaloo excessive. He did not blame us, and he did not tattle on anyone. His notions of fortitude and propriety – which were at the other end of the scale from those of his parents – would not have let him.

When we first arrived in Whitemud the Lazy-S was still a working ranch, with corrals, and calves, and a bunkhouse inhabited by heroes named Big Horn, Little Horn, Slivers, Rusty, and Slippers. There was a Chinese cook named Mah Li, who had been abused in imaginative ways ever since he had arrived back at the turn of the century. In the first district poll for a territorial election, in 1902, someone had taken Mah Li to the polls and enfranchised him on the ground that, having been born in Hong Kong, he could swear that he was a British subject and was not an Indian, and was hence eligible to vote. When I knew him, he was a jabbering, good-natured soul with a pigtail and a loose blue blouse, and I don't suppose a single day of his life went by that he was not victimized somehow. He couldn't pass anybody, indoors or out, without having his pigtail yanked or his shirt tails set on fire. Once I saw the cowboys talk him into licking a frosty doorknob when the temperature was fifteen or twenty below, and I saw the tears in his eyes, too, after he tore himself loose. Another time a couple of Scandinavians tried to get him onto a pair of skis on the North Bench hill. They demonstrated how easy it was, climbed up and came zipping by, and then offered to help his toes into the straps. But Mah Li was too many for them that time. "Sssssssssss!" he said in scorn. "Walkee half a mile back!" When I was ten or eleven Mah Li was a friend of mine. I gave him suckers I caught in the river, and once he made me a present of a magpie he had taught to talk. The only thing it could say was our laundry mark, the number 0 Five, but it was more than any other magpie in town could say, and I had a special feeling for Mah Li because of it. Nevertheless I would have been ashamed not to take part in the teasing, baiting, and candy-stealing that made his life miserable after the Lazy-S closed up and Mah Li opened a restaurant. I helped tip over his backhouse on Hallowe'en; I was part of a war party that sneaked to the crest of a knoll and with .22 rifles potted two of his white ducks as they rode a mud puddle near his shack in the east bend.

The folk culture sponsored every sort of crude practical joke, as it permitted the cruelest and ugliest prejudices and persecutions. Any visible difference was enough to get an individual picked on. Impartially and systematically we persecuted Mah Li and his brother Mah Jim, Jew Meyer and his family, any Indians who came down into the valley in their wobble-wheeled buckboards, anyone with a pronounced English accent or fancy clothes or affected manners, any cry-baby, any woman who kept a poodle dog and put on airs, any child with glasses, anyone afflicted with crossed eyes, St. Vitus's dance, feeble-mindedness, or a game leg. Systematically the strong bullied the weak, and the weak did their best to persuade their persecutors, by feats of courage or endurance or by picking on someone still weaker, that they were tough and strong.

Immune, because they conformed to what the folk culture valued, were people with Texas or Montana or merely Canadian accents, people who wore overalls and worked with their hands, people who snickered at Englishmen or joined the bedevilment of Chinamen, women who let their children grow up wild and unwashed. Indignation swept the school one fall day when the Carpenter kids were sent home by the new teacher from Ontario. She sent a note along with them saying they had pediculosis and should not return to school until they were cured. Their mother in bewildered alarm brought them in to the doctor, and when she discovered that pediculosis meant only the condition of being lousy, she had to be restrained from going over and pulling the smart-alec teacher's hair out. We sympathized completely. That teacher never did get our confidence, for she had convicted herself of being both over-cleanly and pompous.

Honored and imitated among us were those with special skills so long as the skills were not too civilized. We admired good shots, good riders, tough fighters, dirty talkers, stoical endurers of pain. My mother won the whole town because once, riding our flighty mare Daisy up Main Street, she got piled hard in front of Christenson's pool hall with half a dozen men watching, and before they could recover from laughing and go to help her, had caught the mare and remounted and ridden off, tightly smiling. The fact that her hair was red did not hurt: among us, red hair was the sign of a sassy temper.

She was one of the immune, and so was my father, for both had been brought up on midwestern farms, had lived on the Dakota frontier, and accepted without question — though my mother would have supplemented it — the code of the stiff upper lip. She had sympathy for anyone's weakness except her own; he went strictly by the code.

I remember one Victoria Day when there was a baseball game between our town and Shaunavon. Alfie Carpenter, from a river bottom ranch just west of town, was catching for the Whitemud team. He was a boy who had abused me and my kind for years, shoving us off the footbridge, tripping us unexpectedly, giving us the hip, breaking up our hideouts in the brush, stampeding the town herd that was in our charge, and generally making himself lovable. This day I looked up from something just in time to see the batter swing and a foul tip catch Alfie full in the face. For a second he stayed bent over with a hand over his mouth; I saw the blood start in a quick stream through his fingers. My feelings were very badly mixed, for I had dreamed often enough of doing just that to Alfie Carpenter's face, but I was somewhat squeamish about human pain and I couldn't enjoy seeing the dream come true. Moreover I knew with a cold certainty that the ball had hit Alfie at least four times as hard as I had ever imagined hitting him, and there he stood, still on his feet and obviously conscious. A couple of players came up and took his arms and he shook them off, straightened up, spat out a splatter of blood and teeth and picked up his mitt as if to go on with the game. Of course they would not let him – but what a gesture! said my envious and appalled soul. There was a two-tooth hole when Alfie said something; he freed his elbows and swaggered to the side of the field. Watching him, my father broke out in a short, incredulous laugh. "Tough kid!" he said to the man next, and the tone of his voice goose-pimpled me like a breeze on a sweaty skin, for in all my life he had never spoken either to or of me in that voice of approval. Alfie Carpenter, with his broken nose and bloody mouth, was a boy I hated and feared, but most of all I envied his competence to be what his masculine and semi-barbarous world said a man should be.

As for me, I was a crybaby. My circulation was poor and my hands always got blue and white in the cold. I always had a runny nose. I was skinny and small, so that my mother anxiously doctored me with Scott's Emulsion, sulphur and molasses, calomel, and other doses. To compound my frail health, I was always getting hurt. Once I lost both big-toe nails in the same week, and from characteristically incompatible causes. The first one turned black and came off because I had accidentally shot myself through the big toe with a .22 short; the second because, sickly thing that I was, I had dropped a ten-pound bottle of Scott's Emulsion on it.

I grew up hating my weakness and despising my cowardice and trying to pretend that neither existed. The usual result of that kind of condition is bragging. I bragged, and sometimes I got called. Once in Sunday School I said that I was not afraid to jump off the high diving board that the editor of the *Leader* had projected out over the highest cutbank. The editor, who had been a soldier and a hero, was the only person in town who dared use it. It did not matter that the boys who called my bluff would not have dared to jump off it themselves. *I* was the one who had bragged, and so after Sunday School I found myself out on that thing, a mile above the water, with the wind very cold around my knees. The tea-brown whirlpools went spinning slowly around the deep water of the bend, looking as impossible to jump into as if they had been whorls in cement. A half dozen times I sucked in my breath and grabbed my courage with both hands and inched out to the burlap pad on the end of the board. Every time, the vibrations of the board started such sympathetic vibrations in my knees that I had to creep back for fear of falling off. The crowd on the bank got scornful, and then ribald, and then insulting; I could not rouse even the courage to answer back, but went on creeping out, quaking back, creeping out again, until they finally all got tired and left for their Sunday dinners. Then at once I walked out to the end and jumped.

I think I must have come down through thirty or forty feet of air, bent over toward the water, with my eyes out on stems like a lobster's, and I hit the water just so, with my face and chest, a tremendous belly-flopper that drove my eyes out through the back of my head and flattened me out on the water to the thickness of an oil film. The air was full of colored lights; I came to enough to realize I was strangling on weed-tasting river water, and moved my arms and legs feebly toward shore. About four hours and twenty deaths later, I grounded on the mud and lay there gasping and retching, sick for the hero I was not, for the humiliation I had endured, for the mess I had made of the jump when I finally made it — even for the fact that no one had been around to see me, and that I would never be able to convince any of them that I really had, at the risk of drowning, done what I had bragged I would do.

Contempt is a hard thing to bear, especially one's own. Because I was what I was, and because the town went by the code it went by, I was never quite out of sight of self-contempt or the contempt of my father or Alfie Carpenter or some other whose right to contempt I had to grant. School, and success therein, never fully compensated for the lacks I felt in myself. I found early that I could shine in class, and I always had a piece to speak in school entertainments, and teachers found me reliable at cleaning blackboards, but teachers were women, and school was a woman's world, the booby prize for those not capable of being men. The worst of it was that I liked school, and liked a good many things about the womanish world, but I wouldn't have dared admit it, and I could not respect the praise of my teachers any more than I could that of my music teacher or my mother.

"He has the arteestic tempera*ment*," said Madame Dujardin while collecting her pay for my piano lessons. "He's *sensitive*," my mother would tell her friends, afternoons when they sat around drinking coffee and eating Norwegian coffee cake, and I hung around inside, partly for the sake of coffee cake and partly to hear them talk about me. The moment they did talk about me, I was enraged. *Women* speaking up for me, noticing my "sensitivity," observing me with that appraising female stare and remarking that I seemed to like songs such as "Sweet and Low" better than "Men of Harlech", which was *their* sons' favorite — my mother interpolating half with pride and half with worry that sometimes she had to drive me out to play, I'd rather stay in and read Ridpath's *History of the World*. Women giving me the praise I would have liked to get from my father or Slivers or the Assiniboin halfbreed down at the Lazy-S. I wanted to be made of whang leather.

Little as I want to acknowledge them, the effects of those years remain in me like the beach terraces of a dead lake. Having been weak, and having hated my weakness, I am as impatient with the weakness of others as my father ever was. Pity embarrasses me for the person I am pitying, for I know how it feels to be pitied. Incompetence exasperates me, a big show of pain or grief or any other feeling makes me uneasy, affectations still inspire in me a mirth I have grown too mannerly to show. I cannot sympathize with the self-pitiers, for I have been there, or with the braggarts, for I have been there too. I even at times find myself reacting against conversation, that highest test of the civilized man, because where I came from it was unfashionable to be "mouthy".

An inhumane and limited code, the value system of a life more limited and cruder than in fact ours was. We got most of it by inheritance from the harsher frontiers that had preceded ours – got it, I suppose, mainly from our contacts with what was left of the cattle industry.

So far as the Cypress Hills were concerned, that industry began with the Mounted Police beef herd at Fort Walsh, and was later amplified by herds brought in to feed treaty Indians during the starving winters after 1879. In practice, the Indians ate a good deal of beef that hadn't been intended for them; it took a while to teach them that the white man's spotted buffalo were not fair game when a man was hungry. The raiding of cattle and horse herds was never controlled until the Canadian Indians were moved to reservations far north of the Line after 1882. Nevertheless it was the Indians who first stimulated the raising of cattle on that range, and the departure of the Indians which left the Whitemud River country open to become the last great cattle country.

In some ways, the overlapping of the cattle and homesteading phases of the Plains frontier was similar to the overlapping of the horse and gun cultures earlier, and in each case the overlapping occurred latest around the Cypress Hills.

Cattle came in from the south, homesteaders from the east and southeast. Among the homesteaders – Ontario men, Scandinavians, and Americans working up from the Dakotas, and Englishmen, Scots, and Ukrainians straight off the immigrant boats – there was a heavy percentage of greenhorns and city men. Even the experienced dryland farmers from the States were a prosaic and law-abiding lot by comparison with the cowboys they displaced. As it turned out, the homesteaders, by appropriating and fencing and plowing the range, squeezed out a way of life that was better adapted to the country than their own, and came close to ruining both the cattlemen and themselves in the process, but that is a later story. What succeeded the meeting and overlapping of the two cultures was a long and difficult period of adaptation in which each would modify the other until a sort of amalgamation could result. But while the adaptations were taking place, during the years of uneasy meeting and mixture, it was the cowboy tradition, the horseback culture, that impressed itself as image, as romance, and as ethical system upon boys like me. There were both good and bad reasons why that should have been true.

Read the history of the northern cattle ranges in such an anti-American historian as John Peter Turner and you hear that the "Texas men" who brought the cattle industry to Canada were all bravos, rustlers, murderers, gamblers, thugs, and highwaymen; that their life was divided among monte, poker, six-guns, and dancehall girls; and that their law was the gun-law that they made for themselves and enforced by hand. Allow sixty or seventy per cent of error for patriotic fervor, and Mr. Turner's generalizations may be accepted. But it is likewise true that American cow outfits left their gun-law cheerfully behind them when they found the country north of the Line well policed, that they cheerfully co-operated with the Mounted Police, took out Canadian brands, paid for grazing leases, and generally conformed to the customs of the country. They were indistinguishable from Canadian ranchers, to whom they taught the whole business. Many Canadian ranches, among them the 76, the Matador, the Turkey Track, and the T-Down-Bar, were simply Canadian extensions of cattle empires below the border.

So was the culture, in the anthropological sense, that accompanied the cattle. It was an adaptation to the arid Plains that had begun along the Rio Grande and had spread north, like gas expanding to fill a vacuum, as the buffalo and Indians were destroyed or driven out in the years following the Civil War. Like patterns of hunting and war that had been adopted by every Plains tribe as soon as it acquired the horse, the cowboy culture made itself at home all the way from the Rio Grande to the North Saskatchewan. The outfit, the costume, the practices, the terminology, the state of mind, came into Canada ready-made, and nothing they encountered on the northern Plains enforced any real modifications. The Texas men made it certain that nobody would ever be thrown from a horse in Saskatchewan; he would be piled. They made it sure that no Canadian steer would ever be angry or stubborn; he would be o'nery or ringy or on the prod. Bull Durham was as native to the Whitemud range as to the Pecos, and it was used for the same purposes: smoking, eating, and spitting in the eye of a ringy steer. The Stetson was as useful north as south, could be used to fan the fire or dip up a drink from a stream, could shade a man's eyes or be clapped over the eyes of a bronc to gentle him down. Boots, bandanna, stock saddle, rope, the ways of busting broncs, the institution of the spring and fall roundup, the bowlegs in batwing or goatskin chaps — they all came north intact. About the only thing that changed was the name for the cowboy's favorite diversion, which down south they would have called a rodeo but which we called a stampede.

It was a nearly womanless culture, nomadic, harsh, dangerous, essentially romantic. It had the same contempt for the dirt-grubbers that Scythian and Cossack had, and Canadian tillers of the soil tended to look upon it with the same suspicion and fear and envy that tillers of the soil have always expressed toward the herdsmen. As we knew it, it had a lot of Confederate prejudices left in it, and it had the callousness and recklessness that a masculine life full of activity and adventure is sure to produce. I got it in my eyes like stardust almost as soon as we arrived in Whitemud, when the town staged its first stampede down in the western bend. Reno Dodds, known as Slivers, won the saddle bronc competition and set me up a model for my life. I would grow up to be about five feet six and weigh about a hundred and thirty pounds. I would be bowlegged and taciturn, with deep creases in my cheeks and a hide like stained saddle leather. I would be the quietest and most dangerous man around, best rider, best shot, the one who couldn't be buffaloed. Men twice my size, beginning some brag or other, would catch my cold eye and begin to wilt, and when I had stared them into impotence I would turn my back contemptuous, hook onto my pony in one bowlegged arc, and ride off. I thought it tremendous that anyone as small and skinny as Slivers could be a top hand and a champion rider. I don't think I could have survived without his example, and he was still on my mind years later when, sixteen years old and six feet tall and weighing a hundred and twenty-five pounds, I went every afternoon to the university gym and worked out on the weights for an hour and ran wind sprints around the track. If I couldn't be big I could be *hard*.

We hung around the Lazy-S corrals a good deal that first year or two, and the cowpunchers, when they had no one else to pester, would egg us into fights with green cow manure for snowballs; or they would put a surcingle around a calf and set us aboard. After my try I concluded that I would not do any more of it just at that time, and I limped to the fence and sat on the top rail nursing my sprains and bruises and smiling to keep from bawling out loud. From there I watched Spot Orullian, a Syrian boy a couple of years older than I, ride a wildly pitching whiteface calf clear around the corral and half-way around again, and get piled hard, and come up wiping the cow dung off himself, swearing like a pirate. They cheered him, he was a favorite at once, perhaps all the more because he had a big brown birthmark on his nose and so could be kidded. And I sat on the corral rail hunching my winglike shoulder-blades, smiling and smiling and smiling to conceal the black envy that I knew was just under the skin of my face. It was always boys like Spot Orullian who managed to be and do what I wanted to do and be.

Many things that those cowboys represented I would have done well to get over quickly, or never catch: the prejudice, the callousness, the destructive practical joking, the tendency to judge everyone by the same raw standard. Nevertheless, what they themselves most respected, and what as a boy I most yearned to grow up to, was as noble as it was limited. They honored courage, competence, self-reliance, and they honored them tacitly. They took them for granted. It was their absence, not their presence, that was cause for remark. Practicing comradeship in a rough and dangerous job, they lived a life calculated to make a man careless of everything except the few things he really valued.

In the fall of 1906 it must have seemed that the cowboy life was certain to last a good while, for the Canadian range still lay wide open, and stockmen from the western states had prospected it and laid large plans for moving bigger herds across the Line to escape the nesters and sheepmen who had already broken up the Montana ranges. Probably the entire country from Wood Mountain to the Alberta line would have been leased for grazing, at the favorable Canadian rate of a few cents an acre, if the winter of 1906-07 had not happened.

That winter has remained ever since, in the minds of all who went through it, as the true measure of catastrophe. Some might cite the winter of 1886-87, the year of the Big Die-Up on the American range, but that winter did not affect the Whitemud country, where cattle came in numbers only after 1887. Some who had punched cows in Alberta in the early days might cast a vote for the fatal Cochran drive of 1881, when 8,000 out of 12,000 cattle died over by Lethbridge; and some would certainly, just as weather, mention the April blizzard of 1892, or the winter that followed it, or the big May blizzard of 1903. But after 1907 no one would seriously value those earlier disasters. The winter of 1906-07 was the real one, the year of the blue snow. After it, the leases that might have been taken up were allowed to lapse, the herds that might have been augmented were sold for what they would bring – fifteen to twenty dollars a head with suckling calves thrown in. Old cattlemen who had ridden every range from Texas north took a good long look around in the spring and decided to retire.

The ranches that survived were primarily the hill ranches with shelter plus an access to bench or prairie hay land where winter feed could be cut. The net effect of the winter of 1906-07 was to make stock farmers out of ranchers. Almost as suddenly as the disappearance of the buffalo, it changed the way of life of the region. A great event, it had the force in the history of the Cypress Hills country that a defeat in war has upon a nation. When it was over, the protected Hills might harbor a few cowboys, and one or two of the big ranches such as the 76 might go on, but most of the prairie would be laid open to homesteading and another sort of frontier.

That new frontier, of which my family was a part, very soon squeezed out the Lazy-S. The hay lands in the bottoms were broken up into town lots, my father was growing potatoes where whitefaces had used to graze, the punchers were drifting off to Alberta. But while we had them around, we made the most of them, imitating their talk and their walk and their songs and their rough-handed jokes; admiring them for the way they tormented Mah Li; hanging around in the shade of the bunkhouse listening to Rusty, who was supposed to be the second son of an earl, play the mouth organ; watching the halfbreed Assiniboin braid leather or horsehair into halter ropes and hackamores. I heard some stories about the winter of 1906-07, but I never heard enough. Long afterward, digging in the middens where historians customarily dig, I found and read some more, some of them the reminiscences of men I knew. What they record is an ordeal by weather. The manner of recording is laconic, deceptively matter of fact. It does not give much idea of how it feels to ride sixty or eighty miles on a freezing and exhausted pony, or how cold thirty below is when a fifty-mile wind is driving it into your face, or how demoralizing it is to be lost in a freezing fog where north, south, east, west, even up and down, swim and shift before the slitted and frost-struck eyes.

They do not tell their stories in Technicolor; they would not want to seem to adorn a tale or brag themselves up. The calluses of a life of hardship blunt their sensibilities to their own experience. If we want to know what it was like on the Whitemud River range during that winter when the hopes of a cattle empire died, we had better see it through the eyes of some tenderfoot, perhaps someone fresh from the old country, a boy without the wonder rubbed off him and with something to prove about himself. If in inventing this individual I put into him a little of Corky Jones, and some of the boy Rusty whose mouth organ used to sweeten the dusty summer shade of the Lazy-S bunkhouse, let it be admitted that I have also put into him something of myself, the me who sat on a corral bar wetting with spit my smarting skinned places, and wishing I was as tough as Spot Orullian.

QUESTIONS

1. The tone of a writer looking back on his childhood may vary from the deep sadness of Lawrence in "Odour of Chrysanthemums" to the compassionate amusement of O'Connor in "My Oedipus Complex". And many other variations are possible. How would you describe the tone of Wallace Stegner in this essay? Refer to passages in the essay to support your description.

2. The author admits that he was a crybaby, braggart, hypocrite, and self-pitier. How does he temper the account of these weaknesses so that we sympathize with, and perhaps even admire the boy that he was?

3. Stegner implies a set of feelings for his father which stand in contrast to his feelings for his mother. What passages in the essay suggest this contrast?

4. As well as providing a sketch of Stegner as a boy, the essay gives a vivid impression of a frontier community. Refer to the essay to show that both anecdote and historical outline contribute to this impression.

5. In what way does Stegner's self-analysis illustrate Hayakawa's main argument in his essay "How Words Change Our Lives"?

6. "Specifications for a Hero" is a reminiscence of actual, personal experiences, whereas "My Oedipus Complex" is fiction. Nonetheless, the two pieces of writing have some similarities in narrative point of view, tone, and characterization. Compare them in these three respects.

S. I. HAYAKAWA
b. 1906

How words change our lives

The aim of Professor Hayakawa's essay is to alert us to the "meaning of meaning". Things are not always what they seem. Neither are words. It is not easy to say what we mean or mean what we say. As one reads this account of the slipperiness and unreliability of even the simplest words, one surely wonders how any kind of trustworthy communication between human beings is possible at all. Professor Hayakawa is concerned not so much with the different meanings so many words have even in the dictionary, but with the infinite variety of subjective contexts within which words are placed by our emotions, our prejudices, our social and political commitments. He is sensitive, also, to the power of the modern mass media over our response to words and symbols. The essay is a warning against unguarded and crooked responses to meaning. It is also meant as a challenge to forms of thoughtless prejudice which choke words and blind people. Professor Hayakawa, born in Vancouver, studied at the University of Manitoba, McGill University, and the University of Wisconsin. He is now Professor of Language Arts at San Francisco State College. Perhaps his best-known book is *Language in Action* published in 1941.

THE END PRODUCT of education, yours and mine and everybody's, is the total pattern of reactions and possible reactions we have inside ourselves. If you did not have within you at this moment the pattern of reactions which we call "the ability to read English", you would see here only meaningless black marks on paper. Because of the trained patterns of response, you are (or are not) stirred to patriotism by martial music, your feelings of reverence are aroused by the symbols of your religion, you listen more respectfully to the health advice of someone who has "M.D." after his name than to that of someone who hasn't. What I call here a "pattern of reactions", then, is the sum total of the ways we act in response to events, to words, and to symbols.

Our reaction patterns – our semantic habits, as we may call them – are the internal and most important residue of whatever years of education or miseducation we may have received from our parents' conduct toward us in childhood as well as their teachings, from the formal education we may have had, from all the sermons and lectures we have listened to, from the radio programs and the movies and television shows we have experienced, from all the books and newspapers and comic strips we have read, from the conversations we have had with friends and associates, and from all our experiences. If, as the result of all these influences that make us what we are, our semantic habits are reasonably similar to those of most people around us, we are regarded as "well-adjusted", or "normal", and perhaps "dull". If our semantic habits are noticeably different from those of others, we are regarded as "individualistic" or "original", or, if the differences are disapproved of or viewed with alarm, as "screwball" or "crazy".

Semantics is sometimes defined in dictionaries as "the science of the meaning of words" – which would not be a bad definition if people didn't assume that the search for the meanings of words begins and ends with looking them up in a dictionary.

If one stops to think for a moment, it is clear that to define a word, as a dictionary does, is simply to explain the word with more words. To be thorough about defining, we should next have to define the words used in the definition, then define the words used in defining the words used in the definition . . . and so on. Defining words with more words, in short, gets us at once into what mathematicians call an "infinite regress". Alternatively, it can get us into the kind of run-around we sometimes encounter when we look up "impertinence" and find it defined as "impudence", so we look up "impudence" and find it defined as "impertinence". Yet – and here we come to another common reaction pattern – people often act as if words can be explained fully with more words. To a person who asked for a definition of jazz, Louis Armstrong is said to have replied, "Man, when you got to ask what it is, you'll never get to know," proving himself to be an intuitive semanticist as well as a great trumpet player.

Semantics, then, does not deal with the "meaning of words" as that expression is commonly understood. P. W. Bridgman, the Nobel Prize winner and physicist, once wrote, "The true meaning of a term is to be found by observing what a man does with it, not by what he says about it." He made an enormous contribution to science by showing that the meaning of a scientific term lies in the operations, the things done, that establish its validity, rather than in verbal definitions.

Here is a simple, everyday kind of example of "operational" criticism. If you say, "This table measures six feet in length," you could prove it by taking a foot rule, performing the operation of laying it end to end while counting, "One... two... three... four... " But if you say – and revolutionists have started uprisings with just this statement – "Man is born free, but everywhere he is in chains!" – what operations could you perform to demonstrate its accuracy or inaccuracy?

But let us carry this suggestion of "operationalism" outside the physical sciences where Bridgman applied it, and observe what "operations" people perform as the result of both the language they use and the language other people use in communicating to them. Here is a personnel manager studying an application blank. He comes to the words "Education: Harvard University", and drops the application blank in the wastebasket (that's the "operation") because, as he would say if you asked him, "I don't like Harvard men." This is an instance of "meaning" at work – but it is not a meaning that can be found in dictionaries.

If I seem to be taking a long time to explain what semantics is about, it is because I am trying, in the course of explanation, to introduce the reader to a certain way of looking at human behavior. Semantics — especially the general semantics of Alfred Korzybski (1879-1950), Polish-American scientist and educator — pays particular attention not to words in themselves, but to semantic reactions — that is, human responses to symbols, signs, and symbol-systems, including language.

I say *human* responses because, so far as we know, human beings are the only creatures that have, over and above that biological equipment which we have in common with other creatures, the additional capacity for manufacturing symbols and systems of symbols. When we react to a flag, we are not reacting simply to a piece of cloth, but to the meaning with which it has been symbolically endowed. When we react to a word, we are not reacting to a set of sounds, but to the meaning with which that set of sounds has been symbolically endowed.

A basic idea in general semantics, therefore, is that the meaning of words (or other symbols) is not in the words, but in our own semantic reactions. If I were to tell a shockingly obscene story in Arabic or Hindustani or Swahili before an audience that understood only English, no one would blush or be angry; the story would be neither shocking nor obscene — indeed, it would not even be a story. Likewise, the value of a dollar bill is not in the bill, but in our social agreement to accept it as a symbol of value. If that agreement were to break down through the collapse of our Government, the dollar bill would become only a scrap of paper. We do not understand a dollar bill by staring at it long and hard. We understand it by observing how people act with respect to it. We understand it by understanding the social mechanisms and the loyalties that keep it meaningful. Semantics is therefore a social study, basic to all other social studies.

It is often remarked that words are tricky — and that we are all prone to be deceived by "fast talkers", such as high-pressure salesmen, skillful propagandists, politicians or lawyers. Since few of us are aware of the degree to which we use words to deceive ourselves, the sin of "using words in a tricky way" is one that is always attributed to the other fellow. When the Russians use the word "democracy" to mean something quite different from what we mean by it, we at once accuse them of "propaganda", of "corrupting the meanings of words". But when we use the word "democracy" in the United States to mean something quite different from what the Russians mean by it, they are equally quick to accuse us of "hypocrisy". We all tend to believe that the way we use words is the correct way, and that people who use the same words in other ways are either ignorant or dishonest.

Leaving aside for a moment such abstract and difficult terms as "democracy", let us examine a common, everyday word like "frog". Surely there is no problem about what "frog" means! Here are some sample sentences:

"If we're going fishing, we'll have to catch some frogs first." (This is easy.)

"I have a frog in my throat." (You can hear it croaking.)

"She wore a loose, silk jacket fastened with braided frogs."

"The blacksmith pared down the frog and the hoof before shoeing the horse."

"In Hamilton, Ohio, there is a firm by the name of American Frog and Switch Company."

In addition to these "frogs", there is the frog in which a sword is carried, the frog at the bottom of a bowl or vase that is used in flower arrangement, and the frog which is part of a violin bow. The reader can no doubt think of other "frogs".

Or take another common word such as "order". There is the *order* that the salesman tries to get, which is quite different from the *order* which a captain gives to his crew. Some people enter holy *orders*. There is the *order* in the house when mother has finished tidying up; there is the batting *order* of the home team; there is an *order* of ham and eggs. It is surprising that with so many meanings to the word, people don't misunderstand one another oftener than they do.

The foregoing are only striking examples of a principle to which we are all so well accustomed that we rarely think of it; namely, that most words have more meanings than dictionaries can keep track of. And when we consider further that each of us has different experiences, different memories, different likes and dislikes, it is clear that all words evoke different responses in all of us. We may agree as to what the term "Mississippi River" stands for, but you and I recall different parts of the river; you and I have had different experiences with it; one of us has read more about it than the other; one of us may have happy memories of it, while the other may recall chiefly tragic events connected with it. Hence your "Mississippi River" can never be identical with my "Mississippi River". The fact that we can communicate with each other about the "Mississippi River" often conceals the fact that we are talking about two different sets of memories and experiences.

Words being as varied in their meanings as they are, no one can tell us what the correct interpretation of a word should be in advance of our next encounter with that word. The reader may have been taught always to revere the word "mother". But what is he going to do the next time he encounters this word, when it occurs in the sentence "Mother began to form in the bottle"? If it is impossible to determine what a single word will mean on next encounter, is it possible to say in advance what is the correct evaluation of such events as these: (1) next summer, an individual who calls himself a socialist will announce his candidacy for the office of register of deeds in your city; (2) next autumn, there will be a strike at one of your local department stores; (3) next week, your wife will announce that she is going to change her style of hairdo; (4) tomorrow, your little boy will come home with a bleeding nose?

A reasonably sane individual will react to each of these events in his own way, according to time, place, and the entire surrounding set of circumstances; and included among those circumstances will be his own stock of experiences, wishes, hopes, and fears. But there are people whose pattern of reactions is such that some of them can be completely predicted in advance. Mr. A will never vote for anyone called "socialist", no matter how incompetent or crooked the alternative candidates may be. Mr. B-1 always disapproves of strikes and strikers, without bothering to inquire whether or not this strike has its justifications; Mr. B-2 always sympathizes with the strikers because he hates all bosses. Mr. C belongs to the "stay sweet as you are" school of thought, so that his wife hasn't been able to change her hairdo since she left high school. Mr. D always faints at the sight of blood.

Such fixed and unalterable patterns of reaction – in their more obvious forms we call them prejudices – are almost inevitably organized around words. Mr. E distrusts and fears all people to whom the term "Catholic" is applicable, while Mr. F, who is Catholic, distrusts and fears all non-Catholics. Mr. G is so rabid a Republican that he reacts with equal dislike to all Democrats, all Democratic proposals, all opposite proposals if they are also made by Democrats. Back in the days when Franklin D. Roosevelt was President, Mr. G disliked not only the Democratic President but also his wife, children, and dog. His office was on Roosevelt Road in Chicago (it had been named after Theodore Roosevelt), but he had his address changed to his back door on 11th Street, so that he would not have to print the hated name on his stationery. Mr. H, on the other hand, is an equally rabid Democrat, who hates himself for continuing to play golf, since golf is Mr. Eisenhower's favorite game. People suffering from such prejudices seem to have in their brains an uninsulated spot which, when touched by such words as "capitalist", "boss", "striker", "scab", "Democrat", "Republican", "socialized medicine", and other such loaded terms, results in an immediate short circuit, often with a blowing of fuses.

Alfred Korzybski, the founder of general semantics, called such short-circuited responses "identification reactions". He used the word "identification" in a special sense; he meant that persons given to such fixed patterns of response identify (that is, treat as identical) all occurrences of a given word or symbol; they identify all the different cases that fall under the same name. Thus, if one has hostile identification reactions to "women drivers", then all women who drive cars are "identical" in their incompetence.

Korzybski believed that the term "identification reaction" could be generally used to describe the majority of cases of semantic malfunctioning. Identification is something that goes on in the human nervous system. "Out there" there are no absolute identities. No two Harvard men, no two Ford cars, no two mothers-in-law, no two politicians, no two leaves from the same tree, are identical with each other in all respects. If, however, we treat all cases that fall under the same class label as one at times when the differences are important, then there is something wrong with our semantic habits.

We are now ready, then, for another definition of general semantics. It is a comparative study of the kinds of responses people make to the symbols and signs around them; we may compare the semantic habits common among the prejudiced, the foolish, and the mentally ill with those found among people who are able to solve their problems successfully, so that, if we care to, we may revise our own semantic habits for the better. In other words, general semantics is, if we wish to make it so, the study of how not to be a damn fool.

Identification reactions run all the way through nature. The capacity for seeing similarities is necessary to the survival of all animals. The pickerel, I suppose, identifies all shiny, fluttery things going through the water as minnows, and goes after them all in pretty much the same way. Under natural conditions, life is made possible for the pickerel by this capacity. Once in a while, however, the shiny, fluttery thing in the water may happen to be not a minnow but an artificial lure on the end of a line. In such a case, one would say that the identification response, so useful for survival, under somewhat more complex conditions that require differentiation between two sorts of shiny and fluttery objects, proves to be fatal.

To go back to our discussion of human behavior, we see at once that the problem of adequate differentiation is immeasurably more complex for men than it is for pickerel. The signs we respond to, and the symbols we create and train ourselves to respond to, are infinitely greater in number and immeasurably more abstract than the signs in a pickerel's environment. Lower animals have to deal only with certain brute facts in their physical environment. But think, only for a moment, of what constitutes a human environment. Think of the items that call for adequate responses that no animal ever has to think about: our days are named and numbered, so that we have birthdays, anniversaries, holidays, centennials, and so on, all calling for specifically human responses; we have history, which no animal has to worry about; we have verbally codified patterns of behavior which we call law, religion, and ethics. We have to respond not only to events in our immediate environment, but to reported events in Washington, Paris, Tokyo, Moscow, Beirut. We have literature, comic strips, confession magazines, market quotations, detective stories, journals of abnormal psychology, bookkeeping systems to interpret. We have money, credit, banking, stocks, bonds, checks, bills. We have the complex symbolisms of moving pictures, paintings, drama, music, architecture, and dress. In short, we live in a vast human dimension of which the lower animals have no inkling, and we have to have a capacity for differentiation adequate to the complexity of our extra environment.

The next question, then, is why human beings do not always have an adequate capacity for differentiation. Why are we not constantly on the lookout for differences as well as similarities instead of feeling, as so many do, that the Chinese (or Mexicans, or ballplayers, or women drivers) are "all alike"? Why do some people react to words as if they were the things they stand for? Why do certain patterns of reaction, both in individuals and in larger groups such as nations, persist long after the usefulness has expired?

Part of our identification reactions are simply protective

mechanisms inherited from the necessities of survival under earlier and more primitive conditions of life. I was once beaten up and robbed by two men on a dark street. Months later, I was again on a dark street with two men, good friends of mine, but involuntarily I found myself in a panic and insisted on our hurrying to a well-lighted drugstore to have a soda so that I would stop being jittery. In other words, my whole body reacted with an identification reaction of fear of these two men, in spite of the fact that "I knew" that I was in no danger. Fortunately, with the passage of time, this reaction has died away. But the hurtful experiences of early childhood do not fade so readily. There is no doubt that many identification reactions are traceable to childhood traumas, as psychiatrists have shown.

Further identification reactions are caused by communal patterns of behavior which were necessary or thought necessary at one stage or another in the development of a tribe or nation. General directives such as "Kill all snakes", "Never kill cows, which are sacred animals", "Shoot all strangers on sight", "Fall down flat on your face before all members of the aristocracy", or, to come to more modern instances, "Never vote for a Republican", "Oppose all government regulation of business", "Never associate with Negroes on terms of equality", are an enormous factor in the creation of identification reactions.

Some human beings – possibly in their private feelings a majority – can accept these directives in a *human* way: that is, it will not be impossible for them under a sufficiently changed set of circumstances to kill a cow, or not to bow down before an aristocrat, to vote for a Republican, or to accept a Negro as a classmate. Others, however, get these directives so deeply ground into their nervous systems that they become incapable of changing their responses no matter how greatly the circumstances may have changed. Still others, although capable of changing their responses, dare not do so for fear of public opinion. Social progress usually requires the breaking up of these absolute identifications, which often make necessary changes impossible. Society must obviously have patterns of behavior; human beings must obviously have habits. But when those patterns become inflexible, so that a tribe has only one way to meet a famine, namely, to throw more infants as sacrifices to the crocodiles, or a nation has only one way to meet a threat to its security, namely, to increase its armaments, then such a tribe or such a nation is headed for trouble. There is insufficient capacity for differentiated behavior.

Furthermore — and here one must touch upon the role of newspapers, radio, and television — if agencies of mass communication hammer away incessantly at the production of, let us say, a hostile set of reactions at such words as "Communists", "bureaucrats", "Wall Street", "international bankers", "labor leaders", and so on, no matter how useful an immediate job they may perform in correcting a given abuse at a given time and place, they can in the long run produce in thousands of readers and listeners identification reactions to the words — reactions that will make intelligent public discussion impossible. Modern means of mass communication and propaganda certainly have an important part to play in the creation of identification reactions.

In addition to the foregoing, there is still another source of identification reactions; namely, the language we use in our daily thought and speech. Unlike the languages of the sciences, which are carefully constructed, tailor-made, special-purpose languages, the language of everyday life is one directly inherited and haphazardly developed from those of our prescientific ancestors: Anglo-Saxons, primitive Germanic tribes, primitive Indo-Europeans. With their scant knowledge of the world, they formulated descriptions of the world before them in statements such as "The sun rises." We do not today believe that the sun "rises". Nevertheless, we still continue to use the expression, without believing what we say.

But there are other expressions, quite as primitive as the idea of "sunrise", which we use uncritically, fully believing in the implications of our terms. Having observed (or heard) that *some* Negroes are lazy, an individual may say, making a huge jump beyond the known facts, "Negroes are lazy." Without arguing for the moment the truth or falsity of this statement, let us examine the implications of the statement as it is ordinarily constructed: "Negroes are lazy." The statement implies, as common sense or any textbook on traditional logic will tell us, that "laziness" is a "quality" that is "inherent" in Negroes.

What are the facts? Under conditions of slavery, under which Negroes were not paid for working, there wasn't any point in being an industrious and responsible worker. The distinguished French abstract artist Jean Hélion once told the story of his life as a prisoner of war in a German camp, where, during the Second World War, he was compelled to do forced labor. He told how he loafed on the job, how he thought of device after device for avoiding work and producing as little as possible — and, since his prison camp was a farm, how he stole chickens at every opportunity. He also described how he put on an expression of good-natured imbecility whenever approached by his Nazi overseers. Without intending to do so, in describing his own actions, he gave an almost perfect picture of the literary type of the Southern Negro of slavery days. Jean Hélion, confronted with the fact of forced labor, reacted as intelligently as Southern Negro slaves, and the slaves reacted as intelligently as Jean Hélion. "Laziness", then, is not an "inherent quality" of Negroes or of any other group of people. It is a *response* to a work situation in which there are no rewards for working, and in which one hates his taskmasters.

Statements implying inherent qualities, such as "Negroes are lazy" or "There's something terribly wrong with young people today," are therefore the crudest kind of unscientific observation, based on an out-of-date way of saying things, like "The sun rises." The tragedy is not simply the fact that people make such statements; the graver fact is that they believe themselves.

Some individuals are admired for their "realism" because, as the saying goes, they "call a spade a spade". Suppose we were to raise the question "Why should anyone call it a spade?" The reply would obviously be, "Because that's what it is!" This reply appeals so strongly to the common sense of most people that they feel that at this point discussion can be closed. I should like to ask the reader, however, to consider a point which may appear at first to him a mere quibble.

Here, let us say, is an implement for digging made of steel, with a wooden handle. Here, on the other hand, is a succession of sounds made with the tongue, lips, and vocal cords: "spade". If you want a digging implement of the kind we are talking about, you would ask for it by making the succession of sounds "spade" if you are addressing an English-speaking person. But suppose you were addressing a speaker of Dutch, French, Hungarian, Chinese, Tagalog? Would you not have to make completely different sounds? It is apparent, then, that the common-sense opinion of most people, "We call a spade a spade because that's what it is," is completely and utterly wrong. We call it a "spade" because we are English-speaking people, conforming, in this instance, to majority usage in naming this particular object. The steel-and-iron digging implement is simply an object standing there against the garage door; "spade" is what we *call* it — "spade" is a *name*.

And here we come to another source of identification reactions — an unconscious assumption about language epitomized in the expression "a spade is a spade," or even more elegantly in the famous remark "Pigs are called pigs because they are such dirty animals." The assumption is that everything has a "right name" and that the "right name" names the "essence" of that which is named.

If this assumption is at work in our reaction patterns, we are likely to be given to premature and often extremely inappropriate responses. We are likely to react to names as if they gave complete insight into the persons, things, or situations named. If we are told that a given individual is a

"Jew", some of us are likely to respond, "That's all I need to know." For, if names give the essence of that which is named, obviously, every "Jew" has the essential attribute of "Jewishness". Or, to put it the other way around, it is because he possesses "Jewishness" that we call him a "Jew"! A further example of the operation of this assumption is that, in spite of the fact that my entire education has been in Canada and the United States and I am unable to read and write Japanese, I am sometimes credited, or accused, of having an "Oriental mind". Now, since Buddha, Confucius, General Tojo, Mao Tse-tung, Syngman Rhee, Pandit Nehru, and the proprietor of the Golden Pheasant Chop Suey House all have "Oriental minds", it is hard to imagine what is meant. The "Oriental mind", like the attribute of "Jewishness", is purely and simply a fiction. Nevertheless, I used to note with alarm that newspaper columnists got paid for articles that purported to account for Stalin's behavior by pointing out that since he came from Georgia, which is next to Turkey and Azerbaijan and therefore "more a part of Asia than of Europe", he too had an "Oriental mind".

Our everyday habits of speech and our unconscious assumptions about the relations between words and things lead, then, to an identification reaction in which it is felt that all things that have the same name are entitled to the same response. From this point of view, all "insurance men", or "college boys", or "politicians", or "lawyers", or "Texans" are alike. Once we recognize the absurdity of these identification reactions based on identities of name, we can begin to think more clearly and more adequately. No "Texan" is exactly like any other "Texan". No "college boy" is exactly like any other "college boy". Most of the time "Texans" or "college boys" may be what you think they are: but often they are not. To realize fully the difference between words and what they stand for is to be ready for differences as well as similarities in the world. This readiness is mandatory to scientific thinking, as well as to sane thinking.

Korzybski's simple but powerful suggestion to those wishing to improve their semantic habits is to add "index numbers" to all terms, according to the formula: A_1 is not A_2. Translated into everyday language we can state the formula in such terms as these: Cow_1 is not cow_2; cow_2 is not cow_3; $Texan_1$ is not $Texan_2$; $politician_1$ is not $politician_2$; ham and eggs (Plaza Hotel) are not ham and eggs (Smitty's Café); socialism (Russia) is not socialism (England); private enterprise (Joe's Shoe Repair Shop) is not private enterprise (A.T.&T.). The formula means that instead of simply thinking about "cows" or "politicians" or "private enterprise", we should think as factually as possible about the differences between one cow and another, one politician and another, one privately owned enterprise and another.

This device of "indexing" will not automatically make us wiser and better, but it's a start. When we talk or write, the habit of indexing our general terms will reduce our tendency to wild and woolly generalization. It will compel us to think before we speak – think in terms of concrete objects and events and situations, rather than in terms of verbal associations. When we read or listen, the habit of indexing will help us visualize more concretely, and therefore understand better, what is being said. And if nothing is being said except deceptive windbaggery, the habit of indexing may – at least part of the time – save us from snapping, like the pickerel, at phony minnows. Another way of summing up is to remember, as Wendell Johnson said, that "To a mouse, cheese is cheese – that's why mousetraps work."

QUESTIONS

1. What does the author mean by our "semantic habits"? How, in his view, are these habits formed?
2. What is the "operational" meaning of a term?
3. Explain Korzybski's notion of "semantic reaction".
4. How can we be sure of the correct interpretation of a word?

5. Give three illustrations from Canadian life of how prejudice controls the meaning of words.

6. Explain and illustrate with an example of your own what Korzybski means by "identification reaction".

7. How does the author suggest we can control this kind of reaction?

8. What are the dangers in not being able to control the "identification reaction"? Illustrate with Canadian examples.

9. To what degree and in what ways do radio and television affect our "semantic reactions" to the world in which we live?

WILLIAM FAULKNER

1897-1962

The bear ✤ ✤ ✤

This is a story of coming of age. It tells of a young boy's growth into wisdom through a cultivation of a kind of knowledge, recorded, perhaps, in books and poems, but not to be learned from them. It is a knowledge that must be lived if it is to be learned, and it is a knowledge of the heart, not of the head. The art of this story might be described as "symbolic realism". The narrative, the setting, the handling of detail, the dialogue are in the simple realist tradition. But a sense of mystery pervades the telling, and, while the story takes us through the clearly recognizable world of the woodsman and the hunter, we soon know that we are on the track of the unrecognizable. We tread on facts, but our path leads we know not where. At the end of the path, the young boy is to find – and recognize – himself. (It is a path which very few follow to the end.) In reading this story, study the means by which Faulkner transforms the fact of the bear into a being timeless and vast and inevitable. And notice how the final encounter, longed for yet dreaded, becomes a kind of greeting of like to like at the still and inner heart of things. The fruit of the embrace is manhood. Faulkner's novels, richly poetic in treatment, chronicle the decay of the Old South, and the emergence of a new order bedevilled by greed and race hatred. Among his finest works are *The Sound and the Fury* (1929) and *Intruder in the Dust* (1948).

HE WAS TEN. But it had already begun, long before that day when at last he wrote his age in two figures and he saw for the first time the camp where his father and Major de Spain and old General Compson and the others spent two weeks each November and two weeks again each June. He had already inherited then, without ever having seen it, the tremendous bear with one trap-ruined foot which, in an area almost a hundred miles deep, had earned itself a name, a definite designation like a living man.

He had listened to it for years: the long legend of corncribs rifled, of shotes and grown pigs and even calves carried bodily into the woods and devoured, of traps and deadfalls overthrown and dogs mangled and slain, and shotgun and even rifle charges delivered at point-blank range and with no more effect than so many peas blown through a tube by a boy — a corridor of wreckage and destruction beginning back before he was born, through which sped, not fast but rather with the ruthless and irresistible deliberation of a locomotive, the shaggy tremendous shape.

It ran in his knowledge before he ever saw it. It looked and towered in his dreams before he even saw the unaxed woods where it left its crooked print, shaggy, huge, red-eyed, not malevolent but just big — too big for the dogs which tried to bay it, for the horses which tried to ride it down, for the men and bullets they fired into it, too big for the very country which was its constricting scope. He seemed to see it entire with a child's complete divination before he ever laid eyes on either — the doomed wilderness whose edges were being constantly and punily gnawed at by men with axes and plows who feared it because it was wilderness, men myriad and nameless even to one another in the land where the old bear had earned a name, through which ran not even a mortal animal but an anachronism, indomitable and invincible, out of an old dead time, a phantom, epitome, and apotheosis of the old life at which the puny humans swarmed and hacked in a fury of abhorrence and fear, like pygmies about the ankles of a drowsing elephant: the old bear solitary, indomitable and alone, widowered, childless, and absolved of mortality — old Priam reft of his old wife and having outlived all his sons.

Until he was ten, each November he would watch the wagon containing the dogs and the bedding and food and guns and his father and Tennie's Jim, the Negro, and Sam

Fathers, the Indian, son of a slave woman and a Chickasaw chief, depart on the road to town, to Jefferson, where Major de Spain and the others would join them. To the boy, at seven, eight, and nine, they were not going into the Big Bottom to hunt bear and deer, but to keep yearly rendezvous with the bear which they did not even intend to kill. Two weeks later they would return, with no trophy, no head and no skin. He had not expected it. He had not even been afraid it would be in the wagon. He believed that even after he was ten and his father would let him go too, for those two weeks in November, he would merely make another one, along with his father and Major de Spain and General Compson and the others, the dogs which feared to bay at it and the rifles and shotguns which failed even to bleed it, in the yearly pageant of the old bear's furious immortality.

Then he heard the dogs. It was in the second week of his first time in the camp. He stood with Sam Fathers against a big oak beside the faint crossing where they had stood each dawn for nine days now, hearing the dogs. He had heard them once before, one morning last week — a murmur, sourceless, echoing through the wet woods, swelling presently into separate voices which he could recognize and call by name. He had raised and cocked the gun as Sam told him and stood motionless again while the uproar, the invisible course, swept up and past and faded; it seemed to him that he could actually see the deer, the buck, blond, smoke-colored, elongated with speed, fleeing, vanishing, the woods, the gray solitude, still ringing even when the cries of the dogs had died away.

"Now let the hammers down," Sam said.

"You knew they were not coming here too," he said.

"Yes," Sam said. "I want you to learn how to do when you didn't shoot. It's after the chance for the bear or the deer has done already come and gone that men and dogs get killed."

"Anyway," he said, "it was just a deer."

Then on the tenth morning he heard the dogs again. And he readied the too long, too heavy gun as Sam had taught him, before Sam even spoke. But this time it was no deer, no ringing chorus of dogs running strong on a free scent, but a moiling yapping an octave too high, with something more than indecision and even abjectness in it, not even moving very fast, taking a long time to pass completely out of hearing, leaving then somewhere in the air that echo, thin, slightly hysterical, abject, almost grieving, with no sense of fleeing, unseen, smoke-colored, grass-eating shape ahead of it, and Sam, who had taught him first of all to cock the gun and take position where he could see everywhere and then never move again, had himself moved up beside him; he could hear Sam breathing at his shoulder, and he could see the arched curve of the old man's inhaling nostrils.

"Hah," Sam said. "Not even running. Walking."

"Old Ben!" the boy said. "But up here!" he cried. "Way up here!"

"He do it every year," Sam said. "Once. Maybe to see who in camp this time, if he can shoot or not. Whether we got the dog yet that can bay and hold him. He'll take them to the river, then he'll send them back home. We may as well go back too; see how they look when they come back to camp."

When they reached the camp the hounds were already there, ten of them crouching back under the kitchen, the boy and Sam squatting to peer back into the obscurity where they had huddled, quiet, the eyes luminous, glowing at them and vanishing, and no sound, only that effluvium of something more than dog, stronger than dog and not just animal, just beast, because still there had been nothing in front of that abject and almost painful yapping save the solitude, the wilderness, so that when the eleventh hound came in at noon and with all the others watching — even old Uncle Ash, who called himself first a cook — Sam daubed the tattered ear and the raked shoulder with turpentine and axle grease, to the boy it was still no living creature, but the wilderness which, leaning for the moment down, had patted lightly once the hound's temerity.

"Just like a man," Sam said. "Just like folks. Put off as long as she could having to be brave, knowing all the time that sooner or later she would have to be brave to keep on living with herself, and knowing all the time beforehand what was going to happen to her when she done it."

That afternoon, himself on the one-eyed wagon mule which did not mind the smell of blood nor, as they told him, of bear, and with Sam on the other one, they rode for more than three hours through the rapid, shortening winter day. They followed no path, no trail even that he could see; almost at once they were in a country which he had never seen before. Then he knew why Sam had made him ride the mule which would not spook. The sound one stopped short and tried to whirl and bolt even as Sam got down, blowing its breath, jerking and wrenching at the rein, while Sam held it, coaxing it forward with his voice, since he could not risk tying it, drawing it forward while the boy got down from the marred one.

Then, standing beside Sam in the gloom of the dying afternoon, he looked down at the rotted over-turned log, gutted and scored with claw marks and, in the wet earth beside it, the print of the enormous warped two-toed foot. He knew now what he had smelled when he peered under the kitchen where the dogs huddled. He realized for the first time that the bear which had run in his listening and loomed in his dreams since before he could remember to the contrary, and which, therefore, must have existed in the listening and dreams of his father and Major de Spain and even old General Compson, too, before they began to remember in their turn, was a mortal animal, and that if they had departed for the camp each November without any actual hope of bringing its trophy back, it was not because it could not be slain, but because so far they had no actual hope to.

"Tomorrow," he said.

"We'll try tomorrow," Sam said. "We ain't got the dog yet."

"We've got eleven. They ran him this morning."

"It won't need but one," Sam said. "He ain't here. Maybe

he ain't nowhere. The only other way will be for him to run by accident over somebody that has a gun."

"That wouldn't be me," the boy said. "It will be Walter or Major or — "

"It might," Sam said. "You watch close in the morning. Because he's smart. That's how come he has lived this long. If he gets hemmed up and has to pick out somebody to run over, he will pick out you."

"How?" the boy said. "How will he know — " He ceased. "You mean he already knows me, that I ain't never been here before, ain't had time to find out yet whether I — " He ceased again, looking at Sam, the old man whose face revealed nothing until it smiled. He said humbly, not even amazed, "It was me he was watching. I don't reckon he did need to come but once."

The next morning they left the camp three hours before daylight. They rode this time because it was too far to walk, even the dogs in the wagon; again the first gray light found him in a place which he had never seen before, where Sam had placed him and told him to stay and then departed. With the gun which was too big for him, which did not even belong to him, but to Major de Spain, and which he had fired only once — at a stump on the first day, to learn the recoil and how to reload it — he stood against a gum tree beside a little bayou whose black still water crept without movement out of a cane-brake and crossed a small clearing and into cane again, where, invisible, a bird — the big woodpecker called Lord-to-God by Negroes — clattered at a dead limb.

It was a stand like any other, dissimilar only in incidentals to the one where he had stood each morning for ten days; a territory new to him, yet no less familiar than that other one which, after almost two weeks, he had come to believe he knew a little — the same solitude, the same loneliness through which human beings had merely passed without altering it, leaving no mark, no scar, which looked exactly as it must have looked when the first ancestor of Sam Fathers' Chickasaw predecessors crept into it and looked about, club or stone ax or bone arrow drawn and poised; different only because, squatting at the edge of the kitchen, he smelled the hounds huddled and cringing beneath it and saw the raked ear and shoulder of the one who, Sam said, had had to be brave once in order to live with herself, and saw yesterday in the earth beside the gutted log the print of the living foot.

He heard no dogs at all. He never did hear them. He only heard the drumming of the woodpecker stop short off and knew that the bear was looking at him. He never saw it. He did not know whether it was in front of him or behind him. He did not move, holding the useless gun, which he had not even had warning to cock and which even now he did not cock, tasting in his saliva that taint as of brass which he knew now because he had smelled it when he peered under the kitchen at the huddled dogs.

Then it was gone. As abruptly as it had ceased, the woodpecker's dry, monotonous clatter set up again, and after a while he even believed he could hear the dogs — a murmur, scarce a sound even, which he had probably been hearing for some time before he even remarked it, drifting into hearing and then out again, dying away. They came nowhere near him. If it was a bear they ran, it was another bear. It was Sam himself who came out of the cane and crossed the bayou, followed by the injured bitch of yesterday. She was almost at heel, like a bird dog, making no sound. She came and crouched against his leg, trembling, staring off into the cane.

"I didn't see him," he said. "I didn't, Sam!"

"I know it," Sam said. "He done the looking. You didn't hear him neither, did you?"

"No," the boy said. "I — "

"He's smart," Sam said. "Too smart." He looked down at the hound, trembling faintly and steadily against the boy's knee. From the raked shoulder a few drops of fresh blood oozed and clung. "Too big. We ain't got the dog yet. But maybe someday. Maybe not next time. But someday."

So I must see him, he thought. I must look at him. Otherwise, it seemed to him that it would go on like this forever, as it had gone on with his father and Major de Spain, who was older than his father, and even with old General Compson, who had been old enough to be a brigade commander in 1865. Otherwise, it would go on so forever, next time and next time, after and after and after. It seemed to him that he could never see the two of them, himself and the bear, shadowy in the limbo from which time emerged, becoming time; the old bear absolved of mortality and himself partaking, sharing a little of it, enough of it. And he knew now what he had smelled in the huddled dogs and tasted in his saliva. He recognized fear. So I will have to see him, he thought, without dread or even hope. I will have to look at him.

It was June of the next year. He was eleven. They were in camp again, celebrating Major de Spain's and General Compson's birthdays. Although the one had been born in September and the other in the depth of winter and in another decade, they had met for two weeks to fish and shoot squirrels and turkey and run coons and wildcats with the dogs at night. That is, he and Boon Hoggenbeck and the Negroes fished and shot squirrels and ran the coons and cats, because the proved hunters, not only Major de Spain and old General Compson, who spent those two weeks sitting in a rocking chair before a tremendous iron pot of Brunswick stew, stirring and tasting, with old Ash to quarrel with about how he was making it and Tennie's Jim to pour whiskey from the demijohn into the tin dipper from which he drank it, but even the boy's father and Walter Ewell, who were still young enough, scorned such, other than shooting the wild gobblers with pistols for wagers on their marksmanship.

Or, that is, his father and the others believed he was hunting squirrels. Until the third day, he thought that Sam Fathers believed that too. Each morning he would leave the camp right after breakfast. He had his own gun now, a Christmas present. He went back to the tree beside the bayou where he had stood that morning. Using the compass which old General Compson had given him, he ranged from that point; he was teaching himself to be a better-than-fair woodsman without knowing he was doing it. On the second day he even found the gutted log where he had first seen the crooked print. It was almost completely crumbled now, healing with unbelievable speed, a passionate and almost visible relinquishment, back into the earth from which the tree had grown.

He ranged the summer woods now, green with gloom; if anything, actually dimmer than in November's gray dissolution, where, even at noon, the sun fell only in intermittent dappling upon the earth, which never completely dried out and which crawled with snakes – moccasins and water snakes and rattlers, themselves the color of the dappling gloom, so that he would not always see them until they moved, returning later and later, first day, second day, passing in the twilight of the third evening the little log pen enclosing the log stable where Sam was putting up the horses for the night.

"You ain't looked right yet," Sam said.

He stopped. For a moment he didn't answer. Then he said peacefully, in a peaceful rushing burst as when a boy's miniature dam in a little brook gives way, "All right. But how? I went to the bayou. I even found that log again. I – "

"I reckon that was all right. Likely he's been watching you. You never saw his foot?"

"I," the boy said – "I didn't – I never thought – "

"It's the gun," Sam said. He stood beside the fence motionless – the old man, the Indian, in the battered faded overalls and the five-cent straw hat which in the Negro's race had been the badge of his enslavement and was now the regalia of his freedom. The camp – the clearing, the house, the barn and its tiny lot with which Major de Spain in his turn had scratched punily and evanescently at the wilderness – faded in the dusk, back into the immemorial darkness of the woods. The gun, the boy thought. The gun.

"Be scared," Sam said. "You can't help that. But don't be afraid. Ain't nothing in the woods going to hurt you unless you corner it, or it smells that you are afraid. A bear or a deer, too, has got to be scared of a coward the same as a brave man has got to be."

The gun, the boy thought.

"You will have to choose," Sam said.

He left the camp before daylight, long before Uncle Ash would wake in his quilts on the kitchen floor and start the fire for breakfast. He had only the compass and a stick for snakes. He could go almost a mile before he would begin to need the compass. He sat on a log, the invisible compass in his invisible hand, while the secret night sounds, fallen still at his movements, scurried again and then ceased for good, and the owls ceased and gave over to the waking of day birds, and he could see the compass. Then he went fast yet still quietly he was becoming better and better as a woodsman, still without having yet realized it.

He jumped a doe and a fawn at sunrise, walked them out of the bed, close enough to see them – the crash of undergrowth, the white scut, the fawn scudding behind her faster than he had believed it could run. He was hunting right, upwind, as Sam had taught him; not that it mattered now. He had left the gun; of his own will and relinquishment he had accepted not a gambit, not a choice, but a condition in which not only the bear's heretofore inviolable anonymity but all the old rules and balances of hunter and hunted had been abrogated. He would not even be afraid, not even in the moment when the fear would take him completely – blood, skin, bowels, bones, memory from the long time before it became his memory – all save that thin, clear, immortal lucidity which alone differed him from this bear and from all the other bear and deer he would ever kill in the humility and pride of his skill and endurance, to which Sam had spoken when he leaned in the twilight on the lot fence yesterday.

By noon he was far beyond the little bayou, farther into the new and alien country than he had ever been. He was traveling now not only by the old, heavy, biscuit-thick silver watch which had belonged to his grandfather. When he stopped at last, it was for the first time since he had risen from the log at dawn when he could see the compass. It was far enough. He had left the camp nine hours ago; nine hours from now, dark would have already been an hour old. But he didn't think that. He thought, All right. Yes. But what? and stood for a moment, alien and small in the green and topless solitude, answering his own question before it had formed and ceased. It was the watch, the compass, the stick — the three lifeless mechanicals with which for nine hours he had fended the wilderness off; he hung the watch and compass carefully on a bush and leaned the stick beside them and relinquished completely to it.

He had not been going very fast for the last two or three hours. He went no faster now, since distance would not matter even if he could have gone fast. And he was trying to keep a bearing on the tree where he had left the compass, trying to complete a circle which would bring him back to it or at least intersect itself, since direction would not matter now either. But the tree was not there, and he did as Sam had schooled him — made the next circle in the opposite direction, so that the two patterns would bisect somewhere, but crossing no print of his own feet, finding the tree at last, but in the wrong place — no bush, no compass, no watch — and the tree not even the tree, because there was a down log beside it and he did what Sam Fathers had told him was the next thing and the last.

As he sat down on the log he saw the crooked print — the warped tremendous, two-toed indentation which, even as he watched it, filled with water. As he looked up, the wilderness coalesced, solidified — the glade, the tree he sought, the bush, the watch and the compass glinting where a ray of sunshine touched them. Then he saw the bear. It did not emerge, appear; it was just there, immobile, solid, fixed in the hot dappling of the green and windless noon, not as big as he had dreamed it, but as big as he had expected it, bigger, dimensionless, against the dappled obscurity, looking at him where he sat quietly on the log and looked back at it.

Then it moved. It made no sound. It did not hurry. It

crossed the glade, walking for an instant into the full glare of the sun; when it reached the other side it stopped again and looked back at him across one shoulder while his quiet breathing inhaled and exhaled three times.

Then it was gone. It didn't walk into the woods, the undergrowth. It faded, sank back into the wilderness as he had watched a fish, a huge old bass, sink and vanish into the dark depths of its pool without even any movement of its fins.

He thought, It will be next fall. But it was not next fall, nor the next nor the next. He was fourteen then. He had killed his buck, and Sam Fathers had marked his face with the hot blood, and in the next year he killed a bear. But even before that accolade he had become as competent in the woods as many grown men with the same experience; by his fourteenth year he was a better woodsman than most grown men with more. There was no territory within thirty miles of the camp that he did not know – bayou, ridge, brake, landmark, tree, and path. He could have led anyone to any point in it without deviation, and brought them out again. He knew the game trails that even Sam Fathers did not know; in his thirteenth year he found a buck's bedding place, and unbeknown to his father he borrowed Walter Ewell's rifle and lay in wait at dawn and killed the buck when it walked back to the bed, as Sam had told him how the old Chickasaw fathers did.

But not the old bear, although by now he knew its footprints better than he did his own, and not only the crooked one. He could see any one of the three sound ones and distinquish it from any other, and not only by its size. There were other bears within these thirty miles which left tracks almost as large, but this was more than that. If Sam Fathers had been his mentor and the back-yard rabbits and squirrels at home his kindergarten, then the wilderness the old bear ran was his college, the old male bear itself, so long unwifed and childless as to have become its own ungendered progenitor, was his alma mater. But he never saw it.

He could find the crooked print now almost whenever he

liked, fifteen or ten or five miles, or sometimes nearer the camp than that. Twice while on stand during the three years he heard the dogs strike its trail by accident; on the second time they jumped it seemingly, the voices high, abject, almost human in hysteria, as on that first morning two years ago. But not the bear itself. He would remember that noon three years ago, the glade, himself and the bear fixed during that moment in the windless and dappled blaze, and it would seem to him that it had never happened, that he had dreamed that too. But it had happened. They had looked at each other, they had emerged from the wilderness old as earth, synchronized to the instant by something more than the blood that moved the flesh and bones which bore them, and touched, pledged something, affirmed, something more lasting than the frail web of bones and flesh which any accident could obliterate.

Then he saw it again. Because of the very fact that he thought of nothing else, he had forgotten to look for it. He was still hunting with Walter Ewell's rifle. He saw it cross the end of a long blow-down, a corridor where a tornado had swept, rushing through rather than over the tangle of trunks and branches as a locomotive would have, faster than he had ever believed it could move, almost as fast as a deer even because a deer would have spent most of that time in the air, faster than he could bring the rifle sights up with it. And now he knew what had been wrong during all the three years. He sat on a log, shaking and trembling as if he had never seen the woods before nor anything that ran them, wondering with incredulous amazement how he could have forgotten the very thing which Sam Fathers had told him and which the bear itself had proved the next day and had now returned after three years to reaffirm.

And now he knew what Sam Fathers had meant about the right dog, a dog in which size would mean less than nothing. So when he returned alone in April — school was out then, so that the sons of farmers could help with the land's planting, and at last his father had granted him permission, on his promise to be back in four days — he had the dog. It was his own, a mongrel of the sort called by Negroes a fyce, a ratter, itself not much bigger than a rat and possessing that bravery which had long since stopped being courage and had become foolhardiness.

It did not take four days. Alone again, he found the trail on the first morning. It was not a stalk; it was an ambush. He timed the meeting almost as if it were an appointment with a human being. Himself holding the fyce muffled in a feed sack and Sam Fathers with two of the hounds on a piece of plowline rope, they lay down wind of the trail at dawn of the second morning. They were so close that the bear turned without even running, as if in surprised amazement at the shrill and frantic uproar of the released fyce, turning at bay against the trunk of a tree, on its hind feet; it seemed to the boy that it would never stop rising, taller and taller, and even the two hounds seemed to take a desperate and despairing courage from the fyce, following it as it went in.

Then he realized that the fyce was actually not going to stop. He flung, threw the gun away, and ran; when he overtook and grasped the frantically pinwheeling little dog, it seemed to him that he was directly under the bear.

He could smell it, strong and hot and rank. Sprawling, he looked up to where it loomed and towered over him like a cloudburst and colored like a thunderclap, quite familiar, peacefully and even lucidly familiar, until he remembered: This was the way he used to dream about it. Then it was gone. He didn't see it go. He knelt holding the frantic fyce with both hands, hearing the abashed wailing of the hounds drawing farther and farther away, until Sam came up. He carried the gun. He laid it down quietly beside the boy and stood looking down at him.

"You've done seed him twice now with a gun in your hands," he said. "This time you couldn't have missed him."

The boy rose. He still held the fyce. Even in his arms and clear of the ground, it yapped frantically, straining and surging after the fading uproar of the two hounds like a tangle of wire springs. He was panting a little, but he was neither shaking nor trembling now.

"Neither could you!" he said. "You had the gun! Neither did you!"

"And you didn't shoot," his father said. "How close were you?"

"I don't know, sir," he said. "There was a big wood tick inside his right hind leg. I saw that. But I didn't have the gun then."

"But you didn't shoot when you had the gun," his father said. "Why?"

But he didn't answer, and his father didn't wait for him to, rising and crossing the room, across the pelt of the bear which the boy had killed two years ago and the larger one which his father had killed before he was born, to the bookcase beneath the mounted head of the boy's first buck. It was the room which his father called the office, from which all the plantation business was transacted; in it for the fourteen years of his life he had heard the best of all talking. Major de Spain would be there and sometimes old General Compson, and Walter Ewell and Boon Hoggenbeck and Sam Fathers and Tennie's Jim, too, were hunters, knew the woods and what ran them.

He would hear it, not talking himself but listening – the wilderness, the big woods, bigger and older than any recorded document of white man fatuous enough to believe he had bought any fragment of it or Indian ruthless enough to pretend that any fragment of it had been his to convey. It was of the men, not white nor black nor red, but men, hunters with the will and hardihood to endure and the humility and skill to survive, and the dogs and the bear and deer juxtaposed and reliefed against it, ordered and compelled by and within the wilderness in the ancient and unremitting contest by the ancient and immitigable rules which voided all regrets and brooked no quarter, the voices quiet and weighty and deliberate for retrospection and recollection and exact remembering, while he squatted in the blazing firelight as

Tennie's Jim squatted, who stirred only to put more wood on the fire and to pass the bottle from one glass to another. Because the bottle was always present, so that after a while it seemed to him that those fierce instants of heart and brain and courage and wiliness and speed were concentrated and distilled into that brown liquor which not women, not boys and children, but only hunters drank, drinking not of the blood they had spilled but some condensation of the wild immortal spirit, drinking it moderately, humbly even, not with the pagan's base hope of acquiring the virtues of cunning and strength and speed, but in salute to them.

His father returned with the book and sat down again and opened it: "Listen," he said. He read the five stanzas aloud, his voice quiet and deliberate in the room where there was no fire now because it was already spring. Then he looked up. The boy watched him. "All right," his father said. "Listen." He read again, but only the second stanza this time, to the end of it, the last two lines, and closed the book and put it on the table beside him. "She cannot fade, though thou hast not thy bliss, forever wilt thou love, and she be fair," he said.

"He's talking about a girl," the boy said.

"He had to talk about something," his father said. Then he said, "He was talking about truth. Truth doesn't change. Truth is one thing. It covers all things which touch the heart — honor and pride and pity and justice and courage and love. Do you see now?"

He didn't know. Somehow it was simpler than that. There was an old bear, fierce and ruthless, not merely just to stay alive, but with the fierce pride of liberty and freedom, proud enough of the liberty and freedom to see it threatened without fear or even alarm; nay, who at times even seemed deliberately to put that freedom and liberty in jeopardy in order to savor them, to remind his old strong bones and flesh to keep supple and quick to defend and preserve them. There was an old man, son of a Negro slave and an Indian king, inheritor on the one side of the long chronicle of a people who had learned humility through suffering, and pride through the endurance which survived the suffering and injustice, and on the other side, the chronicle of a people even longer in the land than the first, yet who no longer existed in the land at all save in the solitary brotherhood of an old Negro's alien blood and the wild and invincible spirit of an old bear. There was a boy who wished to learn humility and pride in order to become skillful and worthy in the woods, who suddenly found himself becoming so skillful so rapidly that he feared he would never become worthy because he had not learned humility and pride, although he had tried to, until one day and as suddenly he discovered that an old man who could not have defined either had led him, as though by the hand, to that point where an old bear and a little mongrel of a dog showed him that, by possessing one thing other, he would possess them both.

And a little dog, nameless and mongrel and many-fathered, grown, yet weighing less than six pounds, saying as if to itself, "I can't be dangerous, because there's nothing much smaller than I am; I can't be fierce, because they would call it just a noise; I can't be humble, because I'm already too close to the ground to genuflect; I can't be proud, because I wouldn't be near enough to it for anyone to know who was casting the shadow, and I don't even know that I'm not going to heaven, because they have already decided that I don't possess an immortal soul. So all I can be is brave. But it's all right. I can be that, even if they still call it just noise."

That was all. It was simple, much simpler than somebody talking in a book about youth and a girl he would never need to grieve over, because he could never approach any nearer her and would never have to get any farther away. He had heard about a bear, and finally got big enough to trail it, and he trailed it four years and at last met it with a gun in his hands and he didn't shoot. Because a little dog — But he could have shot long before the little dog covered the twenty yards to where the bear waited, and Sam Fathers could have shot at any time during that interminable minute while Old Ben stood on his hind feet over them. He stopped. His father was watching him gravely across the spring-rife twilight of the room; when he spoke, his words were as quiet as the twilight, too, not loud, because they did not need to be because they would last. "Courage, and honor, and pride," his father said, "and pity, and love of justice and of liberty. They all touch the heart, and what the heart holds to becomes truth, as far as we know the truth. Do you see now?"

Sam, and Old Ben, and Nip, he thought. And himself too. He had been all right too. His father had said so. "Yes, sir," he said.

QUESTIONS

1. How, from the beginning, does Faulkner make the bear at once real and more than "real"?

2. The bear is near or present several times in the course of the story. Identify the times and relate each to the "growing up" of the boy.

3. What is the special significance of the episode in which the bear and not the boy "done the looking"?

4. Explain the importance of Sam's advice "Be scared . . . But don't be afraid".

5. In the look which passes between bear and boy, what is "pledged" and "affirmed"?

6. In the last encounter what does the boy learn from Sam? From the little dog?

7. Why does the father read aloud the poem by Keats? Explain the force for the story of the lines quoted.

HUGH MACLENNAN
b. 1907

Sunset and evening star ✦ ✦ ✦

One of the most dedicated and workmanlike of Canadian writers, himself a university professor and a Ph.D., Hugh MacLennan is in a fine strategic position to observe the effect on young minds of some of the modern movements in poetry itself and of new methods in the criticism and teaching of poetry. He feels that the "liberation from the past" effected by writers like Eliot, Pound, and Joyce has created a cult of joylessness and a whole new vocabulary of clichés. Literature has been reduced to a professional racket and the readers of poetry are now "nobody but other poets and the captive-audiences in English courses". In reading the essay, try to decide whether the situation which Hugh MacLennan describes is the creation of a conspiratorial alliance between writers and professors or whether it is to be understood, ultimately, as a symptom of the state to which our civilization has fallen – or risen. There are those who see in the greater complexity and intensity of modern literature proof of an advance in the culture, of a greater sophistication, and of a genuine ripening of the human spirit. Some would point, as against the early Eliot poems quoted here, to later poems such as *Ash Wednesday* and *Four Quartets* in which Eliot achieves a profound, positive, and religious statement. Others would argue that MacLennan is unfair to university teachers of literature who are a very mixed lot, strenuously independent, and with no allegiance to a single literary creed. The title of the essay is taken from Tennyson's lyric "Crossing the Bar" and strikingly suggests the great difference in tone between our literature and the literature of the nineteenth century. It would be a useful exercise to suggest some of the reasons for this difference. Among Hugh MacLennan's major novels are *Barometer Rising* (1941), *Two Solitudes* (1945), and *The Watch That Ends the Night* (1959).

AFTER A DAY of grey clouds the evening broke glorious. The zenith was dark as doom, but the whole west cracked open into a lake of orange, lemon, and lime-green in which individual clouds lay as still as that eroded sword of Mycenae in which the old bronze glows like rusty fire. Through a stretch of ten miles the sentinel elms on the rim of the hills stood outlined in perfect clarity. A flock of birds, mosquito-small in the distance, swirled across that celestial lake of colour before flying south into the dark.

I came down the road and found some young people I knew. They were boys and girls in their late teens, one or two of them with a year of college behind them, and I thought how wonderful to be a boy with a girl on such a night as this. But after talking with them a few minutes I discovered that this was not the case.

They were bored. It was too cold for the motor boat and their various Dads were using the family cars and there was nothing to do because there was no place to go. They couldn't water-ski on the ridges of the hills facing the rise of the moon and they couldn't drive their fathers' cars over the downs. They couldn't get there without walking so they stayed in the dark of the street near the Neon sign. I left them with the feeling I used to have in the depression when I passed the unemployed on park benches.

For without poetry these youths were poor. Poetry had been stillborn in them, or they had never been exposed to it. They had many advantages unknown twenty-five years ago and they were thoroughly nice young people, but their education had produced in each one of them a fear of being alone and an incapacity to be happy unless there was something to do. It occurred to none of them that "the gang" has always been an infallible symptom of poverty.

Not when I was a boy nor at any time in the past were all young people poets or even consciously fond of poetry. But if they had received any education at all, they were at least aware of it. Ever since the Greeks, poetry had been basic to the education of civilized people. Not all of them may have liked it, but it affected most of them to greater or less degree. It taught them to find a country landscape more interesting than a city alley; it improved their vocabulary; it made it easier for the sensitive among them to sublimate their sexual drives into creative channels; it made them richer.

As the colour died, the evening star appeared and a little later the moon broke the cloud-wrack and the night opened up. I thought how Homer had made Helen the loveliest woman there ever was not by describing her, but by telling how the elders of Troy fell silent when she passed them on a moonlit night along the city walls. I thought of that greater story in Homer which Freud considered so profound: Ulysses stopping the ears of his seamen with wax and having himself bound to what Freud called "the mast of sublimation" while his ship sailed past the Sirens' isle. About the feet of the Sirens lay the bones of the men who had touched them, killed by literality. I thought also of the manner in which beautiful girls are described in popular American literature since the war. Each is set forth like a prize bitch in a dog show, all her points specified and described as though she were a pleasure-machine, so that the reader can be absolutely sure that the writer has not cheated him by leaving anything to his imagination. A beri-beri has come into literature with the desiccation of poetry.

For this condition several circumstances are responsible, but the chief criminal is the educational system. Poetry has been almost excluded from it. In few schools are children any longer required to learn verses by heart; the old choral recitation of verse has been thrown out as "uncreative" because it is unoriginal, and for quite a while there has been an idea abroad that making toy houses and cutting out paper patterns on the floor provide the best possible training for creative personalities. Of course, poetry is on the list of required reading for all English exams, including those set by college entrance boards, and if the pupil is lucky in his teacher the results can be as they always are when poetry and youth encounter each other. But it is in college that the shades of the prison house really close down, for there the unhappy student is almost certain to encounter professors who have been trained to murder poetry as efficiently as the German-trained philologists of fifty years ago murdered the ancient classics. Ground out by the Ph.D. system, they use almost any kind of literature as the raw material of what is called critical scholarship, and the very necessities of their trade compel them to concentrate on poets whose writing is dense, or full of obscure symbols and broken lines, or loaded with cross-references and *double-entendres.* Poetry like this gives them material to teach. But

When shepherds pipe on oaten straws
And merry larks are ploughmen's clocks,
And turtles tread, and rooks, and daws,
And maidens bleach their summer frocks . . .

what can a critic do but tell a youth to read it?

Whenever there is something to sell, there is bound to be a racket somewhere. The vested interest of the power-élite in the poetry world is two-fold: they seek a corner in prestige, and they also seek the economic perquisites which go along with this new species of expertise. Valuable college posts are the rewards of the critic-poet in a society where nobody but other poets and the captive-audiences in English courses read modern verse. The origin of this new power-élite, as almost everyone must know by this time, is the artistic revolution fired in the 1920's by T. S. Eliot, Ezra Pound, James Joyce, and a constantly growing army of camp-followers who have copied their mannerisms, and in addition have elevated their choice of subject-matter to a new kind of cliché. At the end of the nineteenth century it was a cliché that sunsets and roses were poetical, and their presence in a line of verse made that verse look like a poem. Since the success of Eliot — the greatest worldly success, surely, of any poet in the last two centuries — objects usually associated with fear, squalor, and ugliness have replaced the old subject-matter, and God help a young poet who fails to understand this.

Let us go then, you and I,
While the evening is spread out against the sky
Like a patient etherized upon a table.

This celebrated line once struck the traditionalists like a deliberate slap in the face. Here was a new vision, and at the time a great one; here was the shock of truth in a world which Rupert Brooke had lamented had grown old and cold and dreary, its roses no more vital than *pot-pourri,* its sunsets described so often that hardly anyone who had read the poetry of the time could any longer see what a real sunset looked like. Well do I remember the time when it was pointed out to me that this line of T. S. Eliot was the most important single line ever written by an English poet. I also remember the character of the man who introduced me to it.

He was an Englishman in his late twenties, and I thought — probably with truth — that up to then he was the most brilliant man I had ever met. He seemed to know everything. He spoke with fascinating familiarity of "Tom" and "Ezra" and "Wystan", and in his little spare time between his scholarship and long evenings of rabid discussion about art, he himself wrote verse which we understood "Tom" had seen and found promising. Trained in Cambridge by the new school of literary critics (shortly afterwards *émigrés* from this group came to Harvard, Yale, and other Ph.D.-giving universities in America, saw them and conquered them in a decade) this Englishman's attitude towards traditional poetry was that of a communist towards traditional statesmen and economists. He was in on the new ground floor and he knew it. When he mentioned Shelley and Wordsworth it was not because he enjoyed what they had written; it was because they were "important" to their time in the sense that Oliver Cromwell, in the Marxists' book, was important to his. The Romantics had revolted and established a new literary power-élite around the year 1800; now it was their turn to be ousted by still another power-élite led by Eliot, Pound, and Joyce. This Englishman was as alert to heresy as any communist I ever met in the Thirties. For a while even Pound fell under a cloud, not even Auden was really safe, and Yeats redeemed himself only at the end, much like a Menshevik joining the C.P. at the last hour before that wonderful day in October, 1917. But the Lenin of the movement was T. S. Eliot, and the lovesong of Prufrock the speech at literature's Finland Station.

Under the influence of this Englishman, whom I genuinely liked (for in himself he was a fascinating and vivid personality), I began studying the high priests of the new Dialectic. I became acquainted with the critical writings of F. R. Leavis, Cyril Connolly, and a host of authors, including, of course, the Master himself, who quickly found his niche as a critic when his poetical vein ran out. Dutifully I turned my back on the poets I had loved (Shakespeare, for some reason, was exempt) and joined the column that trudged off into the wasteland.

I was young, and if it were not bliss to be alive in that new dawn, it certainly wasn't dull. The depression was making us so angry that the modern youth who call themselves Angry Young Men seem by comparison like comfortable bourgeois. No wonder we worshipped Eliot in those days. Though he seemed to have no real interest in politics outside of literature, in which he was proving himself a master politician, indirectly his influence on practical outlooks was immense. A whole generation of young men and women felt rejected by the social and economic system of the time. Very well. Did not Eliot describe with unparallelled power precisely how hideous that system was, how ugly it had become, how little worth it was?

The winter evening settles down
With the smell of steaks in passageways . . .
or, The morning came to consciousness
Of faint stale smells of beer
From the sawdust of trampled streets . . .
or, Remark the cat which flattens itself in the gutter
Slips out its tongue
And devours a morsel of rancid butter . . .

No question about the power here; no argument about the genius; no doubt about the truth of this vision for the poet who saw it. But in retrospect what is really amazing has been the rapidity with which this new subject-matter became clichéd by the army of Eliot's imitators, and how, in a sense, it is unnatural that the revolution he started should have held its power without a Krushchev coming along to modify it.

For Eliot's vision — humourless, passionate, and intense — is utterly devoid of love of any kind, and even devoid of hate. Despair is in it, but dislike much more so: a critical dislike of life itself most of the time, the unrelieved weariness of a middle-aged man passing through his climacteric. A poetry of the menopause it really is, and the Master himself has described it perfectly as "thoughts of a brain in a dry season".

So the revolution conquered, and in almost no time poetry was reduced from a living force to a museum study among the young, and the evil day drew nigh, quicker than any young man could have guessed who rejoiced in this youth in the 1930's.

Nearly all observers who have revisited countries they once knew, and which since have been captured by a totalitarian revolution, have noted a universal phenomenon: people have become so accustomed to an arid life of thought-control, to the cueing up and the shoddy goods in the stores, that they seem to have forgotten what it was like in the same land only a dozen years before. The world of modern poetry to a large extent has become like that now, with the successful poets ensconced in universities giving courses in literary criticism, and writing at odd moments brief little word-groups which seem like critical cryptograms in broken lines, the thought so subtle or so obscure, that nobody really understands what it signifies. One of the most curious aspects of the revolution in literature has been the discarding of the age-old axiom that unless a book or a poem is a communication, it does not really exist. This new verse, much of it, deliberately avoids communication, which apparently belongs to the dead past which the revolution overthrew. Even more curious — or is it, really? — has been the durability of the revolutionary subject-matter: the Freudian symbols, the cats in the alleys, the frustrated and frustrating half-dreams, half-thoughts, half-lines. Most curious of all is the fact that this subject-matter is often chosen by quite lusty youths who romp with their girls and enjoy the woods and lakes and rivers of the land, and then return to their desks to write cryptograms about how bad it all is. Big Brother is certainly watching.

Now as the moon mounted the sky I heard the hoot of an owl in the gully and recalled that Englishman with his detective's mind who declared that it was the duty of the critic "to liberate poetry from the tyranny of the past". I also recalled the moment when I understood how parochial he was. It was in Russia just before the war, when I used to spend hours looking at the glum faces of the proletariat liberated from the past by the Bolsheviks.

QUESTIONS

1. Explain the significance of the title and the opening description for the argument of the essay.

2. What does MacLennan mean by saying that "without poetry these youths were poor"?

3. In what sense does the author think descriptions of beautiful girls in popular American literature lack poetry? How does this relate to the Ulysses episode?

4. What, according to MacLennan, is the role of the good teacher of literature? How does he think this role has been abused? What do you think constitutes good teaching of a poem?

5. What are the clichés of modern poetry?

6. What does MacLennan believe to be wrong about his young Englishman's approach to the literature of the nineteenth century?

7. How does MacLennan account for Eliot's early popularity and for the vogue which he created?

8. Why does MacLennan think that the new poetry was "reduced from a living force to a museum study among the young"? Has this reduction indeed taken place?

9. Why do you think modern poets "deliberately avoid communication"?

10. Explain what MacLennan means by the sentence "Big Brother is watching".

JOHN MILTON

1608-1674

Excerpts from *Areopagitica*

In every debate affecting the rights of the human person, particularly his right to freedom of thought and expression, the voices of two men are still heard – John Milton and John Stuart Mill: the first, the great poet and pamphleteer of the Puritan Revolution of the seventeenth century; the second, the leading exponent of political liberalism in the nineteenth century. Whether the issue is the censorship of a new book or play or painting, or whether it involves the right of men to express unpopular opinion in public, champions of human freedom still take as their basic texts Milton's *Areopagitica* and Mill's great essay *On Liberty*. We are including here significant and characteristic passages from both of these great works. John Milton understands liberty in Christian terms. Man must be free because man is created in the image of God. True, man lives in a world which abounds in evil, and man himself, because of Adam's disobedience, inherits a strong inclination toward evil. But man has been redeemed by Christ. He is thus capable of choosing between good and evil and he must be allowed his right to make the choice. If he is prevented from exercising his power of choice he loses his dignity, his very humanity. Evil cannot be overcome without a clear knowledge of what it is, nor can it be overthrown by men whose moral muscles have never been exercised in acts of choice. "That which purifies us is trial and trial is by what is contrary." *Areopagitica* was published in 1644. Milton wrote it, he said "in order to deliver the press from the restraints with which it was encumbered" (Parliament the year before had passed a censorship law which seemed to threaten all freedom of expression). The theme of Christian liberty is later to inform Milton's great poems *Paradise Lost, Paradise Regained,* and *Samson Agonistes.*

1

. . . I DENY NOT but that it is of greatest concernment in the church and commonwealth to have a vigilant eye how books demean themselves as well as men; and thereafter to confine, imprison, and do sharpest justice on them as malefactors. For books are not absolutely dead things, but do contain a potency of life in them to be as active as that soul was whose progeny they are; nay, they do preserve as in a vial the purest efficacy and extraction of that living intellect that bred them. I know they are as lively and as vigorously productive as those fabulous dragon's teeth; and being sown up and down, may chance to spring up armed men. And yet, on the other hand, unless wariness be used, as good almost kill a man as kill a good book: who kills a man kills a reasonable creature, God's image; but he who destroys a good book, kills reason itself, kills the image of God, as it were, in the eye. Many a man lives a burden to the earth; but a good book is the precious lifeblood of a master spirit, embalmed and treasured up on purpose to a life beyond life. 'Tis true, no age can restore a life, whereof perhaps there is no great loss; and revolutions of ages do not oft recover the loss of a rejected truth, for the want of which whole nations fare the worse. We should be wary, therefore, what persecution we raise against the living labours of public men, how we spill that seasoned life of man preserved and stored up in books; since we see a kind of homicide may be thus committed, sometimes a martyrdom; and if it extend to the whole impression, a kind of massacre, whereof the execution ends not in the slaying of an elemental life, but strikes at that ethereal and fifth essence, the breath of reason itself, slays an immortality rather than a life.

2

. . . Good and evil we know in the field of this world grow up together almost inseparably; and the knowledge of good is so involved and interwoven with the knowledge of evil, and in so many cunning resemblances hardly to be discerned, that those confused seeds which were imposed on Psyche as an incessant labour to cull out and sort asunder, were not more intermixed. It was from out the rind of one apple tasted, that the knowledge of good and evil, as two twins cleaving together, leaped forth into the world. And perhaps this is that doom which Adam fell into of knowing good and evil, that is to say, of knowing good by evil.

As therefore the state of man now is, what wisdom can there be to choose, what continence to forbear without the knowledge of evil? He that can apprehend and consider vice with all her baits and seeming pleasures, and yet abstain, and yet distinguish, and yet prefer that which is truly better, he is the true warfaring Christian. I cannot praise a fugitive and cloistered virtue, unexercised and unbreathed, that never sallies out and sees her adversary, but slinks out of the race where that immortal garland is to be run for, not without dust and heat. Assuredly we bring not innocence into the world, we bring impurity much rather: that which purifies us is trial, and trial is by what is contrary. That virtue therefore which is but a youngling in the contemplation of evil, and knows not the utmost that vice promises to her followers, and rejects it, is but a blank virtue, not a pure; her whiteness is but an excremental whiteness; which was the reason why our sage and serious poet Spenser, whom I dare be known to think a better teacher than Scotus or Aquinas, describing true temperance under the person of Guyon, brings him in with his palmer through the cave of Mammon and the bower of earthly bliss, that he might see and know, and yet abstain.

Since therefore, the knowledge and survey of vice is in this world so necessary to the constituting of human virtue, and the scanning of error to the confirmation of truth, how can we more safely and with less danger scout into the regions of sin and falsity than by reading all manner of tractates and hearing all manner of reason? And this is the benefit which may be had of books promiscuously read.

3

. . .For if they fell upon one kind of strictness, unless their care were equal to regulate all other things of like aptness to corrupt the mind, that single endeavour they knew would be but a fond labour; to shut and fortify one gate against corruption, and be necessitated to leave others round about wide open. If we think to regulate printing, thereby to rectify manners, we must regulate all recreations and pastimes, all that is delightful to man. No music must be heard, no song be set or sung, but what is grave and Doric. There must be licensing dancers, that no gesture, motion, or deportment be taught our youth, but what by their allowance shall be thought honest; for such Plato was provided of. It will ask more than the work of twenty licensers to examine all the lutes, the violins, and the guitars in every house; they must not be suffered to prattle as they do, but must be licensed what they may say. And who shall silence all the airs and madrigals that whisper softness in chambers? The windows also, and the balconies must be thought on; there are shrewd books, with dangerous frontispieces, set to sale; who shall prohibit them? Shall twenty licensers?

QUESTIONS

1. Summarize Milton's view of the "potency of a good book". Does the book enjoy the same kind of prestige today? What do you think of the notion that television has, in a real sense, replaced the book?

2. Do you agree with Milton that a virtue which has not been put to the test "is but a blank virtue" – no virtue at all? Can you give an illustration to support your view?

3. How do books aid in the acquisition of real virtue?

4. Are there any kinds of literature which you think should be censored? Should there be censorship of books, films, and television programs now available to children? Would Milton make the same argument in defence of television that he makes in defence of books?

5. Note Milton's fear that censorship of books will quickly spread to censorship of all the arts. Can you think of any modern instances of this wider kind of censorship?

JOHN STUART MILL

1806-1873

Excerpts from *On Liberty* ✤ ✤ ✤

As passionate as John Milton in his defense of man's right to freedom of thought and expression, Mill did not, as Milton did, ground his convictions in Christianity. In the excerpt which follows from his long essay *On Liberty* (1859), he refers to the principles of "utility". The philosophy of utility (or utilitarianism) had been developed by his father's friend, Jeremy Bentham (1748-1832). Young John Stuart Mill was brought up in strict accordance with the Benthamite doctrines. These doctrines had no place for religion or the supernatural. Later, Mill was to sum up the philosophy of utility in these words: "The creed which accepts as the foundation of morals utility, or the greatest happiness principle, holds that actions are right in proportion as they tend to promote happiness, wrong as they tend to produce the reverse of happiness. By happiness is intended pleasure and the absence of pain: by unhappiness, pain and the privation of pleasure." John Stuart Mill was never to treat pleasure and pain in the narrow physical animalistic sense. Like Bentham, he worked for "the greatest good of the greatest number" as a social goal, but included in "the good" the pleasures of mind and spirit. Nevertheless, and unlike Milton, he thought of "goods" like freedom as natural possibilities without need of supernatural sanction and capable of being actualized by intelligent calculation and suitable social action.

. . . THE OBJECT of this Essay is to assert one very simple principle, as entitled to govern absolutely the dealings of society with the individual in the way of compulsion and control, whether the means used be physical force in the form of legal penalties, or the moral coercion of public opinion. That principle is, that the sole end for which mankind are warranted, individually or collectively, in interfering with the liberty of any of their number, is self-protection. That the only purpose for which power can be rightfully exercised over any member of a civilized community, against his will, is to prevent harm to others. His own good, either physical or moral, is not a sufficient warrant. He cannot rightfully be compelled to do or forbear because it will be better for him to do so, because it will make him happier, because, in the opinion of others, to do so would be wise, or even right. These are good reasons for remonstrating with him, or reasoning with him, or persuading him, or entreating him, but not for compelling him, or visiting him with any evil in case he do otherwise. To justify that, the conduct from which it is desired to deter him must be calculated to produce evil to some one else. The only part of the conduct of any one, for which he is amenable to society, is that which concerns others. In the part which merely concerns himself, his independence is, of right, absolute. Over himself, over his own body and mind, the individual is sovereign.

It is, perhaps, hardly necessary to say that this doctrine is meant to apply only to human beings in the maturity of their faculties. We are not speaking of children, or of young persons below the age which the law may fix as that of manhood or womanhood. Those who are still in a state to require being taken care of by others must be protected against their own actions as well as against external injury. For the same reason, we may leave out of consideration those backward states of society in which the race itself may be considered as in its nonage. The early difficulties in the way of spontaneous progress are so great, that there is seldom any choice of means for overcoming them; and a ruler full of the spirit of improvement is warranted in the use of any expedients that will attain an end, perhaps otherwise unattainable. Despotism is a legitimate mode of government in dealing with barbarians, provided the end be their improvement, and the means justified by actually effecting that end. Liberty, as a principle, has no application to any state of things anterior to the time when mankind have become capable of being improved by free and equal discussion. Until then, there is nothing for them but implicit obedience to an Akbar or a Charlemagne, if they are so fortunate as to find one. But as soon as mankind have attained the capacity of being guided to their own improvement by conviction or persuasion (a period long since reached in all nations with whom we need here concern ourselves), compulsion, either in the direct form or in that of pains and penalties for non-compliance, is no longer admissible as a means to their own good, and justifiable only for the security of others.

It is proper to state that I forego any advantage which could be derived to my argument from the idea of abstract right, as a thing independent of utility. I regard utility as the ultimate appeal on all ethical questions; but it must be utility in the largest sense, grounded on the permanent interests of a man as a progressive being. Those interests, I contend, authorize the subjection of individual spontaneity to external control, only in respect to those actions of each, which concern the interest of other people. If any one does an act hurtful to others, there is a *prima facie* case for punishing him, by law, or, where legal penalties are not safely applicable, by general disapprobation. There are also many positive acts for the benefit of others, which he may rightfully be compelled to perform; such as to give evidence in a court of justice; to bear his fair share in the common defence, or in any other joint work necessary to the interest of the society of which he enjoys the protection; and to perform certain acts of individual beneficence, such as saving a fellow-creature's life, or interposing to protect the defenceless against ill-usage, things which whenever it is obviously a man's duty to do, he may rightfully be made responsible to society for not doing. A person may cause evil to others not only by his actions but by his inaction, and in either case he is justly accountable to them for the injury. The latter case, it is true, requires a much more cautious exercise of compulsion than the former. To make any one answerable for doing evil to others is the rule; to make him answerable for not preventing evil is, comparatively speaking, the exception. Yet there are many cases clear enough and grave enough to justify that exception. In all things which regard the external relations of the individual, he is *de jure* amenable to those whose interests are concerned, and, if need be, to society as their protector. There are often good reasons for not holding him to the responsibility; but these reasons must arise from the special expediencies of the case: either because it is a kind of case in which he is on the whole likely to act better, when left to his own discretion, than when controlled in any way in which society have it in their power to control him; or because the attempt to exercise control would produce other evils, greater than those which it would prevent. When such reasons as these preclude the enforcement of responsibility, the conscience of the agent himself should step into the vacant judgment seat, and protect those interests of others which have no external protection; judging himself all the more rigidly, because the case does not admit of his being made accountable to the judgment of his fellow-creatures.

But there is a sphere of action in which society, as distinguished from the individual, has, if any, only an indirect interest; comprehending all that portion of a person's life and conduct which affects only himself, or if it also affects others, only with their free, voluntary, and undeceived consent and participation. When I say only himself, I mean directly, and in the first instance, for whatever affects himself, may affect others through himself, and the objection which may be grounded on this contingency, will receive consideration in the sequel. This, then, is the appropriate region of human liberty. It comprises, first, the inward domain of consciousness; demanding liberty of conscience in the most comprehensive sense; liberty of thought and feeling; absolute freedom of opinion and sentiment on all subjects, practical or speculative, scientific, moral, or theological. The liberty of expressing and publishing opinions may seem to fall under a different principle, since it belongs to that part of the conduct of an individual which concerns other people, but being almost of as much importance as the liberty of thought itself, and resting in great part on the same reasons, is practically inseparable from it. Secondly, the principle requires liberty of tastes and pursuits; of framing the plan of our life to suit our own character; of doing as we like, subject to such consequences as may follow: without impediment from our fellow-creatures, so long as what we do does not harm them, even though they should think our conduct foolish, perverse, or wrong. Thirdly, from this liberty of each individual, follows the liberty, within the same limits, of combination among individuals; freedom to unite, for any purpose not involving harm to others: the persons combining being supposed to be of full age, and not forced or deceived.

No society in which these liberties are not, on the whole, respected, is free, whatever may be its form of government; and none is completely free in which they do not exist absolute and unqualified. The only freedom which deserves the name, is that of pursuing our own good in our own way, so long as we do not attempt to deprive others of theirs, or impede their efforts to obtain it. Each is the proper guardian of his own health, whether bodily, *or* mental and spiritual. Mankind are greater gainers by suffering each other to live as seems good to themselves, than by compelling each to live as seems good to the rest.

Though this doctrine is anything but new, and, to some persons, may have the air of a truism, there is no doctrine which stands more directly opposed to the general tendency of existing opinion and practice. Society has expended fully as much effort in the attempt (according to its lights) to compel people to conform to its notions of personal as of social excellence. The ancient commonwealths thought themselves entitled to practise, and the ancient philosophers countenanced, the regulation of every part of private conduct by public authority, on the ground that the State had a deep interest in the whole bodily and mental discipline of every one of its citizens; a mode of thinking which may have been admissible in small republics surrounded by powerful enemies, in constant peril of being subverted by foreign attack or internal commotion, and to which even a short interval of relaxed energy and self-command might so easily be fatal that they could not afford to wait for the salutary permanent effects of freedom. In the modern world, the greater size of political communities, and, above all, the separation between spiritual and temporal authority (which placed the direction of men's consciences in other hands than those which controlled their worldly affairs), prevented so great an interference by law in the details of private life; but the engines of moral repression have been wielded more strenuously against divergence from the reigning opinion in self-regarding, than even in social matters; religion, the most powerful of the elements which have entered into the formation of moral feeling, having almost always been governed either by the ambition of a hierarchy, seeking control over every department of human conduct, or by the spirit of Puritanism. And some of those modern reformers who have placed themselves in strongest opposition to the religions of the past, have been no way behind either churches or sects in their assertion of the right of spiritual domination: M. Comte, in particular, whose social system, as unfolded in his *Système de Politique Positive,* aims at establishing (though by moral more than by legal appliances) a despotism of society over the individual, surpassing anything contemplated in the political ideal of the most rigid disciplinarian among the ancient philosophers.

Apart from the peculiar tenets of individual thinkers, there is also in the world at large an increasing inclination to stretch unduly the powers of society over the individual, both by the force of opinion and even by that of legislation; and as the tendency of all the changes taking place in the world is to strengthen society, and diminish the power of the individual, this encroachment is not one of the evils which tend spontaneously to disappear, but, on the contrary, to grow more and more formidable. This disposition of mankind, whether as rulers or as fellow-citizens, to impose their own opinions and inclinations as a rule of conduct on others, is so energetically supported by some of the best and by some of the worst feelings incident to human nature, that it is hardly ever kept under restraint by anything but want of power, and as the power is not declining, but growing, unless a strong barrier of moral conviction can be raised against the mischief, we must expect, in the present circumstances of the world, to see it increase.

QUESTIONS

1. Would John Milton agree that "over himself, over his own body and mind, the individual is sovereign"?

2. Mill would not apply his definition of liberty to the very young, or to "backward" peoples. Would exponents of liberty nowadays wish to go further than Mill? Should there be no censorship at all? Should all undeveloped areas of the world be given self-rule at once and with no further preparation? Give examples of this problem from current affairs.

3. What limits does Mill put to the liberty of mature persons and peoples?

4. What areas of personal life and conduct must be left free and uncontrolled? Why?

5. To what extent do these areas coincide with those delineated by Milton?

6. From what direction comes the threat to this kind of liberty? In Mill's day? In our own?

7. Would Mill's argument be strengthened or weakened by the support of Milton's religious view of man's nature and destiny?

Notes

WHAT I BELIEVE

p. 2	*Erasmus:*	Desiderius Erasmus (1466-1536), humanist scholar of the Renaissance.
p. 2	*Montaigne:*	Michel de Montaigne (1533-1592), French essayist and sceptic.
p. 2	*Moses:*	prophet and lawgiver, founder of the faith of Israel.
p. 2	*St. Paul:*	theologian and Christian missionary of the first century.
p. 2	*Mount Moriah:*	the mountain on which Abraham offered Isaac (Genesis XXII.2).
p. 2	*Elysian Field:*	in classical mythology, the place of the blessed spirits after death.
p. 2	*"Lord, I disbelieve . . ."*	a significant variation on the passage from St. Mark IX.24: "Lord, I believe; help thou my unbelief."
p. 3	*Dante:*	Dante Alighieri (1265-1321), Italian poet of the late Middle Ages.
p. 3	*Brutus and Cassius:*	The leaders of the conspiracy that murdered Caesar suffer endless punishment in Dante's *Inferno*.

p. 4 *"even Love, the Beloved Republic":* The line is from Swinburne's poem *Hertha.*

p. 4 *Home Office:* the British Government Department in charge of police, the prison system, and immigration.

p. 5 *Nibelung's Ring:* Richard Wagner's opera sequence *The Ring of the Nibelung* consists of four operas: *The Rhine Gold* (1869), *The Valkyrie* (1870), *Siegfried* (1876), and *The Twilight of the Gods* (1876). From this highly symbolic and complex work E. M. Forster abstracts elements which parallel and illustrate the situation in Europe in 1939. Fafnir, the giant, turns himself into a serpent (the figure of evil) to guard the stolen Rhine Gold (a symbol of power). The believers in force would bring the struggle for power into the open at once. Wotan, King of the Gods, prepares by buying time until he can meet force with force. The Valkyries, daughters of Wotan and Earth, seek human fulfilment, life and love, in the midst of crisis and in the face of doom. Brünnhilde, whom Wotan loves best of the Valkyrie maidens, epitomizes the eternal and necessary value of love even in the teeth of doom. In other words, Forster sees in Wagner's symbols a hope for the endurance of the deepest human values despite the dark presence in life of greed, envy, and malice. And it is a subtle stroke on Forster's part to pit Wagner against Hitler. For Wagner was Hitler's favourite composer.

p. 6 *Nietzscheans:* adherents of the Superman philosophy of Friedrich Nietzsche (1844-1900).

p. 7 *Sophocles:* (495-406 B.C.), Greek dramatist. Only seven of his plays survive in their entirety.

p. 7 *Horace:* Quintus Horatius Flaccus (65-8 B.C.), Roman poet.

p. 10 *Jacopone da Todi:* (c.1230-1306), medieval Italian poet.

p. 11 *Naked I came into the world . . .* cf. the Book of Job I.21.

MARRAKECH

p. 13 *Marrakech:* city in Morocco, North Africa. Morocco gained its independence in 1956, but at the time Orwell wrote it was a French dependency.

p. 14 *Arab navvy:* Arab labourer. "Navvy" is a British colloquialism.

p. 18 *farthing:* a small English coin, now obsolete; in our currency worth about a third of a cent.

p. 19 *screw-gun batteries:* The screw-gun was a double-barrelled artillery piece, its barrels screwed together.

THAT DAY AT HIROSHIMA

p. 25 *Asano family:* a prominent family in Hiroshima whose residence there dates back to at least 1619. The leader of the Forty-seven Ronin was an Asano.

p. 25 *Forty-seven Ronin:* Ronin were masterless feudal warriors. These forty-seven had lost their place in feudal society when their overlord had fallen into disgrace and committed suicide. After avenging his disgrace, the forty-seven also committed suicide.

p. 25 *tabi socks:* socks that are made rather like mittens. The sandal thong fits into the separation between the big toe and the other toes.

p. 26 *shamisen:* a stringed instrument by which the geisha accompanies her singing.

p. 26 *B-29's:* large bombers, the "flying fortresses" of the United States Army Air Corps in the Second World War.

p. 36 *rigor mortis:* Latin phrase meaning the rigidity of death.

p. 36 *risus sardonicus:* Latin phrase meaning scornful laughter.

THE KILLERS

p. 43 *from a saloon to a lunch-counter:* The story is set in the United States in the 1920's when it was illegal to manufacture or distribute alcoholic beverages. Much of the gangsterism of the period was related to the illegal manufacture and distribution of alcohol.

ONE, TWO, THREE LITTLE INDIANS

p. 57 *the five Dionney kids:* the five daughters born to Mr. and Mrs. Oliva Dionne at Callander, Ontario, on May 28, 1934. They were a tourist attraction during the 1930's and 1940's.

THE ROCKPILE

p. 68 *the Bronx:* The Bronx is a borough of New York City separated from the island of Manhattan by the Harlem River. The name Harlem is given to the part of Manhattan immediately below the Harlem River.

HA'PENNY

p. 79	*Potchefstroom Road, Baragwanath crossroads, Van Wyksrus Road:*	roads in the environs of the South African city of Johannesburg.
p. 79	*Durban, Port Elizabeth, etc.:*	cities and towns in South Africa.
p. 80	*meneer:*	the Afrikaans for "Sir". Afrikaans is the language of the Boers and is derived from Dutch.
p. 82	*Mosuto:*	a black African tribe.
p. 82	*coloured:*	Mrs. Maarman was of mixed blood.

THE MACBETH MURDER MYSTERY

p. 87	*She fixed me with a glittering eye:*	a humorous reference to Coleridge's poem *The Ancient Mariner*. At the beginning of the poem a wedding guest is hypnotized and made to listen to a long narrative by the ancient mariner who "holds him with his glittering eye".

MY OEDIPUS COMPLEX

p. 91	*Oedipus Complex:*	a psychological condition, especially evident between ages four and five, in which a boy loves his mother intensely. The term arises from Oedipus, the hero of Greek mythology who unwittingly slew his father and married his own mother.
p. 92	*Gurkha knives:*	The Gurkhas are a warlike people from Nepal. In the First World War many Gurkhas fought in the British army and were noted for prowess with their knives in close combat.

p. 92	*button-sticks:*	soldiers' appliance for cleaning brass buttons without soiling the cloth of the uniform.
p. 92	*seventeen and six:*	about two dollars and sixty cents in present Canadian currency, but worth more in 1918.
p. 94	*a wax:*	a fit of anger.
p. 100	*codded me:*	fooled me, netted me. The cod is the deepest recess of a net.

MY DISCOVERY OF ENGLAND

p. 120	*Thotmes II:*	Thotmes or Tuthmosis was an Egyptian Emperor of the sixteenth century B.C.
p. 120	*a light . . . in the tall Clock Tower:*	The light indicates that the House of Commons is in session. Leacock has his own notion of where the Members of the House actually congregate.
p. 121	*House of Lords:*	the Upper House of the British Parliament. Its membership consists of the higher ranks of the hereditary aristocracy, bishops of the established Church, and, recently, non-hereditary "life" peers appointed by the government.

AMERICA AT LAST

p. 124	*Julie Andrews and Richard Burton:*	popular stage and film stars.
p. 124	*Camelot:*	Broadway musical show based on White's book about King Arthur, *The Once and Future King.*
p. 124	*Gustave Doré:*	(1832-1883), French artist famous for his illustration of Dante's *Inferno.*

p. 124	*King Kong:*	an over-size monster in a horror film of the 1930's.
p. 125	*Santa Sofia:*	The Church of the Holy Wisdom built in Constantinople in 561. After the conquest by the Turks in 1453 it became a mosque.
p. 125	*Gothic:*	medieval architectural style whose main structural feature was the pointed arch.
p. 125	*Cherokees:*	one of the largest of American Indian tribes. They inhabited the area of the southern Alleghenies.
p. 127	*L.A.:*	Los Angeles.
p. 127	*sticky:*	unresponsive.
p. 129	*Carson:*	Kit Carson (1809-1868) was a famous American hunter, frontier scout, and Indian agent.
p. 129	*Frémont:*	John Charles Frémont (1813-1860), American explorer, soldier, and political leader.
p. 129	*Mme. Nhu:*	Her husband Ngo Dinh Nhu and her brother-in-law Ngo Dinh Diem, head of the government of South Vietnam, were assassinated on November 1, 1963.
p. 130	*forty-niners:*	the people who participated in the 1849 Gold Rush to California.
p. 131	*Lex and Pax Romana:*	Roman law and Roman peace. The phrases are usually applied to the period of the early empire under Augustus.
p. 131	*S.P.Q.R.:*	Senatus populusque Romanus, the senate and the Roman people, i.e. the authority of the Roman state.
p. 132	*Marlowe:*	Christopher Marlowe (1564-1593), Elizabethan dramatist.
p. 132	*Webster:*	John Webster (c.1575-c.1624), Jacobean dramatist.

p. 132	*Ford:*	John Ford (1586-c.1639), Jacobean dramatist.
p. 132	*the Borgias:*	a ruling family of Central Italy in the fifteenth century. Lucrezia Borgia, the Duke Cesare Borgia, and Pope Alexander VI were its most famous members.
p. 132	*the Duchess of Malfi:*	the central character in the play of the same name by John Webster.
p. 133	*Ku Klux Klan:*	a white terrorist organization in the Deep South of the United States.

THE UNFADING BEAUTY: A WELL-FILLED MIND

p. 135	*Anatole France:*	(1844-1924), French novelist, essayist, historian, and poet.
p. 136	*7:45 local:*	The reference is to commuter trains linking the suburbs to the downtown areas of cities like New York and Chicago.
p. 136	*"To see life steadily and see it whole":*	The author has adapted a line from Matthew Arnold's poem "To a Friend" in which he acclaims the Greek dramatist Sophocles as one "who saw life steadily and saw it whole". Arnold regarded Sophocles as typical of the Greek humanist spirit in the Golden Age.
p. 137	*Aristotle:*	(384-322 B.C.), philosopher of ancient Greece.
p. 137	*Chaucer:*	Geoffrey Chaucer (c.1344-1400), English poet, author of the *Canterbury Tales.*
p. 137	*Phi Beta Kappa key:*	Membership in the Greek-letter fraternity is based on high academic standing. The key is worn as a sign of membership.

p. 137	*Ivy League:*	a term applied to the older, ivy-covered colleges and universities of the Eastern Seaboard of the United States, among them Harvard, Yale, Princeton, Cornell, Dartmouth.
p. 138	*Greek aorist:*	a past tense of Greek verbs denoting an action and indicating whether the action is completed, continued, or repeated.
p. 138	*Latin ablative absolute:*	a phrase that contains a noun or pronoun and a participle and has a logical but not a grammatical connection with the clause upon which it depends.
p. 139	*Plato:*	(428 or 427-348 or 347 B.C.), Greek philosopher.
p. 139	*Yeats:*	William Butler Yeats (1865-1939), Irish poet, dramatist, and critic. The quotation is from Yeats' "Sailing to Byzantium".
p. 140	*. . . at his thrombosis:*	Ciardi alludes to the high rate of heart attacks among business executives.
p. 141	*Hemingway:*	Ernest Hemingway (1898-1961), American novelist and short story writer.
p. 141	*Marlene Dietrich:*	popular German-American film star.
p. 141	*P.T.A.:*	Parent-Teacher Association.
p. 141	*Salvador Dali:*	(b. 1904), contemporary Spanish painter.
p. 141	*Frost:*	Robert Lee Frost (1875-1963), the greatest of modern American poets.
p. 142	*Catherine Drinker Bowen:*	(b. 1897), popular American biographer.
p. 142	*Aldous Huxley:*	(1894-1963), English novelist and essayist.
p. 142	*Wallace Stevens:*	(1879-1955), American poet.

p. 143 *John Donne:* (c.1571-1631), English poet and churchman.

p. 143 *Penelope:* wife of Ulysses, King of Ithaca, and celebrated in Homer's *Odyssey*.

p. 143 *Cleopatra:* (69-30 B.C.), Queen of Egypt, heroine of Shakespeare's *Antony and Cleopatra.*

p. 143 *Ophelia:* the daughter of Polonius in Shakespeare's *Hamlet.*

p. 143 *Du Barry:* Comtesse du Barry (1746-1793), mistress of Louis XV of France.

p. 143 *Emma Bovary:* the heroine of Flaubert's novel *Madame Bovary.*

p. 143 *Anna Karenina:* the heroine of Tolstoi's novel of the same name.

p. 143 *"Age cannot wither her . . .":* from Shakespeare's *Anthony and Cleopatra,* Act II, Scene 2.

p. 144 *Mozart:* Wolfgang Amadeus Mozart (1756-1791), Austrian composer.

ODOUR OF CHRYSANTHEMUMS

p. 146 *Selston:* Selston, Underwood, and Brinsley are villages in Nottinghamshire.

p. 147 *pit-bank:* a heap of shale brought up from the mine, but not usable as coal. It is burned to reduce its bulk.

p. 147 *headstocks:* framework to support the winding machine.

p. 149 *mash:* mix or stir (the tea-leaves).

p. 149 *'Lord Nelson':* Like the 'Yew Tree' and 'Prince o'Wales' mentioned later, it is a public house, a tavern.

p. 151	*to get some ripping done:*	to behave like a wastrel.
p. 152	*wafflin' it about:*	moving it about.
p. 152	*crozzled:*	burnt.
p. 156	*squab:*	a couch.
p. 157	*loose-all:*	the signal to stop work.
p. 157	*next bantle:*	the next load.
p. 158	*butty:*	workmate.
p. 158	*nine o'clock deputy:*	nine o'clock shift.
p. 161	*butties:*	members of his work gang.
p. 161	*under th' face:*	the coal face, the vertical surface that the miners dig out. He was undermining this surface when the collapse occurred behind him.

THE WEDDING GIFT

p. 170	*Port Marriott:*	a fictitious name given to one of the early settlements on the east coast of Nova Scotia. The same is true for Bristol Creek and Scrod Harbour mentioned later.
p. 171	*Lady Huntingdon's Connexion:*	Connexion was a term used by the Methodists in England to denote a local association of people sharing their religious practices. Lady Huntington subsidized this particular group. Methodists emphasized austerity in daily life and in worship.
p. 178	*flint and steel:*	objects for making a fire. They were carried together with dry, inflammable material in a tinderbox. The steel was struck against the flint to make a spark which ignited the tinder.

DR. HEIDEGGER'S EXPERIMENT

p. 189 *folios . . . black-letter quartos . . . duodecimos:* books of various sizes. The folio is the largest, its pages being half the size of a full printer's sheet. The pages of the duodecimo are one twelfth the size of a full sheet. Black-letter is a form of type used by early printers.

p. 192 *Ponce de Leon:* (c.1460-1522), the Spanish discoverer of Florida. He came upon it searching for a land which, Indian legend told him, contained a fountain with marvellous curative powers.

THE PERFUME SEA

p. 202 *Parsee:* member of a religious sect in India, descendants of Persians who settled in India in the 8th century.

p. 202 *kenkey:* dough-balls made of corn-meal, a staple dish in Ghana.

p. 202 *hashish:* the tops or leaves of Indian hemp, chewed or smoked for narcotic effect.

p. 206 *Barbera:* an elongated, red, acid fruit.

p. 211 *elephant grass:* a tall perennial resembling sugar cane.

p. 211 *casuarina trees:* hardwood trees, seventy to eighty feet high, found in Australia, southeast Asia, and tropical Africa.

p. 211 *paw-paw:* a tree bearing a small fleshy fruit.

p. 211 *hibiscus and bougainvillaea:* flowering shrubs.

p. 212 *frangipani tree:* a tree with fragrant blossoms from which perfume is made.

p. 212 *gecko:* a small lizard.

p. 212	*puff-adder:*	a venomous African snake.
p. 212	*chameleon:*	a lizard with the power of changing the colour of its skin.
p. 213	*Pagliacci:*	*The Players,* Leoncavallo's opera, first performed in 1892.
p. 214	*Haroun al Raschid:*	(763-809), Caliph of Baghdad in its "Golden Age" of the *Arabian Nights* tales.
p. 215	*phrenology:*	the study of the conformation of the skull based on the theory that its shape indicates mental powers and characteristics.
p. 215	*creme-de-cacao:*	a chocolate-flavoured liqueur.
p. 217	*Ashanti:*	the people of a former British colony in West Africa of the same name, now part of Ghana.
p. 218	*ouija board:*	a board with letters and words which, when touched by a spiritualist medium, is supposed to give answers, messages, etc.
p. 219	*aura:*	a distinctive spiritual envelope which is said by spiritualists to surround every person.
p. 219	*African highlife:*	a popular modern dance form of West Africa.
p. 221	*niim tree:*	or nim, neem, a tree about eighty feet high with a dense crown, native to India but found now throughout West Africa. Its wood resembles mahogany.

THE BIRD AND THE MACHINE

p. 230	*Hobbes:*	Thomas Hobbes (1588-1679), English philosopher whose writings elaborate the mechanistic view of the universe that Eiseley rejects. The *Leviathan,* a political treatise, is his most famous work.

THE HINT OF AN EXPLANATION

p. 249	*Pennine tunnels:*	tunnels through the Pennine Chain in England.
p. 250	*"back":*	the area behind a building.
p. 251	*anthropomorphic:*	ascribing human characteristics to God or the gods.
p. 255	*De Bello Gallico:*	Julius Caesar's account of the Gallic Wars.
p. 255	*Cyclops:*	in Greek mythology a race of lawless giants with but one eye in the middle of the forehead.
p. 256	*cruet:*	a small glass bottle containing water that is to be mixed with wine in the course of the Mass.
p. 257	*Confession . . . Consecration:*	two stages in the action of the Mass, the first when the sins of the faithful are confessed, the second when the priest consecrates the bread and wine on the altar.
p. 257	*last Sacrament:*	Extreme Unction, the anointing with oil of the sick or dying.
p. 257	*Host:*	the consecrated bread or wafer in the celebration of the Mass.

PIGEON FEATHERS

p. 262	*P. G. Wodehouse:*	(b. 1881), English humourist and novelist.
p. 263	*Green Mansions:*	romantic nature novel by American novelist W. H. Hudson (1841-1922).
p. 263	*Manuel Komroff:*	(b. 1890), American novelist. *I, the Tiger* is one of his historical novels.
p. 263	*Galsworthy:*	John Galsworthy (1867-1933), English novelist.

p. 263	*Ellen Glasgow:*	(1874-1945), American novelist.
p. 263	*Irvin S. Cobb:*	(1876-1944), American humourist and novelist.
p. 263	*Sinclair Lewis:*	(1885-1951), American novelist.
p. 263	*"Elizabeth":*	pen-name of Mary Annette Russell (1866-1947), American novelist.
p. 269	*the crabs on the shore in The Time Machine:*	Towards the end of the book the dying earth is described as being occupied by monstrous red crabs.
p. 279	*Plato:*	(428 or 427-348 or 347 B.C.), Greek philosopher and disciple or Socrates (c.469-399 B.C.). Plato wrote *The Republic*, a work of philosophy, in the form of a dialogue between Socrates and some friends.
p. 279	*The Parable of the Cave:*	In Book VII of *The Republic* Socrates tries to explain the unchanging reality behind changing appearance. He says that most men live like prisoners in a cave with their backs to the light. Instead of real objects, they see only flickering shadows of them on the cave wall. These they take for reality.

SPECIFICATIONS FOR A HERO

p. 291	*territorial election in 1902:*	Saskatchewan did not become a province until 1905.
p. 297	*the Line:*	the border dividing American Montana from Canadian territory.
p. 298	*John Peter Turner:*	author of *The North-West Mounted Police*, a book that includes a history of the transition period, 1873-1893, in the Canadian West.
p. 298	*monte:*	Spanish-American card game.

p. 299 *Scythian and Cossack:* The Scythians were warlike nomads of ancient times who roamed the regions to the northeast of the Black Sea and the Caucasus. Like the more modern Cossacks, they were skilled horsemen.

p. 300 *Confederate prejudices:* prejudices brought from the rebellious confederacy of the southern states.

HOW WORDS CHANGE OUR LIVES

p. 307 *Louis Armstrong:* (b. 1900), popular Negro jazz band leader and trumpet soloist.

p. 307 *P. W. Bridgman:* (1882-1961), Harvard professor who received the Nobel Prize in physics in 1946.

p. 309 *frog:* an ornamental braiding on a jacket or coat; a triangular elastic horny pad in the middle of the sole of a horse's foot; a device permitting wheels on one rail of a track to cross an intersecting rail.

p. 316 *Jean Hélion:* (b. 1904), French painter of the Modernist School.

p. 317 *Tagalog:* the language of one of the native peoples of the Philippines.

p. 318 *Buddha:* Gautama Buddha was the founder of a religion which arose in the sixth century B.C. in India and spread throughout the Orient.

p. 318 *Confucius:* (551 or 550-479 or 478 B.C.), Chinese philosopher and ethical teacher.

p. 318 *General Tojo:* (1884-1948), Japanese general and political leader in World War II.

p. 318 *Mao Tse-tung:* (b. 1894), the head of the Chinese Communist Party.

p. 318 *Syngman Rhee:* (1875-1965), Korean political leader, President of South Korea 1948-1960.

p. 319 *Wendell Johnson:* (b. 1906), author and Professor of Speech Pathology at the University of Iowa.

THE BEAR

p. 322 *Priam:* King of Troy, an old man at the time of the Trojan war (see Homer's *Iliad* XXIV).

p. 323 *Chickasaw:* an Indian tribe of the northern Mississippi.

p. 329 *healing:* To heal is a dialect word of the southern United States meaning to cover with earth.

p. 336 *"She cannot fade though thou hast not thy bliss . . .":* a line from the *Ode to a Grecian Urn* by John Keats.

SUNSET AND EVENING STAR

p. 340 *Mycenae:* one of the most ancient cities of Greece. As early as the fourteenth century B.C. its craftsmen were skilled in pottery, bronze, glass, ivory, and gold.

p. 341 *Homer:* the name applied to the author of the Greek epics *Iliad* and *Odyssey.* Estimates of his birth-date vary from 685 B.C. to 1159 B.C.

p. 341 *Freud:* Sigmund Freud (1865-1939), the Viennese founder of psychoanalysis.

p. 342 *German-trained philologists:* The author refers to a tradition of scientific language study which ignored literary values.

p. 342 *"When shepherds pipe . . .":* The passage is from Shakespeare's *Love's Labour's Lost,* Act V, Scene 2.

p. 342 *T. S. Eliot:* (1888-1965), American-born poet, high priest of the modern movement.

p. 342 *Ezra Pound:* (b. 1885), American poet associated with Eliot and Joyce.

p. 342 *James Joyce:* (1882-1941), Irish novelist who revolutionized the form of the novel.

p. 342 *"Let us go then . . .":* from Eliot's poem "Prufrock" (1917).

p. 343 *Rupert Brooke:* (1887-1915), Georgian lyric poet.

p. 343 *"Tom":* Thomas Stearns Eliot.

p. 343 *"Wystan":* Wystan Hugh Auden (b. 1907), English-born poet (now an American citizen).

p. 343 *Oliver Cromwell:* (1599-1658), the leader of the English "middle-class" revolution in the seventeenth century.

p. 343 *Mensheviks joining the C.P.:* From 1903 until the Bolshevik revolution in 1917 the Mensheviks were the moderate wing of the Socialist Party in Russia. The Bolsheviks formed the extremist wing which later became the Communist Party.

p. 344 *Lenin . . . Finland Station:* Lenin returned from exile in Switzerland, arriving in a sealed car in April 1917 at the Finland Station, Petrograd (now Leningrad). His arrival provided the Bolsheviks with a leader for their successful revolution in October 1917.

p. 344 *Prufrock:* "The Love Song of J. Alfred Prufrock". This poem and the 1917 volume in which it appeared are regarded by MacLennan as the works which precipitated the modern revolution in poetry.

p. 344 *Dialectic:* Karl Marx, the father of Communism, used the term to describe his own theory of movement and change in social and economic forms. Dialectic is the study of contradictions that result in change.

p. 344 *F. R. Leavis:* (b. 1895), Cambridge professor and literary critic.

p. 344 *Cyril Connolly:* (b. 1903), British journalist and critic.

p. 344 *the Master:* T. S. Eliot.

p. 344 *the wasteland:* Eliot's *The Waste Land,* with its theme of decay and despair, came to characterize a whole period of modern civilization between the wars.

p. 344 *Angry Young Men:* a group of English writers of the 1950's, headed by John Osborne and Kingsley Amis, who protested against conventional social and moral values.

p. 344 *The winter evening settles down:* from Eliot's poem *Preludes* (I).

p. 344 *The morning came to consciousness:* from Eliot's *Preludes* (II).

p. 344 *Remark the cat which flattens itself . . .* from Eliot's *Rhapsody on a Windy Night.*

p. 345 *Khrushchev:* the Soviet premier and chairman of the Communist Party, who fell from power in 1964.

AREOPAGITICA

p. 348 *Areopagitica:* The title is from the court, Areopagus, which sat on the hill of Ares in ancient Athens.

p. 349 *fabulous dragon's teeth:* Cadmus, King of Thebes, sowed the teeth of a dragon before his enemies, and they

		magically changed into a host of armed warriors.
p. 349	*that ethereal and fifth essence:*	aether, the substance of the stars and heaven, superior to the four elements, earth, air, fire, and water, which compose our planet. This notion of a fifth element comes, probably, from Ovid's description of the creation in *Metamorphoses* and can be traced back as far as Aristotle.
p. 349	*Psyche . . . to cull out and sort asunder:*	According to the ancient mythological story Venus, jealous of Cupid's love for Psyche, forces her to sort out the different kinds of grain in a mountain-like mass of grains. Industrious and friendly ants come to her rescue and do the sorting for her.
p. 349	*one apple tasted:*	the apple of the Tree of the Knowledge of Good and Evil in the Garden of Eden.
p. 350	*that immortal garland:*	the wreath with which the Olympic runner is crowned, used by Milton as a metaphor for the crown of righteousness earned by the Christian.
p. 350	*blank virtue:*	colourless virtue.
p. 350	*excremental:*	external.
p. 350	*Spenser:*	Edmund Spenser (1552-1559) was an Elizabethan poet best known for his epic *The Faerie Queene.*
p. 350	*Scotus:*	John Duns Scotus (c.1265-c.1308), a medieval philosopher of the Franciscan order. He was of Scottish birth.
p. 350	*Aquinas:*	St. Thomas Aquinas (c.1225-1274), theologian and philosopher of the Dominican order, whose *Summa Theologica* is one of the mightiest achievements in the history of Christian thought.

p. 350 *Guyon ... Mammon:* In Spenser's *Faerie Queene*, Book II, Sir Guyon, the temperate man, withstands the temptation of Mammon (wealth, power) and abstains from the temptations of the flesh in the Bower of Bliss, a garden filled with the prospect of sensual pleasure. The Palmer (so called because he has earned the palm for his pilgrimage to the Holy Land) is Guyon's companion in most of the episodes of Book II. He represents the restraint of reason. Milton is mistaken, however, in saying that the Palmer accompanies Guyon through the Cave of Mammon.

p. 350 *fond:* foolish.

p. 351 *Doric:* the music of the Dorians, a people of ancient Greece, was reputed to be able to strengthen the virtues because of its manly vigour.

p. 351 *honest:* decent.

p. 351 *Plato:* Plato in the *Laws* suggested that no music be permitted in the good city which does not do proper praise to the gods and the great heroes of the past.

p. 351 *shrewd:* wicked.

p. 351 *frontispieces:* A frontispiece is an illustrated or decorated first page of a book.

ON LIBERTY

p. 354 *Akbar:* an Indian Mogul Emperor who reigned from 1556 to 1605. His authority was absolute but he ruled wisely and instituted many reforms.

p. 354	*Charlemagne:*	Charles the Great (c.742-814), King of the Franks and Emperor of the Romans, advanced the cause of Christianity throughout much of Europe.
p. 354	*utility:*	see the foreword to this essay.
p. 354	*prima facie:*	at first sight.
p. 355	*de jure:*	responsible by law.
p. 357	*Comte . . . Système de Politique Positive:*	Auguste Comte (1798-1857) was a French philosopher whose major work, *Système de Politique Positive* (published in several volumes between 1851 and 1854), under the guise of reform and social harmony, advocated a highly regimented and totalitarian social order.

4 5 6 7 8 Bry 74 73 72 71